ALASTAIR SAWDAY'S
SPECIAL PLACES TO STAY

£14.99/$23.95

£14.99

£14.99/$23.95

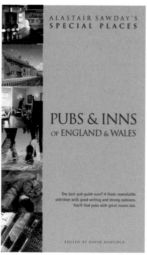

£13.99/$23.95

Sixth edition
Copyright © 2007
Alastair Sawday Publishing Co. Ltd

Published in 2007
Alastair Sawday Publishing,
The Old Farmyard,
Yanley Lane, Long Ashton
Bristol BS41 9LR
Tel: +44 (0)1275 395430
Fax: +44 (0)1275 393388
Email: info@specialplacestostay.com
Web: www.specialplacestostay.com

The Globe Pequot Press
P. O. Box 480, Guilford,
Connecticut 06437, USA
Tel: +1 203 458 4500
Fax: +1 203 458 4601
E-mail: info@globepequot.com
Web: www.globepequot.com

Design:
Caroline King

Maps & Mapping:
Maidenhead Cartographic Services Ltd

Printing:
Butler & Tanner, Frome, UK

UK Distribution:
Penguin UK, 80 Strand, London

ISBN 978-1-901970-81-4

A catalogue record for this book is
available from the British Library.

Paper and Printing: We have sought the lowest
possible ecological 'footprint' from the production
of this book, using super-efficient machinery,
vegetable inks and high environmental standards.
Our printer is ISO 14001-registered.

The publishers have made every effort to
ensure the accuracy of the information
in this book at the time of going to
press. However, they cannot accept
any responsibility for any loss, injury
or inconvenience resulting from the
use of information contained therein.

ALASTAIR SAWDAY'S
SPECIAL PLACES TO STAY

IRELAND

Contents

Back Page

Photo stockbyte

Alastair Sawday Publishing

Our main aim is to publish beautiful guidebooks but, for us, the question of who we are is also important. For who we are shapes the books, the books shape your holidays, and thus are shaped the lives of people who own these 'special places'. So we are trying to be a little more than 'just a publishing company'.

New eco offices

In January 2006 we moved into our new eco offices. With super-insulation, underfloor heating, a wood-pellet boiler, solar panels and a rainwater tank, we have a working environment benign to ourselves and to the environment. Lighting is low-energy, dark corners are lit by sun-pipes and one building is of green oak. Carpet tiles are from Herdwick sheep in the Lake District.

Environmental & ethical policies

We make many other gestures: company cars run on gas or recycled cooking oil; kitchen waste is composted and other waste recycled; cycling and car-sharing are encouraged; the company only buys organic or local food; we don't accept web links with companies we consider unethical; we bank with the ethical Triodos Bank.

We have used recycled paper for some books but have settled on selecting paper and printing for their low energy use. Our printer is British and ISO14001-certified and together we will work to reduce our environmental impact.

In 2005 we won a Business Commitment to the Environment Award and in April 2006 we won a Queen's Award for Enterprise in the Sustainable Development category. All this has boosted our resolve to promote our green policies. Our flagship gesture, however, is carbon offsetting; we calculate our carbon emissions and plant trees to compensate. In future we will support projects overseas that plant trees or reduce carbon use.

Carbon offset

SCAD, in South India supports the poorest of the poor. The money we send to offset our carbon emissions will be used to encourage village tree planting and, eventually, low-carbon technologies. Why India? Because the money goes a long way and admin costs are very low.
www.salt-of-the-earth.org.uk

Ethics

But why, you may ask, take these things so seriously? You are just a little publishing company, for heaven's sake! Well, is there any good argument for not taking them seriously? The world, by the admission of the vast majority of scientists, is in trouble. If we do not change our ways urgently we will

Who are we?

doom the planet and all its creatures – whether innocent or not – to a variety of possible catastrophes. To maintain the status quo is unacceptable. Business does much of the damage and should undo it, and provide new models.

Pressure on companies to produce Corporate Social Responsibility policies is mounting. We are trying to keep ahead of it all, yet still to be as informal and human as possible – the antithesis of 'corporate'.

The books – and a dilemma
So, we have created fine books that do good work. They promote authenticity, individuality and good local and organic food – a far cry from corporate culture. Rural economies, pubs, small farms, villages and hamlets all benefit. However, people use fossil fuel to get there. Should we aim to get our readers to offset their own carbon emissions, and the B&B and hotel owners too?

We are gradually introducing green ideas into the books and onto our web site: the Fine Breakfast scheme that highlights British and Irish B&B owners who use local and organic food; celebrating those who make an extra environmental effort; gently encouraging the use of public transport, cycling and walking. This year we are publishing *Green Places*

to Stay focusing on responsible travel and eco-properties around the globe.

Our Fragile Earth series
The 'hard' side of our environmental publishing is the Fragile Earth series: *The Little Earth Book, The Little Food Book* and *The Little Money Book*. They consist of bite-sized essays, polemical, hard-hitting and well researched. They are a 'must have' for anyone who seeks clarity about some of the key issues of our time. This year we have also published *One Planet Living*.

Lastly – what is special?
The notion of 'special' is at the heart of what we do, and highly subjective. We discuss this in the introduction. We take huge pleasure from finding people and places that do their own thing – brilliantly; places that are unusual and follow no trends; places of peace and beauty; people who are kind and interesting – and genuine.

We seem to have touched a nerve with thousands of readers; they obviously want to stay in special places rather than the dull corporate monstrosities that have disfigured so many of our cities and towns. Life is too short to be wasted in the wrong places. A night in a special place can be a transforming experience.

Alastair Sawday

Acknowledgements

Exploring, and inspecting, Ireland's hotels and other places to stay has always been one of the editorial treats of the job. So convivial, so generous are the Irish hosts that inspectors have to assume that time will take on new shapes. Schedules slip, slide, decay with imprecision and delay. Yet these books have somehow always emerged, as full of 'specialness' as any. Ann Cooke-Yarborough hesitated for not a moment in taking on this role again. She has a particular affection for interesting people and places. Ireland is a wonderful stamping ground for people like her.

So this latest edition has been created, with energy and panache, by a woman of considerable gifts who has created many other fine books for us. Thank you, Ann, again and again. This book is yours.

Alastair Sawday

Series Editor Alastair Sawday

Editor Ann Cooke-Yarborough

Editorial Director Annie Shillito

Writing Ann Cooke-Yarborough

Inspections Susan Alcorn, Rosie Bunbury, Sinead Connelly, Ann Cooke-Yarborough, Lorely Forrester, Nicola Hamilton, Annabel Hewat, Fred & Herta Rigney, Maureen Thornton

Accounts Bridget Bishop, Jessica Britton, Christine Buxton, Sandra Hasell, Sally Ranahan

Editorial Jackie King, Jo Boissevain, Florence Oldfield, Maria Serrano, Rebecca Stevens, Danielle Williams

Production Julia Richardson, Rachel Coe, Tom Germain, Rebecca Thomas, Allys Williams

Sales & Marketing & PR Siobhán Flynn, Andreea Petre Goncalves, Sarah Bolton

Web & IT Russell Wilkinson, Chris Banks, Joe Green, Brian Kimberling

Previous Editors Simon Greenwood, Stephen Tate

History of Ireland Turtle Bunbury

Advice and support Emily Dixon, Brendan Flanagan

And many thanks to those people who did just one or two inspections.

A word from Alastair Sawday

A recent trip to Dublin revealed a different place from the one I had last seen a few years ago. The city heaves with modern life, with pavement cafés and cosmopolitan buzz – not surprising with hundreds of thousands of East Europeans now adding their vitality, and help, to Ireland's own. The economic boom after Ireland's entry into the euro-zone has settled down a bit (this book has over 70 places charging £70 or less for a double room with breakfast) but the extent to which the Irish 'hospitality' business is dependent on outsiders is astonishing. I was charmed by Latvians in Wicklow and by Poles in Dublin. Eighty per cent of hotel workers come from abroad. I fear for Ireland if they ever go home.

For all the changes, most that is familiar remains. The North is still an area that cries out to be explored by travellers who have for so long ignored its wild loveliness. There is bucolic beauty, there is remoteness and there is history in glittering quantity. Forget the 'troubles' – they are far away and remote, too. Up there you will find a warmth and ease of welcome that is matchless, and the boom has not reached into the crevices of daily life as it has elsewhere.

This wonderful book also shows you thirty special holiday homes to rent,

Photo Tom Germain

from rambling seaside houses to country mansions, to a wee hideaway for two. And you don't always need a car; more than half of our owners will arrange transport from the nearest bus stop or railway station. Go on – break free!

Irish hotel (and B&B) prices are now more attractive than you might suppose. Apparently, developers of housing estates have been required to erect hotels too, as a sort of 'planning gain'. As development has proceeded apace, so the hotels have mushroomed. They have to fight for their share of visitors and have thus sparked a bizarre price war. You are the beneficiaries, though I do feel sorry for family hotels and B&Bs. Do go and support them.

Alastair Sawday

Introduction

THIS BOOK GATHERS TOGETHER A WIDE VARIETY OF PLACES TO STAY THAT BUCK THE DEPERSONALISING TREND

Readers have written many things since the last edition of *Special Places to Stay in Ireland* – praises, grumbles, recommendations, holiday diaries. An example:

"One of the best days we spent in Ireland was in this delightful house. Its best features must be the lack of TV & radio in every room, no trouser press, and the long six-foot bath in the rose bathroom. Breakfasts were a delight with fresh fruits and full Irish fry, then tea in front of the peat fire in the afternoon and evening. We will go back and we hope that Lucy and Gary are left alone by the Tourist bureaucrats for as long as possible."

Researching this edition, we have met owners of a small cottage on half a dozen acres putting huge effort into qualifying for inclusion in the local conservation area; owners who keep a *"very friendly lazy big Empress of Blanchings pig who will probably never see the abattoir"*; and several hosts who find that meetings of minds are the source of real riches and are determined not to increase their capacity simply to make more **money**, knowing that the effect will be to make them less close to **people**.

So things aren't all bad in the world of Irish accommodation, the Irish people aren't all *"becoming materialistic like people in other countries,"* as local Cassandras would have us believe. True, the price of staying at a special B&B or small hotel has gone up, because fuel and insurance costs have rocketed, taking services and food with them. Most owners are deeply disturbed by these economics.

And it's true that the 'special places to stay' scene in the Republic has changed in the last few years, at both ends of the scale. As a result of a tax-credit scheme, new low-cost hotels have sprouted up all over the country, little old hotels have added big new extensions and there is a glut of rooms on the market. The corporate world is better equipped

Photo right Westcove House, entry 119
Photo left Johnny's Cottage, entry 32

Introduction

to stack 'em high and sell 'em cheap than the family running a modest B&B who cannot compete with loss-leader promotions, despite all their qualities of character, personal attention and history.

At the top end we used only to find that marvellous emblem of the Irish countryside, the history-laden Georgian country house – farmhouse or stately home – whose owners were often descendents of the original builders. They have been welcoming paying guests to sleep in their four-posters, dine off their fine china and enjoy their occasionally hair-raising histories for many years. Now the young educated professionals who

Photo Castle Leslie, entry 47

represented half their business are suddenly following other sirens and patronising the trendy new spa hotels and 'resorts'. The effect is so powerful that even simple B&Bs are installing hot tubs in their gardens while the grand old houses are casting round for new ideas to attract these fickle golden boys and girls back to their rich old stones.

The booming Irish labour market has drawn many bright young East Europeans and Asians, particularly to the hospitality and health industries. All our societies are becoming multi-cultural; Ireland started later than most and has now gone ahead.

These are the trends. This book gathers together a wide variety of places to stay that buck the depersonalising trend and retain their individuality, even quirkiness, that makes for a memorable encounter, however short. There are thousands of people out there whose true Irish ease of contact, sense of humour and gentle courtesy do much to restore one's faith in humanity. So don't let the acceleration distract you. As one owner put it, "*Take the time to spend time with Ireland's greatest treasure, its people. There is no substitute for meeting the locals, sampling the food, listening to the traditional music live in the local pub. We are a nation of storytellers, everyone has a tale to tell, every tale is worth hearing*".

Go with an open heart, a warm sweater and plenty of time: the real people of Ireland are still out there and still ready to 'pass the time of day' with you.

The owners

Young or old, long-established landowners on their estates, ex-townies newly-converted to doing B&B out in the wilds or, vice-versa, couples from the country launching trendy little city guest houses, they are passionate about history – local and all-Irish – often holding very definite views, often deeply knowledgeable and thoughtful citizens. They also love talking about their old stones, old codgers, old heroes and old ancestors. They are a wonderfully mixed bag so do read carefully, between the lines too, in order to find those who will really suit you.

Where and when to go

Spring and autumn can be luminous but the weather is always changeable, though the south-west is milder than the rest of the country. July and August are best avoided. Tourists flood into Kerry, Cork, Connemara and the Giant's Causeway at that time. In particular, tour buses thunder anti-clockwise round the Ring of Kerry, from Killarney to Kenmare. If you have no choice but to be there in high summer, you should do the same, otherwise you will be meeting them head-on round some dangerous bends.

Include Ulster if you can, it has so much to discover, from the stunning beauty of the coast of Donegal and the glens of Antrim to the lively medieval walled city of Derry, the quirky personality of the gardens at Mount Stewart, fabulous coarse fishing and innumerable historic ruins.

What's in the book?

This guide covers all types of places to stay in the island of Ireland – as long as they have something special – classified under the four historic

Photo Rathmullan House, entry 35

Introduction

provinces of Ulster (north), Connacht (west), Leinster (east) and Munster (south). Within the provinces, counties follow each other organically for ease of planning, and all categories of places to stay, from grand hotels to farmhouse B&Bs and self-catering places, are listed by area. Thus, you may be looking for a family house to rent for two weeks and a B&B or small hotel where grandparents or friends can spend a weekend nearby: you will find both described in the same section of the book.

How we choose our special places
We search for the best of everything and write a book without fixed boundaries. We include places where hospitality is practised with flair, good humour and commitment. We visit each property and judge it on its own merits, not by comparison. We like people who do their own thing, though being eccentric is no excuse for unclean rooms. The key considerations are atmosphere and value for money. Good views are more important to us than a trouser press, good walks more important than a fitness centre. Irish houses vary from extremely grand to deliciously modest, Irish hotels from high luxury to welcoming simplicity. I trust you will find your special place – or places – to stay, meet these warm-hearted people, perhaps make new friends.

Photo Knockeven House, entry 150

Subscriptions
Owners pay to appear in this guide. Their fee goes towards the high costs of inspecting and producing an all-colour book and maintaining a sophisticated web site. We only include places that we like and find special for one reason or another. It is not possible for anyone to buy their way onto these pages.

Maps
Each property is flagged with its entry number on the maps at the front. Holiday homes are marked in red, the rest in blue. Places offering both overnight and self-catering have flags in two colours. Please don't use these maps as anything other than a general guide or a good starting point for planning your trip. Use a good detailed road map for real navigation. Most places will send you detailed instructions once you have booked your stay.

How to make your choice
Above all, read the entry carefully. A simple B&B will be here because its owners are lovely people, be they artists, farmers, cooks or teachers, but the price they charge is an indication of level of service and comfort: don't expect designer bathrooms or a tea kettle in your room. A wayside hotel will be charming but won't offer laundry service or sundry smellies. If such things are important to you then

Introduction

check when you book and in all cases fit your expectations into the price range.

Types of places to stay
Hotels come in all sorts here, from the country-house hotel with touches of luxury and lots of services, even golf, to the little modern place in town where the emphasis is on intimacy and hands-on attention. We even have a vast family hotel – with remarkable eco-credentials and a superior contemporary art collection.

B&Bs The range of B&Bs in Ireland is astonishing, though prices have been creeping up in popular destinations. You may find the larger houses are more guest houses than family B&Bs, they may have a receptionist and they often concentrate on providing first-class food.

Inns and restaurants with rooms also focus on the quality of their food and offer the well-fed guest a decent place to lay his head for the night. They will be busy in the evenings, often with live music and extended opening hours. This is part of their charm and those wanting peace and quiet should take it into account.

Self-catering addresses
A good number of our entries are houses, gate lodges, cottages and castles that you can rent for yourselves, friends and families. Unless otherwise stated, the price includes linen, heating and electricity but always check when booking. Owners may charge extra for turfs or logs for the fire. Three of these self-catering entries have been included in partnership with the Irish Landmark Trust whose admirable conservation work is described at the back of the book. Also, a number of B&Bs mention their self-catering after their B&B prices and are flagged with double colours on the map.

Green entries and environmental awareness
We have chosen, very subjectively, seven places that are making a particular effort to be eco-friendly and have given them a 'green' double-page spread with extra photographs to illustrate what they are doing.

Photo Cahernane House Hotel, entry 111

This does not mean there are no other places in the guide taking green initiatives. A number of estates are REPS registered: the Rural Environment Protection Scheme requires five years 'probation' before a farm/estate can be rewarded (financially) for environmentally friendly farming/management practices. Other owners are committed members of the Slow Food Movement (see pages 302-303). And everyone recycles diligently.

Rooms

We state whether rooms are double, twin, twin/double (ie. zip-link beds), single, family, triple or a suite. Assume rooms have either bath or shower en suite unless another arrangement is mentioned. A 'separate' or 'shared' bathroom means that it is not en suite and will have either a shower or a bath, a wc and a basin next door, across the landing, or elsewhere in the house. 'Separate' means for the sole use of that room's occupants. If you'd like your child in your room, ask when booking if you may have a cot or a foldaway bed and what the charge will be.

Prices

In Northern Ireland, prices are in sterling (£); in the Republic they are in euros (€). There's a conversion indicator at the end of the book. We quote the lowest to the highest price for a double room with breakfast. The prices we print are presumed to be valid for the year of publication. However, they are not binding and owners may change them at any time; do confirm on booking. It is fairly common for hotels to up their prices for Bank Holiday weekends, and beyond the year of publication you should always expect things to have changed. Larger places may add 10%-15% to your bill 'in lieu of all gratuities' and some may add VAT. However, lots of places offer reductions for longer stays and in the less tourist-ridden seasons; always enquire when booking.

Meals

Breakfast

The Irish know how to do a good breakfast. There are often several courses with a choice of main dishes. Fruit and yogurt are

Photo Sliabh gCua Farmhouse, entry 165

Introduction

increasingly provided but the traditional fry, often including black and white pudding, remains a favourite. We have introduced our Fine Breakfast scheme in Ireland. You will find a description of the scheme at the back of the book.

Dinner

Ireland now has a well-founded reputation for caring about good food. The range of good cooking is phenomenal, with chefs using the natural larder on their doorstep to produce excellent, fresh-tasting, locally-sourced food. The seafood, the meat, the milk and the vegetables here taste outstanding. No wonder the Slow Food ethos comes naturally (see pages 302-303). Owners who don't do dinner will recommend somewhere nearby.

Symbols

There's an explanation of our symbols on the last page of the book. Use them as a guide rather than a statement of fact. If an owner doesn't have a symbol that you are looking for, it's still worth asking whether they would be prepared to accommodate you.

Children

Our 🐥 symbol shows places which are happy to accept children of all ages, not that they will necessarily have all the equipment for children, so check when booking. A few places will do high tea/early supper but the symbol does mean there may be children at dinner so if you dislike this combination then avoid dining at these places.

Pets

Our 🐕 symbol is given to places where your pet can sleep in your bedroom but not on your bed. If you cannot warm to dog friendliness at breakfast or the possibility of doggy aromas in your bedroom, take note. Similarly, our 🐈 symbol is for owners who keep animals, be it a horse, a parrot or a family of cats.

Smoking

Smoking is forbidden in bars, restaurants, dining and sitting rooms in the Republic but paradoxically bedrooms are exempt from the law so ask about non-smoking rooms in

Photo above Ulusker House & Mossie's Restaurant, entry 123
Photo right Rathmullan House, entry 35

hotels if it is important to you. B&Bs where the owners smoke may be more relaxed about this rule on the grounds that they are in their own house, preparing the food and doing the housework rather than employing others.

Booking, deposits and cancellation
Do think ahead... and then do what you said you would do. Most places will take bookings by post, fax or email but many like a telephone contact too. Some will ask for a deposit – often non-refundable if you cancel and they cannot re-let. Many require a credit card number or possibly full payment several weeks before you arrive and if you cancel you will be charged the set amount.

If you are asked to pay a deposit by a place that does not take credit cards, you no longer need send a cheque, with possible delivery anxieties, or go to your bank to order a direct transfer. The new trend is for the owner to give you his IBAN (international banking) number and from your home computer banking account you can simply deliver the sum from your account to his.

Do let your host know roughly when you will be arriving and call if you are badly delayed. B&B owners will generally want to be there when you arrive and to spend some time with you. It's important to be punctual if you have booked an evening meal.

Payment
All our owners take cash and local currency cheques with a cheque card. If they take credit cards, we have given them the 📇 symbol. If you have a Diners, an American Express or a lesser-known card, check whether the owner can accept it before you arrive. If you plan to pay by credit card, inform your bank. Owners have found that guests give a card number, the electronic transaction takes time, the guests leave and the owner is left with a truncated payment because the bank's ceiling on that card is £100. It is laborious and embarrassing to have to recover the difference after the event.

Photo Gregans Castle Hotel, entry 86

Practical matters
North/South differences

Nothing announces any change of any sort when you cross The Border between Northern Ireland and the Republic. However, there are certain consequences of this two-country situation:
• Two currencies: sterling is often accepted in the South, euros in the North, but it's better to have some of both if you plan to cross over
• Two telephone systems: phonecards from one side do not work in slots on the other
• Two insurance systems: your car-hire insurance may not cover you for travelling in the other part of Ireland unless you specifically ask for it

Driving in Ireland

Expect to take twice as long as 'normal' to drive from one place to another – and enjoy it. There are few motorways, main roads tend to go through old town centres, country roads are narrow lanes with high hedges, surprise bends and dogs sleeping in patches of sun.

As part of the United Kingdom, the North uses miles, the Republic uses kilometres. You drive on the left and speed limits are:
• 110kph (70mph) on some stretches of motorway
• 100kph (60mph) on most motorways and other dual carriageways

Photo Mount Vernon, entry 87

• 50/60kph (30/40mph) through villages and towns.
A good map is the Michelin 1/400,000 map of Ireland

The boom has seen an increase in traffic and house building on the main roads, so plan your route along minor ones. This is the way to discover the old and timeless Ireland that you are probably looking for.

Telephoning

The country code for the Republic is 353, for Northern Ireland it is 44. We have included the country codes in the listings: dial your international access and the number as printed ignoring the bracketed (0). When telephoning from within the country, just dial the national number including the first bracketed (0).

Introduction

Our partners
The Irish Landmark Trust

Three of our self-catering entries are included in association with the Irish Landmark Trust, a not-for-profit charitable trust whose purpose is to rescue smaller buildings that are part of Ireland's heritage, north and south. It restores the buildings given into its care to ensure their survival and makes them available as short-let holiday homes. This lightweight use protects the fabric of the building from the excessive alterations that might be needed for permanent living and gives more people the chance to experience living in a faithfully restored building representative of an old way of life. Income from bookings contributes to the upkeep of these very special places, of course.

Many of the properties would be lost without the Trust's intervention, all are restored with style, integrity and respect for their original character. When restoring, the Trust promotes traditional skills among the local workforce who may learn old crafts

such as lime-painting, stone wall building or medieval woodwork restoration. The social and architectural history of each building is researched and a modern interpretation of the way people once inhabited and used it is encouraged.

To discover what other places they have for short-term rent, consult www.irishlandmark.com or contact them at info@irishlandmark.com or by telephone +353 (0)1 670 4733.

Tailormade Ireland

Tailormade Ireland is an established bespoke tour company based in Ireland and specialising in sporting and cultural itineraries throughout the island of Ireland. From initial concept to departure they consider and manage every fine detail. "*Our clients enjoy access to a 'hidden' Ireland and with our knowledge and experience, together with Alastair Sawday's special places to stay, we ensure you enjoy a truly tailormade experience.*"
Consult their web site www.tailormade-ireland.com or contact Emily Dixon on info@tailormade-ireland.com or by telephone +353 (0)59 916 1473.

Internet

www.specialplacestostay.com has online pages for all the special places featured here and from all our other books - around 5,000 in

Photo Tailormade Ireland

total. There's a searchable database, a taster of the write-ups and colour photos. And look out for our dedicated self-catering web site, www.special-escapes.co.uk. For more details, see the back of the book.

Disclaimer
We make no claims to pure objectivity in choosing our Special Places. They are here because we like them. Our opinions and tastes are ours alone and this book is a statement of them; we hope that you will share them. We have done our utmost to get our facts right and we apologise unreservedly for any errors that may have crept in.

We do not check such things as fire alarms, swimming pool security or any other regulation with which owners of properties receiving paying guests should comply. This is the responsibility of the owners.

Feedback
Feedback from you is invaluable and we always act upon comments, which may be sent by letter or email to info@sawdays.co.uk. Or you can visit our web site and write to us from there. With your help and our own inspections we can maintain our reputation for dependability - and do bear with us at busy times; it's difficult to respond immediately. Poor reports are followed up with the owners in question: we need to

hear both sides of the story. Really worrying reports lead to incognito visits, after which we may exclude a place. As a general rule, do mention any problems that may arise to the relevant people during your stay; they should want to resolve them on the spot.

Owners are informed when we receive substantially positive reports about them, and recommendations are followed up with inspection visits where appropriate. If your recommendation leads us to include a place, you receive a free copy of the edition in which it first appears.

So tell us if your stay has been a joy or not, if the atmosphere was great or stuffy, whether the owners or staff were cheery or bored. We aim to celebrate human kindness, fine architecture, real food, history and landscape, and hope that these books may be a passport to memorable experiences.

Ann Cooke-Yarborough

Historical snippet
From about 1845, the Dunbrody, one of the so-called Famine Ships, sailed between Ireland and Canada three times a year for 20 years. On the outward journey it carried Irish emigrants fleeing the devastation of the great potato famine; on the return journey it carried Canadian timber for the wealthy, who wanted for nothing, to build or extend their mansions because Ireland did not produce enough good timber for their purpose.

Key to general map

The Regions of Ireland: Colour coded opposite:
Ulster • Connacht • Munster • Leinster •

Ulster (entries 1-49)

Londonderry
Antrim
Down
Armagh
Fermanagh
Tyrone
Donegal
Monaghan
Cavan

Munster (85-187)

Clare
Limerick
Kerry
Cork
Waterford
Tipperary

Connacht (50-84)

Sligo
Leitrim
Roscommon
Mayo
Galway

Leinster (188-247)

Wexford
Kilkenny
Carlow
Laois
Wicklow
Dublin
Kildare
Offaly
Longford
Meath
Westmeath
Louth

General map

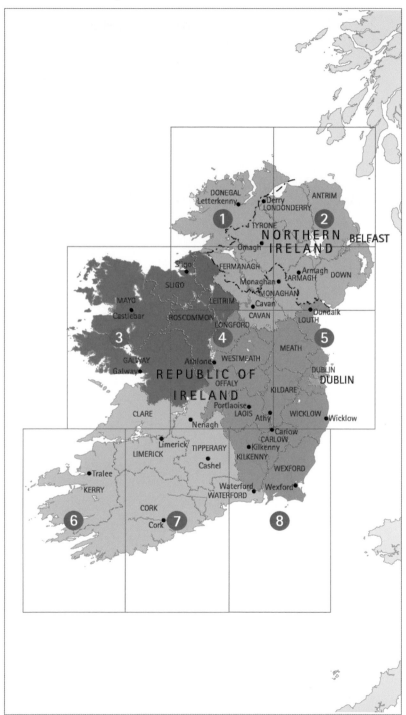

Map 1

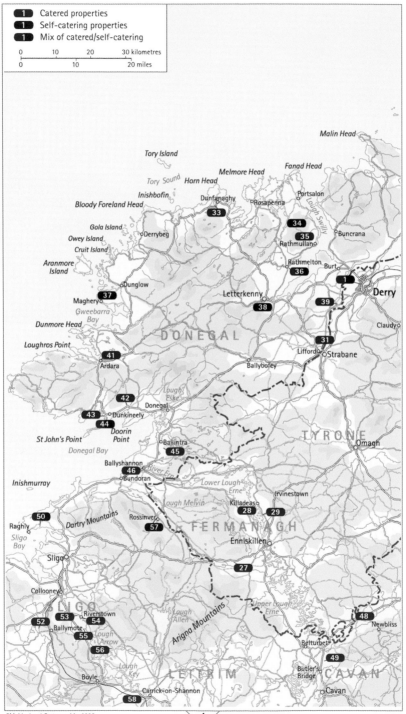

Catered properties
Self-catering properties
Mix of catered/self-catering

0   10   20   30 kilometres
0   10   20 miles

Malin Head

Tory Island

Tory Sound   Horn Head   Melmore Head   Fanad Head

Inishbofin   Dunfanaghy   Portsalon

Bloody Foreland Head   Rosapenna   Lough Swilly

33

Gola Island   Derryberg   34

Owey Island   Buncrana

Cruit Island   35

Aranmore   Rathmullano
Island
Rathmelton   Burt

Dunglow   36

Maghery   37   1   Derry

Gweebarra   39
Bay
Letterkenny   Claudy

Dunmore Head   38

Loughros Point   31

Ardara   41   Lifford   Strabane

Ballybofey

Lough
Eske   42   TYRONE

Donegal   Omagh

43   Dunkineely

44   Doorin

St John's Point   Point

Donegal Bay   Ballintra

45

Ballyshannon

46   River Erne

Inishmurray   Bundoran   Lower Lough
Erne

Lough Melvin   Irvinestown

50   Dartry Mountains   Rossinver   Killadeas

Raghly   57   28   29

Sligo
Bay   FERMANAGH

Sligo   Enniskillen

Collooney   27

SLIGO   Upper Lough
Erne

53   Riverstown   48

52   54   Newbliss

Ballymote   Lough
Arrow   Belturbet

55

56   Arigna Mountains

Lough   49
Key

Boyle   LETRIM   Butler's   CAVAN
Bridge

Carrick-on-Shannon   Cavan

58

Map 2

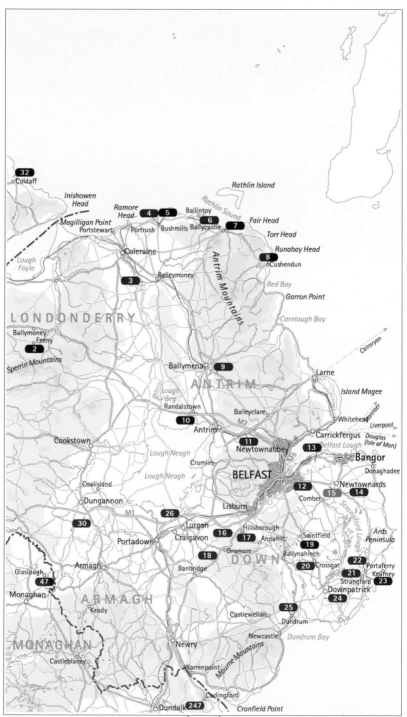

Map 3

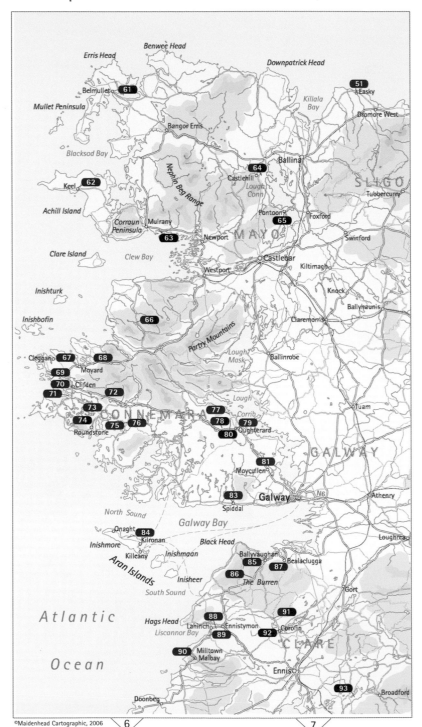

Map 4

29

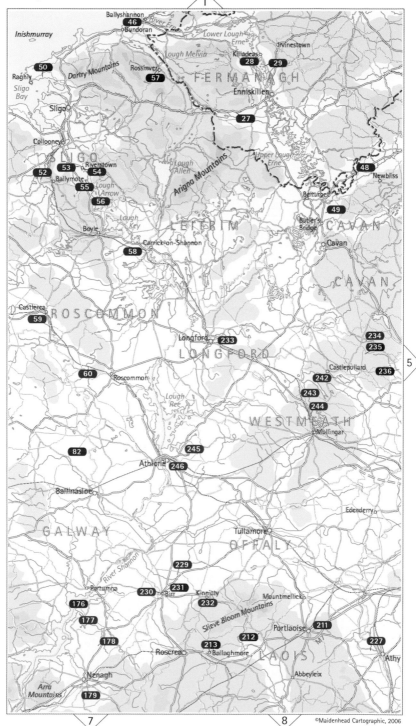

Map 5

Map 6

31

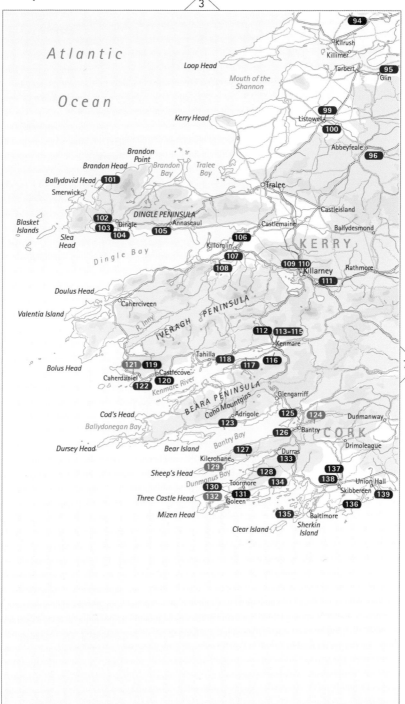

Map 7

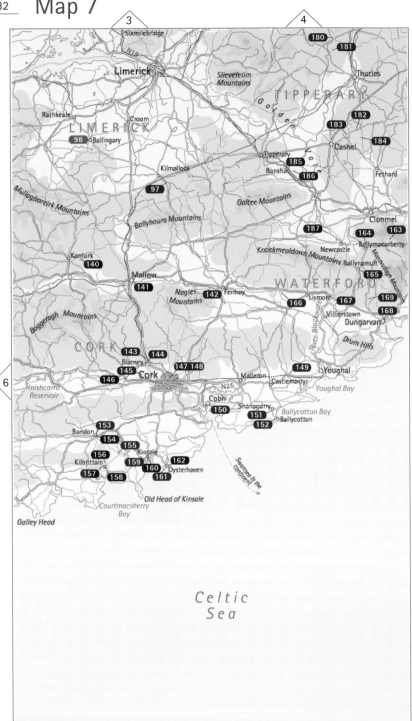

3

4

180
181

Sixmilebridge

N18

Slievefelim
Mountains

Limerick

Thurles

TIPPERARY

Rathkeale

Croom

Golden

182

LIMERICK

183

Cashel

184

98 Ballingary

Kilmallock

Tipperary

185

Mullaghareirk Mountains

97

Banshee

186

Fethard

Ballyhoura Mountains

Galtee Mountains

187

Clonmel

164 163

Knockmealdown Mountains

Newcastle

Ballymacarberry

Kanturk

Ballynamult

Mooncullagh Mountains

140

Mallow

WATERFORD

141

Nagles
Mountains

142 Fermoy

165

Lismore

166

167

169

Boggeragh Mountains

Villierstown

168

Dungarvan

CORK

143 144

Drum Hills

River Blackwater

Blarney

145

Cork

147 148

149

Youghal

6

146

Midleton

Castlemartyr

Inishcarra
Reservoir

N25

Youghal Bay

Cobh

Shanagarry

150

151

Ballycotton Bay

152

Ballycotton

153

Bandon

154

155

Kinsale

156

159

162

Kilbrittain

160

Oysterhaven

157

158

161

Old Head of Kinsale

Courtmacsherry
Bay

Galley Head

Celtic
Sea

Swansea & the
Continent

Map 8

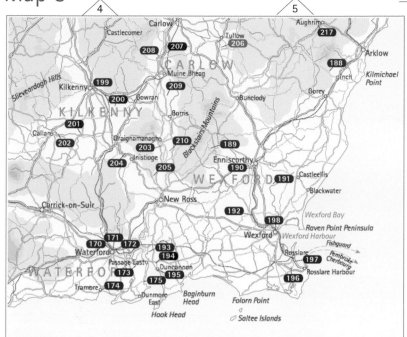

Castlecomer

Carlow

4   5

Tullow
206
Aughrimo
217

208 **207**

CARLOW

Arklow

Muine Bheag
188
Kilmichael
Point

Slieveardagh Hills

Kilkenny
199

209

Inch

Bowran
200

Bunclody

Gorey

KILKENNY

Borris

Blackstairs Mountains

201

Callan

Graignamanagh

189

202

203

210

Inistioge

Enniscorthy

204

205

190

191

Castleellis

WEXFORD

Blackwater

Carrick-on-Suir

New Ross

192

198

Wexford Bay

Wexford

Raven Point Peninsula

Wexford Harbour

Fishguard

171

193

Rosslare

Pembroke

170

172

194

197

Cherbourg

Waterford

Duncannon

Passage East

173

195

Rosslare Harbour

WATERFORD

175

196

Tramore

174

Dunmore
East

Baginburn
Head

Folorn Point

Hook Head

Saltee Islands

*Celtic
Sea*

Ulster

Photo Northern Ireland Tourist Board

The Merchant's House

16 Queen Street, Derry, Co. Londonderry BT48 7EQ

Do visit Derry, Ireland's best-preserved walled city. Fascinating because of its position at the core of Northern Ireland's turbulent 20th century, it also has St Columb's Cathedral in the Planter Gothic style to blow its trumpet, and the Verbal Arts Centre to celebrate the Irish oral tradition. The real find, though, is the Merchant's House, an 1868 townhouse built in the Georgian style and lovingly, simply, naturally restored by Joan and Peter, two of the most unusual and civilised people you are likely to meet. After travelling in Latin America, they came back to Ireland, buying the house in 1993 while Peter was still teaching history at the University of Ulster in Derry. They join a colourful list of previous owners who include a Justice of the Peace, a grocer, two rectors and a butcher. Edward VII is said to have had tea in the dining room where breakfast is now served round a large wooden table. The bedrooms are full of period furniture, including a gorgeous half-tester bed, and the first-floor living room has the glorious generosity of the Georgian ideal. *Handy for Derry airport.*

rooms	4 + 2: 1 double with sep. bath; 1 twin with sep. shower; 1 double, 1 twin, sharing bath. 2 apts for 4 & 8.
price	£45-£60. Singles from £25-£35. Apts £350-£550 per week.
meals	Restaurants in Derry.
closed	Rarely.
directions	From Derry Airport, A2 to Derry over Craigavon Bridge, 2nd bridge over river, right for centre. Over 2 r'bouts, past Tesco, left Lower Clarendon St, 1st right after lights.

B&B & Self-catering

Joan & Peter Pyne

tel	+44 (0)2871 269691
fax	+44 (0)2871 266913
email	saddlershouse@btinternet.com
web	www.thesaddlershouse.com

Map 1 Entry 1

Drumcovitt House Cottages
704 Feeny Road, Feeny, Co. Londonderry BT47 4SU

No wonder poets and writers love Drumcovitt, its atmosphere is like no other, earthy and diaphanous, hands-on hard work and landed grandeur. The original workaday farmhouse on the hill shrank from sight in 1796 when a lofty declaration of Georgian wealth was stretched across its face but the useful parts remained, stalwart as ever, hidden behind the makeover. Here, in the solid old stone barns beneath the towering trees, are three sweet little cottages, each with its own stretch of terrace. With excellent materials and workmanship and lots of colour, they have been converted into welcoming, family-friendly spaces. There's nothing luxurious or fragile, just deep armchairs, easy wooden floors and good simple kitchens. The view will gather you up, on misty mornings, when only the highest peaks and the spire of Banagher church are visible. Walks in the glens may bring sightings or hearings of rare birds, up in the woods you will discover a prehistoric ring-fort and back 'home' are three generations of genuinely lovely people should you need anything. *One cottage has wheelchair access.*

rooms	3 cottages for 4 (1 double, 1 twin, 1 bath).
price	£305-£425 per week.
meals	Self-catering.
closed	Christmas & New Year.
directions	From Derry A6 for Belfast 10 miles; right B74 to Feeny. Through village, house 0.5 miles on left.

The Sloan Family
tel	+44 (0)2877 781224
fax	+44 (0)2877 781224
email	drumcovitt.feeny@btinternet.com
web	www.drumcovitt.com

Self-catering

Map 2 Entry 2

Harmony Hill Country House
Balnamore, Ballymoney, Co. Antrim BT53 7PS

The picture tells half the story: Harmony Hill, one of the earliest dry spinning mills, is neither what it looks nor what its name says. The country house bit is invisible from the add-on front – one bay window lights the intimate sitting room – but the blue drawing room behind is as high, moulded and grand as you could wish, full of restrained good taste, aromatic turf fires and enticingly soft sofas. Trish occasionally plays the grand piano, wisteria blooms by the veranda, the path leads under the rookery to the millpond. Richard and Trish's reason for being here is their much-appreciated restaurant that meanders darkly round the little plant-climbed courtyard, oozing saloon vibes from its wooden cubicles and low beams. Two high-class chefs work simple wonders with the freshest seafood and vegetables grown right here. But the Wilson family's open, intelligent welcome of house guests will make you feel one of them. Bedrooms are unexpectedly rustic in a log cabin fashion, with pine-slat panelling, meringue plaster, each with a cosy turf fire, two with steep ladders to children's sleeping lofts.

rooms	4: 2 twins/doubles, 2 family rooms with bunk beds.
price	£79. Singles £49. Extra person sharing, £20.
meals	Dinner £25-£30, 6.30pm-9.30pm (Wed-Sat only). Sunday lunch.
closed	Christmas & New Year.
directions	From Ballymoney ringroad A26 for Coleraine; 3rd left for Balnamore, over r'way; left at T-junc.; 3rd right on tight bend.

Restaurant with rooms

Trish Wilson

tel	+44 (0)2827 663459
fax	+44 (0)2827 663740
email	webmaster@harmonyhill.net
web	www.harmonyhill.net

Map 2 Entry 3

Bushmills Inn Hotel

9 Dunluce Road, Bushmills, Co. Antrim BT57 8QG

Bushmills is always that step ahead. Now in care for our environment. Roy Bolton, who wants guests to have and be the best, gives you the chance to learn how easy it is to re-use and recycle in his rich-rustic rooms and bathrooms (water-saving devices coming soon). He creates a cosy feel despite the hotel's size. The sense of settled age is remarkable in the Mill House extension where rooms are big and quietly luxurious (illustrated). But the original warren-like 17th-century coaching inn lives on in masses of timber – panelling, partitions, beams, and wooden booths ('snugs' in Irish) in the restaurant where the stables once were. There are multifarious sitting spaces, some with traditional gaslights, welcoming turf fires, flagstones, oil lamps and rural bric-a-brac. Something for everyone, in fact, in a warm atmosphere of relaxed indulgence. James McKendry paintings of the Giant's Causeway coastline lead upstairs to comfortable cottage-style bedrooms, each different from the next. Many come for the golf, the coastline or the world's oldest distillery up the road – raise your glass to Ireland.

rooms	32: 5 doubles, 1 twin, 20 twins/doubles, 4 singles, 2 family rooms.
price	£98-£268. Singles from £68.
meals	Dinner, à la carte, about £30. Day menu, until 6pm, £5-£25.
closed	Christmas Day.
directions	From A26 at Ballymoney B66 then right B17 to Bushmills & Giant's Causeway. In town, hotel entrance before bridge near River Bush.

	Roy Bolton
tel	+44 (0)2820 733000
fax	+44 (0)2820 732048
email	mail@bushmillsinn.com
web	www.bushmillsinn.com

Hotel

Map 2 Entry 4

The Drum Gate Lodge, Bushmills, Co. Antrim

Contact: 25 Eustace Street, Temple Bar, Dublin 2

A most intriguing 'cottage'. As you arrive along the deeply quiet country road, you will be greeted by friendly donkeys; they make the miniature castellated tower even more unexpected against its bucolic backdrop. Built in 1800, inhabited until 1962, it guarded the tradesmen's entrance to Ballylough estate and carries many memories of the harshness of life in rural Ireland. Skilfully restored and adapted by the Irish Landmark Trust, it now has a discreet little extension, linked to the drum by a very fitting curved passage. The circular living room with its pot stove and gothic windows really does feel like a medieval tower – tiny wee for two with a couple of good armchairs, a well-stocked bookcase and no television. The stairs curl upwards from beside the fireplace to the circular bedroom: three more gothic windows and a generous double bed. The extension, in perfect proportion to the drum, contains a neat little modern kitchen and bathroom; heating is underfloor throughout. So near yet so far from the Giant's much-tramped coastal trail, the Drum is a sweet curvy hideaway for two.

rooms	Lodge for 2 (1 double, 1 bathroom).
price	£353-£441 per week.
	Weekend & mid-week breaks possible.
meals	Self-catering.
closed	Never.
directions	Directions given on booking.

Self-catering

The Irish Landmark Trust

tel	+353 (0)1 670 4733
fax	+353 (0)1 670 4887
email	bookings@irishlandmark.com
web	www.irishlandmark.com

Map 2 Entry 5

Whitepark House

Whitepark Bay, Ballintoy, Co. Antrim BT54 6NH

Bob is amazing, a friendly and fastidious host, he cannot do enough for you, organising bathroom and breakfast times so that everyone is happy, helping you plan your day, turning on your bedside light before you come back. No wonder he was 'UK Landlady of the Year 2003'. The incongruously castellated frontage opens onto an eye-stretching gathering of beatific buddhas, prickly cacti, orderly elephants and manifold pictures among a mass of indoor vegetation. Bob and Siobhán created all this from trips to India, Sri Lanka and further east. Whitepark House, first built in 1735, is in a superb position looking right out to sea. On clear days you can see Rathlin lighthouse, Islay and Jura. The bedrooms ooze splendour, especially the big double at the end of the upstairs corridor. The one bathroom is big, warm and welcoming. Breakfast by the window in the large open-plan hall and plot your walk along the coast. Bob will drop you off at the Giant's Causeway – the eight-mile cliff walk back to base is surely one of the reasons cameras were invented. *No smoking in bedrooms. Children over 12 welcome.*

rooms	3: 2 doubles, 1 twin, sharing bathroom & extra wc.
price	£70. Singles £40.
meals	Restaurants nearby.
closed	Rarely.
directions	From Bushmills A2 coast road to Whitepark Bay. Entrance on right, 100 yds past youth hostel.

Bob & Siobhán Isles
tel   +44 (0)2820 731482
email   bob@whiteparkhouse.com
web   www.whiteparkhouse.com

B&B

Map 2 Entry 6

Bath Lodge

16 Carrickmore Road, Ballycastle, Co. Antrim BT54 6QS

Perched at the end of half a mile of golden sand – waves lapping hungrily, gulls mewing overhead, the heart-stopping view to Rathlin Island and Scotland all yours – Bath Lodge is a quaint, lovable family house, a warren of level changes, rambling staircase, corners, crannies and a comfortable mix of furniture. There's nothing posh or scary: bring the children, their friends and all the gear without fear for the ancient floorboards or well-worn rugs. The grown-ups will grab the deep-seated view-filled sitting room; the big downstairs 'dormitory' doubles as a fine playroom, the lawns are great for games, the walled garden for sheltered peace. Originally five 18th-century miners' cottages whose tiny attics were thrown up to create lofty ceilings, it has old bones and the essential modernities. In the large kitchen/breakfast room the Aga fights the huge refrigerator for centre stage, the scullery hides any mess. Bedrooms have the same old-style comfort of mixed antiques, good beds, space. Rabbits crop the clifftop of the wild garden in peace yet the town is just behind you. Brilliant for a family holiday.

rooms	House for 11 (1 double, 2 triples, 1 suite for 3, 3 bathrooms). Overflow garden room for 3 with bathroom.
price	£300–£800 per week.
meals	Self-catering. Restaurants within walking distance.
closed	Rarely.
directions	Directions given on booking.

Self-catering

Dr Sarah Mills

tel	+44 (0)2078 345839
mobile	+44 (0)7717 597904
email	sarah@mills158.co.uk

Map 2 Entry 7

Drumkeerin

201a Torr Road, Cushendun, Co. Antrim BT44 0PU

What a remarkable couple, gently retired into an early taste of paradise, strong-minded and active, both artists and art historians. Mary takes centre stage with her love of life and people, her sparkling talk of art and artists, Ireland and the Irish, her life and times. Joe quietly fills all the other roles with his strength, humour and wisdom, tends the hens and introduces you to his special love, the Moyle Arts Forum for putting sculpture into landscape. They chose this house for the heart-stopping view, of course, and rebuilt the inside. That sky floods a mixture of modern and antique furniture with changing light; personal treasures of all sorts, pots and paintings catch the eye. Except in the breakfast room where only the window calls for attention: "we are working with the scenery" they say, and you can only tear yourself away by walking out into it. Bedrooms are palely, softly restful, even the tellys are white. A tamed garden leads to woodland and a rushing stream. A house of heart and humanity against an overawing backdrop of natural power and beauty. *Painting & walking breaks organised.*

rooms	3 + 1: 1 double, 2 family rooms. Annexe for 10.	
price	£50-£60. Singles £30-£35. Annexe £50 (for 2). Reduction for families sharing.	
meals	Restaurants in village.	
closed	Rarely.	
directions	From Larne A2, or from Ballymena A43, to Cushendall; continue A2 to Cushendun; continue to Torr Road junc.; right for 50yds, left into lane, house signposted.	

	Joe & Mary McFadden	
tel	+44 (0)2821 761554	
email	drumkeerin@zoom.co.uk	**B&B & Self-catering**
web	www.drumkeeringuesthouse.com	

Map 2 Entry 8

Marlagh Lodge

71 Moorfields Road, Ballymena, Co. Antrim BT42 3BU

A couple of young musicians take on a Victorian house, devote intense energy to saving and painstakingly restoring it all (bar the headless ghost): fine proportions, original fireplaces, 'servants' quarters' (where they now live), the old garden… and declare themselves "Victorians at heart". Voracious readers, Rachel and Robert prefer long walks and good food to television. Passionate about their house, they have treated it to stacks of books, antique pianos, prints, furniture and ornaments, set off by most beautiful William Morris wallpapers. After strong colours and a certain formality downstairs, a lighter, quirkier touch informs the luxurious bedrooms: salvaged baths with character, imperfections and the view; lovely furniture, fabrics and linens. These delightful, energetic people do all the decorating themselves, have invented Ballymarlagh Tummy Warmer porridge, among other breakfast marvels, and beyond the pretty courtyard, where the bell-tower still crowns the stables, have planted herbs at the foot of the fabulous monkey-puzzle tree. You soon forget the busy road in their wonderful universe.

rooms	3: 1 double, 1 four-poster; 1 twin with separate bath.
price	£70-£80.
meals	Dinner £31.50.
closed	Rarely.
directions	From Belfast A26 to Ballymena until signs for Larne; at 2nd r'bout, A36 for Larne 0.75 miles (end of crawler lane); right Rankinstown Road, drive immed'ly left.

B&B

Rachel & Robert Thompson

tel	+44 (0)2825 631505
fax	+44 (0)2825 641590
email	info@marlaghlodge.com
web	www.marlaghlodge.com

Map 2 Entry 9

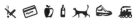

Ballealy Cottage, Lough Neagh, Co. Antrim

Contact: 25 Eustace Street, Temple Bar, Dublin 2

Down the twisty lane, past the ancient hedgerows, and there, set in a woodland glen, is a fairytale cottage: half-hipped roofs, crooked gables, octagonal chimneys – could it be the Gingerbread House? A stream slips noiselessly past, three gnarled apple trees stand guard. No witch lived here but Lord O'Neill's deerkeeper, his boots wearing the scrapers outside and the original flags in the hall, his hand polishing the smooth oak bannisters, his children's feet scuffing the cobbles visible under a patch of floorboards. The caring workmanship, the heavy period furniture, the old washroom with its cast-iron pot, set you squarely back in simpler times. The cosy kitchen/diner holds the tone with chunky pottery and cutlery; so do the old wing chairs and sofas round the sitting room fire. Bedding on the old iron bedsteads is new with modern duvets, the big bright bathroom beside the master bedroom upstairs has a roll-top bath, the small shower room for the connecting downstairs bedrooms is adequate, the cooking galley is new and practical, and there's central heating! A fascinating unusual hideaway.

rooms	Cottage for 5-7 (1 double, 1 suite for 3, 1 double sofabed; 1 bath, 1 shower).
price	£364-£546 per week. Weekend & mid-week breaks possible.
meals	Self-catering.
closed	Never.
directions	Directions given on booking.

The Irish Landmark Trust

tel	+353 (0)1 670 4733
fax	+353 (0)1 670 4887
email	bookings@irishlandmark.com
web	www.irishlandmark.com

Self-catering

Map 2 Entry 10

The Moat Inn

12 Donegore Hill, Templepatrick, Co. Antrim BT41 2HW

Thelma, new to B&B, bakes the bread, makes the jam, irons the sheets, and enjoys every minute of it. Full of ebullient charm, slight and strong, she puts her considerable energy into welcoming you to this delightful example of a small Irish house. Built as a coaching inn up against the medieval motte, it is part of a darling little hamlet, hidden away from the modern world. Inside, past the fireplace where the mistress would have cooked her sodabreads (the crock still hangs there), it ducks and dives into a series of cute and cosy rooms with a colourful Victorian feel. William Morris wallpaper, a lace cloth, a comfortable wing chair by the glowing fire in the drawing room; red walls and mahogany in the dining room where Thelma serves an elegant, intimate breakfast by candle and firelight; lovely Irish/French linen and antiques in the bedrooms, one blue, one red; good little shower rooms lined with evocative pictures of 1950s Paris. And everywhere works by Ross Wilson, one of Ulster's foremost living artists. Ulster's history hangs in the very air. *Ten-minute drive from Belfast Airport.*

rooms	2 doubles.
price	£70–£80. Singles £45–£50.
meals	Dinner £22.50. By arrangement only. Packed lunch £5. Afternoon tea £5.
closed	Christmas.
directions	From Belfast International airport A57 for Belfast, past Templeton Hotel, left at Templepatrick r'bout for Donegore; follow sign over m'way; 1st right Donegore Hill; inn on left opp. church.

B&B

Thelma McCausland

tel	+44 (0)2894 432923
fax	+44 (0)2894 433726
email	thelma@themoatinn.co.uk
web	www.themoatinn.co.uk

Map 2 Entry 11

Ravenhill House

690 Ravenhill Road, Belfast, Co. Antrim BT6 0BZ

Belfast has a buoyant, contemporary cultural life and staying at Ravenhill will connect you to those vibes. The centre is 10 minutes by bus and there's lots of life within walking distance, the Real Music Club for example. Running this bright and well-loved B&B in a leafy district of smart Victorian houses, the Nicholsons are a young and enthusiastic couple. Roger, from the north of England, loves the buzz of his adopted city and is glad to share its sights and secrets. Olive, from Westmeath, is warm and friendly, faultlessly juggling the B&B and three energetic children. Ravenhill has a cheerful lived-in atmosphere, people come and go, kids play here and there, the city moves past the window. Good-sized bedrooms are done with soothing greens, crisp linen, the odd Barbara Allen print and locally-made ash and oak furniture with purple heart trim. There's a sitting room with books, a piano, log fire and internet connection. Entirely local or organic, breakfast is mouth-watering: Roger is proud of his authentic Ulster breakfasts with homemade bread and marmalade a speciality – not to be hurried.

rooms	5: 2 twins/doubles, 1 twin, 1 single, 1 family room.
price	£70. Singles £45. Family room £80 for 3.
meals	Restaurants within walking distance.
closed	Christmas & New Year.
directions	From city centre, A24 Ormeau road for Newcastle & Downpatrick; over bridge; 500 yds further, left at r'bout; house 50 yds on right.

	Olive & Roger Nicholson
tel	+44 (0)2890 207444
fax	+44 (0)2890 282590
email	relax@ravenhillhouse.com
web	www.ravenhillhouse.com

B&B

Map 2 & 5 Entry 12

Beech Hill Country House

23 Ballymoney Road, Craigantlet, Holywood, Co. Down BT23 4TG

If you don't believe in ground-hugging grandeur, be converted. In this pastoral setting, Victoria's grandmother built a memory of the house she grew up in: Georgian proportions and family elegance, all on one floor. The drawing room is pure landed gentry with Grandmother's cameos, paintings and antiques, lightened by Victoria's superb strong colour touches on the fireside armchairs and cushions; breakfast is a magnificent scene, fine fruits among the silverware, mahogany, walnut and Crown Derby. After years in the catering trade, Victoria is a natural host with lots of local knowledge who clearly enjoys chatting to visitors. You will be greeted by a clutch of happy dogs and offered tea and delicious cakes, possibly in the marvellously floral conservatory between old terracotta tiles and floods of sky. Bedrooms are eminently, seductively comfortable in gently-defined colours, well-chosen fabrics and good furniture. All rooms have French windows onto the peaceful garden and bathrooms are both pretty and immaculate. A most gracious house. *Children over ten welcome.*

rooms	3 + 1: 2 doubles, 1 twin. Cottage for 2-3.
price	£70-£80. Singles £50. Cottage £300-£380 p.w.
meals	Restaurants in Holywood & Belfast.
closed	Rarely.
directions	From Belfast A2 for Bangor. Bypass Holywood; right up Ballymoney Rd at sign to Craigantlet; house 1.75 miles on left.

Country house & Self-catering

Victoria Brann

tel	+44 (0)2890 425892
fax	+44 (0)2890 425892
email	info@beech-hill.net
web	www.beech-hill.net

Map 2 Entry 13

Edenvale House

130 Portaferry Road, Newtownards, Co. Down BT22 2AH

Up from the main road by the lapping waters of Strangford Lough, the long narrow lane brings you to Edenvale, a fine Georgian house steeped in rural peace. Diane is a gas, as they say here, a 100-mph dynamo whom everyone seems to know and like. She will welcome you with friendly exuberance, tea and cakes in the beautiful drawing room or the bright sunroom with its views of the brooding Mourne Mountains. Gordon has a quick humour, too, and is quite prepared to take over welcome duties as the occasion requires. Large, immaculate bedrooms are well proportioned with luxuriously big beds, pelmets and hangings. There are some unusual pieces of furniture: old 'Flemish' bedheads, an inlaid dressing table and its fine oval-mirrored wardrobe. A lot of effort goes into each aspect of the Edenvale experience, and that includes superb and varied breakfasts. The garden, as well as happy flourishing roses, has a jungle full of trees for climbing, shrubberies for hiding and croquet for cunning on the lawn – a paradise for children. Gentle, playful dogs, too. *20 minutes from Belfast City Airport.*

rooms	3: 1 double, 1 twin, 1 family.
price	£75–£80. Singles £45.
meals	Restaurants in Bangor & Newtownards.
closed	Christmas & New Year.
directions	From Newtownards A20 for Portaferry 2 miles; entrance on left up drive.

Diane & Gordon Whyte
tel   +44 (0)2891 814881
email   edenvalehouse@hotmail.com
web   www.edenvalehouse.com

Country house

Map 2 & 5 Entry 14

Anna's House

Tullynagee, 35 Lisbarnett Road, Comber, Newtownards, Co. Down BT23 6AW

A fascinating house of contrast and talent. Anna's love is the astounding gardens beyond Ken's workshop: pine wood with hammock, secret lily pond, orchard, veg patch with gazebo, voluptuous borders, all risen to maturity in 30 years, her son's terracotta characters giving the finishing touch. Ken the steel-builder and music-lover has designed a soaring 'concert hall' extension to their old farmhouse. Actually a new 30-foot-high living space with a musician's gallery and acoustics for oratorios: steel struts, polished granite floor, a wall of glass to tip you into the serenity of unlandscaped natural beauty and the lake, it is an unmitigated success, a "wow!" at first sight and a real pleasure to be in, be it for a quiet read or the magic of music. Quietly dedicated and cosmopolitan, Anna loves cooking and baking (all organic, naturally): one guest told of "breakfasts like wedding feasts". Bedrooms, one on the ground floor, two off the new gallery, are simply pretty with white and pine backgrounds, beautiful linen, mahogany doors, good showers and private balconies. Rural seclusion just 20 minutes from Belfast.

That field spread before the house provides geothermal heating (only the pump is electric) and Ken has installed solar panels for hot water. Anna's two-acre organic garden grows fruit and veg galore, flowers to lift your heart and corners for contemplation, wildlife flourishes in thick hedges along fields and lake. She uses only organic paints and natural fabrics in the bedrooms and drives the best hybrid car. True believers, they put quantities of creative energy into their green crusade and are the only accommodation providers in Northern Ireland to have signed the Soil Association's Code of Conduct.

rooms	3: 2 double, 1 twin.
price	£70-£85.
meals	Pub-restaurant 0.5 miles.
closed	Christmas & New Year.
directions	From Belfast A22 for Downpatrick; 3 miles after Comber, pass petrol station & pub on right; right Lisbarnett Rd 0.5 mile; right into private lane to end.

	Ken & Anna Johnson
tel	+44 (0)2897 541566
fax	+44 (0)2897 541566
email	anna@annashouse.com
web	www.annashouse.com

SPECIAL
GREEN ENTRY
see page 16

B&B

Map 2 & 5 Entry 15

Sylvan Hill House

76 Kilntown Road, Dromore, Co. Down BT25 1HS

One of the most enjoyable couples you could hope to meet, Elise and Jimmy are full of zest and interest. She travels, adventurously, intelligently, to wild places in wild ways (huskies to ice hotels in the Arctic, horses round Patagonia, legs in the Himalaya) – not bad for a grandmother. He prefers his home comforts and is happy seeking adventure over dinner with friends while Elise is away. Horses are a shared passion, they are involved in the annual Balmoral Show in Belfast and have lots of remarkable racing memorabilia. It is a harmonious, human old house of calm character which they have extended over the years and dressed in good plain fabrics plus some colourful ethnic touches: Andean shawls rather than chintz, good furniture, hunting prints. They almost always dine with their guests, in summer in the little conservatory overlooking the Mourne and Dromara Mountains, in winter in the deliciously cosy living room. Elise is a self-trained chef and loves cooking. Breakfast is a treat, too. The immaculate rooms are soft, pretty, individual and deeply restful. A happy family lives here. *Pets by arrangement. Vegetarian meals available.*

rooms	3: 1 twin, 1 triple; 1 twin/double with separate bathroom.
price	£60. £56 for two nights.
meals	Dinner with wine, £16.
closed	Rarely.
directions	From Dromore B2 to Lurgan; 0.5 mile after red houses, right Kilntown Rd for Moira 1.5 miles; house at top of hill on right.

Country house

	Elise & Jimmy Coburn
tel	+44 (0)2892 692321
email	sylvanhillhouse@hotmail.com

Map 2 & 5 Entry 16

Fortwilliam Country House

210 Ballynahinch Road, Hillsborough, Co. Down BT26 6BH

Tall, friendly and ever-elegant, Mavis loves chatting with you over tea and homemade cakes or the most generous breakfast round a comfortable table in her country-style Aga kitchen where baskets hang from oak beams. Four-square Fortwilliam is 300 years old with 1930s bay windows. Daring carpet colours, hunting prints and glass ornaments contrast with antique furniture of great character: fine 1930s coordinates in the Garden room where a window seat looks over the daisy-strewn lawn, gleaming mahogany in the Victorian room, fabulous Irish carved beds in the Primrose room. Each is individually draped with velvet, brocade or patchwork while bathrooms have thoughtful extras "to pamper yourself with". Terry is a busy farmer tending a suckling herd on 70 acres with help from two friendly dogs; plus his hobby, the thoroughbred brood mares. Curl up beside the fire in the snug sitting room or relax in the tranquil walled garden and enjoy the view of the hills. Nothing is too much trouble here, the Dunlops have won guest-house awards – rightly so. Your welcome could not be more Irish.

rooms	3: 1 double en suite; 2 doubles, each with separate bathroom.
price	£65. Singles £40.
meals	Restaurant in Hillsborough.
closed	Rarely.
directions	From Hillsborough B177 for Ballynahinch 3.5 miles. House on hill on right, up steep drive.

	Terry & Mavis Dunlop
tel	+44 (0)2892 682255
fax	+44 (0)2892 689608
email	info@fortwilliamcountryhouse.com
web	www.fortwilliamcountryhouse.com

Country house

Map 2 & 5 Entry 17

Clanmurry

16 Lower Quilly Road, Dromore, Co. Down BT25 1NL

Long before the age of steam, John's ancestors carried Irish emigrants to America in square-rigged clippers. Clanmurry celebrates the brave beauty of these ships and their crews and John is a mine of enthralling historical fact. The tumult of the handy Dublin/Belfast A1 fades at the gates as the gentle air of this fine garden and 1820s house takes over. Inside, friendly country pieces sit well among original marble fireplaces, gracious arches and moulded ceilings. Bedrooms, traditionally-furnished like the rest of the house, are full of light and garden views; two can connect for families; their daughter's old room is fresh yellow and still shelters a tribe of fluffy friends. Your warm and kindly hosts delight in telling those seafaring tales, helping guests plan their Irish travels or talking gardening. They have put their own stamp on the marvellous mature garden, laid out in the 1960s by a passionate gardener – it deserves more than a passing saunter. And their speciality is coddling eggs for breakfast: they had their first coddled egg on their African honeymoon and have been coddling ever since.

rooms	3 twins sharing 2 bathrooms.
price	£60. Singles £40.
meals	Restaurant 3 miles.
closed	Christmas & New Year.
directions	From Belfast M1 south then A1 south to Dromore for exactly 8 miles; 1st right after only road bridge over Dromore bypass; entrance 1st on right.

	Sara & John McCorkell
tel	+44 (0)2892 693760
fax	+44 (0)2892 698106
email	mccorkell@btinternet.com
web	www.clanmurry.com

Country house

Map 2 & 5 Entry 18

The Hermitage Cottage
14 Drumnaconnell Road, Saintfield, Co. Down BT24 7NB

Deeply different... What is special here is the genuinely soulful environment Sally has created on her 20 acres: a walking labyrinth, a fire pit that is ceremonially lit to welcome in the seasons, a bridge over quiet waters, seated buddhas, meditation corners. Yes, Sally is pretty special, too. With a deep-seated innocence and a love of her Native American culture she came to Tibetan Buddhism and is involved with the local inter-faith forum working to heal some of Northern Ireland's wounds. In this atmosphere, her weeny 'cottage' — a glorified lean-to attached to her family house — is aptly named: decked in Tibetan prayer flags, defended by a brass dragon door knocker, it is perfect for one frugal person in search of a week's birdsung serenity. Inside, you find basic living spaces: a single/double cell-like bedroom with high roughly-hewn white walls, flagstones and a small desk, a windowless shower room, a neat little kitchen. The approach past someone else's scrapyard is anything but appealing, the furnishing is monastically spartan, the space minimal — the people and the paradise garden are exceptional.

rooms	Cottage for 1-2.
price	£200-£300 per week.
meals	Self-catering.
	Restaurants in Saintfield, 1.5km.
closed	Rarely.
directions	From Saintfield for Ballynahinch. After speed limit ends, left into Drumnaconnell Road; at scrapyard, left up lane behind; 1st house on right. (Owners will collect from station or airport.)

	Sally Taylor
tel	+44 (0)2897 510232
email	sally.taylor803@btopenworld.com
web	www.thehermitagecottage.com

Self-catering

Map 2 & 5 Entry 19

Dufferin Coaching Inn

33 High Street, Killyleagh, Co. Down BT30 9QF

The new owners of the Dufferin Inn, a well-travelled sister team, run it with fresh and friendly enthusiasm: they both love meeting new people. Rooms have been brightened up and the big new lounge is a summery festival of leaf green, yellow and wine-red round the wood-burning stove; breakfast is now prettily arranged in the light of the ground floor. Lush patchwork quilts on four-posters in wrought iron and wood make for colourful, tempting bedrooms, some big, others snugger. The light flows in through floral-framed windows over walls decked in William Morris onto superior pine furniture. The spotless bathrooms are big and square and… different, be it spriggy wallpaper, blood-red panelling or, in one case, the bath in the bedroom. This solid old former bank has a banqueting hall with licensed bar down below (the gents' is in the old strongroom) and, as well as tailored receptions, Leontine and Sabina are planning casino nights, Oktoberfest, murder mystery and private dinner parties. The Dufferin Arms next door has a lovely timeworn atmosphere, live music on Saturdays and excellent food.

rooms	6: 1 double, 1 twin, 4 four-posters.
price	£50-£70. Singles £35-£45. Low season reductions.
meals	Dinner at Dufferin Arms next door.
closed	Rarely.
directions	From Belfast A22 for Downpatrick to Saintfield; bear left to Killyleagh 18 miles; right at mural on wall, follow one-way system. Inn on left, 100 yds from castle.

Inn

	Leontine & Sabina Callow
tel	+44 (0)2844 821134
fax	+44 (0)2844 821102
email	info@dufferincoachinginn.com
web	www.dufferincoachinginn.com

Map 2 & 5 Entry 20

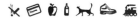

Strangford Cottage

41 Castle Street, Strangford, Co. Down BT30 7NF

Poised above the waters at the entrance to Lough Strangford, roses framing its Georgian windows, this is one of a glorious row of 200-year-old houses. Maureen matches her house: both are instantly friendly. Walls are hung with paintings, some of them hers; objects catch your eye at every glance; antique and modern sofas lounge by the fire in the guest sitting room; curtains fall luxuriously to the floor and all the bedrooms have windows to let the light in from the living, moving lough. In the big creamy-rich suite, two wicker armchairs turn their backs on the sumptuous mountain of a bed to contemplate that magical view. The period pink room has a collection of paintings and a claw-footed bath in the room, designer-fashion, backed by Maureen's plant mural, so what matter that your loo is across the landing? And the sun is always out in the third room, glowing in its citrus colours and vibrant hanging. Maureen is an attentive host: treats await you in your room and her refined breakfasts, in the pretty dining room or by the pond in the gorgeous walled garden, are out of this world.

rooms	3: 2 doubles, 1 suite.
price	£110-£140. Singles £75-£90. Advance booking advised.
meals	Choice in village.
closed	October-March except by arrangement.
directions	From Downpatrick A25 to Strangford 12 miles. House in village centre. Detailed directions given on booking.

Maureen Thornton

tel	+44 (0)2844 881208
fax	+44 (0)2844 881246
email	moethornton@hotmail.com

B&B

Map 2 & 5 Entry 21

The Narrows

8 Shore Road, Portaferry, Co. Down BT22 1JY

The new owners of this shoreside inn are aimiable, eager and very attentive. They plan to nurture the lean young reputation of The Narrows while adding a degree of cosiness that it definitely lacked. Two deep sofas in the little reception area are the first sign, the rich raspberry-fool and black of the restaurant are the second. There's a warm fire and thick tapestry curtains so you can linger over the mouth-watering dishes: "adding colour to the freshest fish and veg without disguising identity" is the chef's aim. The setting is beautiful, looking across a sliver of water to Strangford village opposite. Ferries chug to and fro and boats pass left and right, heading into deep ocean or returning to the calmer waters of the lough. Bedrooms are bright, modern, comfortable: magnolia-soft walls, low patchwork-quilted beds, coir matting, local art. The attic rooms are especially cosy and attractive. Children love the walled garden. The road that disappears on the other side leads down the coast through the unspoilt and almost French harbour village of Killough to the Mourne Mountains. Terrific.

rooms	13: 12 twins/doubles, 1 single.
price	From £90. Singles from £45-£70. Half-board £62.50 p.p.
meals	Lunch from £8. Dinner, à la carte, £18-£25.
closed	Rarely.
directions	From Belfast, A20 south for 28 miles to Portaferry. Inn on shore front.

Inn

Ian & Gillian Killan

tel	+44 (0)2842 728148
fax	+44 (0)2842 728105
email	info@narrows.co.uk
web	www.narrows.co.uk

Map 2 & 5 Entry 22

Barr Hall Barns
31 Barr Hall Road, Portaferry, Co. Down BT22 1RQ

If you drive along this shore when the tide is out you can watch the grey seals basking on the rocks like fat lazy bananas. It's a magical area, the rolling hills on one side of the water, the dark Mournes rising above the mist on the other, mostly owned by the National Trust. And Barr Hall Barns fit perfectly: stone and brick for the Barn and Cottage, limewash for the haybarn Loft with its floor-to-ceiling window and wow-provoking interior. The gracious, talented owners have converted these once tumbledown outhouses brilliantly and Maureen's creative flair and needlework skills are obvious: vibrant colours, a set of Russian dolls here, a quilt hanging over an internal balcony there. Quality counts too: open-plan kitchens with oil-fired Esse stoves, Le Creuset pots and sharp knives; soft-cushioned sitting areas warmed by cast-iron gas fires. Light pours in through well-placed windows onto original timbers and stonework, pale walls and good furniture. It is all clean-cut, vivid and welcoming, the communal garden, laundry and barbecues making the ideal final flourish.

rooms	Barn for 6-8 (1 double, 2 twins, 1 sofabed, 1 bath, 1 shower). Cottage for 4 (1 double, 1 twin, 1 bath). Loft for 2 (1 twin, 1 shower).
price	£200-£480 per week. Ask about short breaks (minimum 3 nights).
meals	Self-catering. Restaurants 3.5 miles.
closed	Rarely.
directions	Directions on booking.

	Dr Maureen Edmondson
tel	+44 (0)2842 729895
fax	+44 (0)2842 728053
email	info@barrhallbarns.com
web	www.barrhallbarns.com

Self-catering

Map 2 & 5 Entry 23

Ballymote House
Killough Road, Downpatrick, Co. Down BT30 8BJ

You may feel you have entered a whirlwind: let yourself be swept up by this vibrant young family. Nicola runs the place with gusto and seemingly boundless energy, poaching nectarines for breakfast one moment, conversing with great erudition the next, then out to feed the horses, dogs in tow. They run an insurance business here, too. A genuine no-frills, intelligent and organised family. Neither grand nor lowly, Ballymote stands in an undisturbed pocket of historic monuments, deserted beaches and rolling countryside. A short drive or bike ride leads to the dolmens, castles, healing wells and 10th-century churches left by earlier inhabitants. One of the area's first unfortified houses, this place has wonderful charm, its graceful 1730s Georgian looks framed by a fine park laid out by 19th-century plantsman George Carter. The sight of mature ash and sycamore lifts any morning. The house has natural style, hugely comfortable, easy country-house bedrooms, and there's an odd Landseer glass sculpture of two polar bears. Killough village is near, walks in the Mourne Mountains are stupendous.

rooms	3: 1 double, 1 single; 1 double with separate bath.
price	From £70. Singles from £40.
meals	Meals by arrangement. Pubs & restaurants 2 miles.
closed	23-30 December.
directions	From Downpatrick B176 for Killough; house 1 mile on left after town.

Country house

	James & Nicola Manningham-Buller
tel	+44 (0)2844 615500
fax	+44 (0)2844 612111
email	bandb@ballymotehouse.com
web	www.ballymotehouse.com

Map 2 & 5 Entry 24

The Carriage House

71 Main Street, Dundrum, Co. Down BT33 0LU

Maureen is the perfect host and her new-old house will seduce you with its redesigned interior and eclectic collection of furniture, art and animals. Delicate antique wardrobes mix easily with retro and modern pieces; lovely oils, prints, tapestries, carvings and, unforgettably, the life-size horse in the yard, decorate the uncluttered open space; a gang of quirky wooden parrots perches in the rubber plants trying to talk to the fat cat, the patient labrador or Humphrey the hedgehog as he strolls round Maureen's pretty walled garden, delighting her grandchildren. She has taste, a good eye, a huge heart, tends her guests as carefully as her window boxes and gives her modestly luxurious rooms the little extras that turn them into indulgent guest rooms. The gorgeously plump bed was made with the finest cotton sheets, its pillows piled high and soft, rather like the local mountains, all designed to counter any traffic nuisance (one room is at the back). And next morning, prepare for as dainty or as hearty a feast as you choose: spiced plums, just-made fruit salad, herby sausages, homemade scones.

rooms	3: 1 double, 2 twins/doubles.
price	£60. Singles £40.
meals	Buck's Head restaurant next door.
closed	Rarely.
directions	From Belfast A24 through Ballynahinch & Clough to Dundrum. House in village centre, painted rich blue, name etched in fanlight.

	Maureen Griffith
tel	+44 (0)2843 751635
email	inbox@carriagehousedundrum.com
web	www.carriagehousedundrum.com

B&B

Map 2 & 5 Entry 25

Newforge House

58 Newforge Road, Magheralin, Craigavon, Co. Armagh BT67 0QL

Beautifying, restoring, then inviting the world to share it is a splendid way to save an old family house. John's ancestors, who owned the local linen mill, built this elegantly generous mansion 200 years ago. After two years of deep and respectful restoration, he and Louise have hung up their tools, opened the door and put their creative talents at the service of people wanting gentle young style, lovely rooms and good fresh home-cooked food in season, be they independent travellers, wedding parties or business events. The Mathers love this house and its history, at every turn there's an old family photograph (don't miss the downstairs loo), a linen history memento, an original wall hanging. The blend of antique and modern gives the house easy charm, soft colours are mixed for serenity – peach, green, all the beiges -, perfect foils for the lustrous furniture. Superb modern bathrooms and IT connections are unobtrusive extras. You won't easily forget Louise's lilting Scottish accent or John's fine food. Nor his father's tireless pursuit of perfection outside: the formal garden is deservedly listed.

rooms	6: 3 twins/doubles, 2 doubles, 1 four-poster.
price	£100–£140. Singles £65–£90. Discounts groups & over 2 nights.
meals	Dinner £27.50 Tue to Sat. Give 24 hrs notice. Light supper Sun & Mon.
closed	Christmas & New Year.
directions	From Belfast M1 west, exit 9 for Lurgan 3 miles; in Magheralin left at Byrne's pub: Newforge Road 0.5 mile; 1st left after speed limit.

Country house

		The Mathers Family
tel		+44 (0)2892 611255
fax		+44 (0)2892 612823
email		enquiries@newforgehouse.com
web		www.newforgehouse.com

Map 2 & 5 Entry 26

Abocurragh

Letterbreen, Enniskillen, Co. Fermanagh BT74 9AG

Bernie is so open, thoughtful and dynamic, you will like her immediately. And find it impossible to believe she has three adult children. 15 years ago, the Mullallys built onto and over their original basic bungalow to produce this house, including the big flounced sitting room… and two extra rooms. So Bernie took up B&B and has loved it ever since. She still does a bit of midwifery but is ever making sure her pretty, pinky rooms are immaculate, the cushions just so, the water on the tray, the high-class showers sparkling. Good lighting is another caring detail, modern pine furniture adds to the cleancut feel, an old chest of drawers reminds you this is the country. Gerry runs the big farm, dashing on his quadbike from yard to field and occasionally dropping by to say a cheery hallo and grab a coffee: Abocurragh is busy living its productive life. The front 'pleasure garden' with its tinkling pond and prettiness is as carefully manicured as the house and on warm mornings you may even enjoy Bernie's delicious fresh-fruit breakfast starter on the terrace, otherwise in the shelter of the flowery conservatory.

rooms	3: 1 double, 2 family.
price	£50–€60. Singles £30–£35.
meals	Dinner £18. BYO wine.
closed	Rarely.
directions	From Enniskillen A4 for Sligo; through Letterbreen; 2 miles on, left at sign to end of road.

The Mullally Family

tel	+44 (0)2866 348484
fax	+44 (0)2866 348288
email	abocurragh@yahoo.com
web	www.abocurragh.com

B&B

Map 1 & 4 Entry 27

Old Glebe House

Killadeas, Irvinestown, Enniskillen, Co. Fermanagh BT94 1NZ

Climb the drive then look back: the old rectory stands on its own green hillock that falls down past rhododendrons, lilacs and fine trees to the busy-ish road and then, if it could, into Lough Erne – a commanding position and a lovely garden. Inside, Irene will greet you with anxious delight and show you into her very blue-carpeted drawing room full of colourful seats and intriguing treasures; the gilt mirrors are superb. Then up the gentle stairs, greeting Sir Walter Scott on the way, to either the beautifully-decorated four-poster room with its view of the lough – each item is luscious, the medallioned bed, the pale yellow and soft brown covers, the soft-stripe silk curtains, all on Irene's perfect choice of scorched-earth painted boards – or the very different, sober triple whose fine great inlaid mahogany bed stands like a throne before the same view. Next morning, the dining room's remarkably ornate Irish-Georgian antiques may grab all your attention but Irene teaches catering and knows about good breakfasts, so do concentrate. You will be well cared for.

rooms	2: 1 four-poster, 1 triple.
price	£50. Singles £30.
meals	Two restaurants within 0.5 miles.
closed	Christmas & New Year.
directions	From Enniskillen A32 for Omagh 3 miles; fork left B82 for Kesh 4 miles. In Killadeas, house on right on bend just past lay-by.

B&B

	Irene & Ronnie Chambers
tel	+44 (0)2868 621537

Map 1 & 4 Entry 28

Rossfad House

Killadeas, Ballinamallard, Co. Fermanagh BT94 2LS

Built in 1776, Georgian Rossfad stands on the shore of Lower Lough Erne in a lakeland fringed with forest, castle ruins and ancient monastic towers. The 1870s Victorian guest wing has its own entrance and bright sitting room, its south-facing bedrooms enjoying long views of the garden, the lake, the mountains beyond. Irish sport horses graze in rolling meadows, spring lambs kick their heels in daffodils beneath the stately oaks; later, azalea and rhododendron bloom joyously. Rooms are simply done but comfortable. Lois's lovely smile welcomes you. John and Lois's easy-going lifestyle immediately puts you at ease. Full of stories, she'll guide you to all Fermanagh's history and treasures: stately homes, scenery, the best sausages from Miss Northern Ireland – and Rossfad House. Breakfast lingers by the French windows, open on sunnier days, the lake view draws you out for a stroll, there are lots of books, comfy sofas and a log fire in winter. Croquet and badminton can be played in the garden. Swim in the lake if the mood takes you, or just sit and gaze over its intricate maze of islands.

rooms	2: 1 twin/double; 1 twin/double with separate bathroom.
price	From £50. Singles from £30.
meals	Restaurants in Enniskillen.
closed	December-March.
directions	From Enniskillen A32 for Omagh 3 miles; fork left B82 3 miles; avenue opp. road to Whitehill (look for trees at end of unsurfaced road to house). Don't go to Ballinamallard.

	John & Lois Williams
tel	+44 (0)2866 388505
fax	+44 (0)2866 388505
email	rossfadhouse@aol.com

Country house

Map 1 & 4 Entry 29

Grange Lodge Country House

7 Grange Road, Dungannon, Co. Tyrone BT71 7EJ

People come a long way for Norah's cooking: she writes in the local paper, gives popular 'Cook with Norah' classes, has added a second dining room to Grange Lodge. She and Ralph are efficient, natural hosts with Ralph front of house spinning yarns as he serves and Norah in the kitchen producing memorable food and winning hatfuls of awards. Many of her vegetables, herbs and fruit are home grown and served in season. After a dinner that would satisfy a giant, coffee is taken in the antique- and trinket-filled pale green and pink drawing room or, on wet, wintry evenings, around an open fire in the cosy 'den'. The bedrooms are all different with thick carpets, feminine frills, pot-pourri, more trinkets and ivy-clad windows. On its round knoll of manicured lawns beneath the giant chestnut tree, this proud old house has been extended ever since it was built in 1698; the result is a harmonious whole, although telltale floorboard creaks and ceilings that vary in height point to different eras. The breakfast special of porridge and Irish whiskey is astounding. *Children over 12 welcome.*

rooms	5: 3 doubles, 1 twin, 1 single.
price	£78. Singles £55-£59.
meals	Dinner from £26.
closed	Mid-December to 1 February.
directions	From M1 junc. 15, A29 for Armagh & Moy 1 mile; left at Grange Lodge sign then 1st right. House on right through white-walled entrance.

B&B

Norah & Ralph Brown

tel	+44 (0)2887 784212
fax	+44 (0)2887 784313
email	stay@grangelodgecountryhouse.com
web	www.grangelodgecountryhouse.com

Map 2 & 5 Entry 30

Carricklee House
Strabane, Co. Tyrone BT82 9SE

Come on a horse and put him to bed in supreme elegance in the listed stables. Between lyrical stable and solid-set manse your feet may be ambushed by friendly hounds, your ears by rowdy rooks: this is real country living. Now that only third-world labour is competitive, James may be the last of many Herdmans to have spun fine linen yarn at Sion Mills but the old grandeur lives on in this house. The great drawing room, decorated in the 1940s for his mother by the fashionable Lennigan & Morant team, is still remarkable in its ochre-brown walls, superb matching carpet with pinky bits, original chair coverings and an astonishing rococo filigree mirror which they gave the lady of the house to thank her for the contract. Penny is a lively, intelligent host who loves this house and its rambling garden, knows all the history and tells it well; James will fill in any gaps with his personal reminiscences, then get back to work. Deeply comfortable bedrooms – an orange half-tester in one, blue Jouy print in another, perfect little granny single – and always garden views. Ideal for Donegal sights, golf and fishing.

rooms	3: 1 double, 1 twin, 1 single, sharing 2 bathrooms.
price	£60-£80. Singles £40.
meals	Restaurant 2 miles.
closed	December-February; winter bookings by arrangement.
directions	From Strabane A5 for L'Derry; left at 2nd lights B85 for Clady 0.5 mile; fork left Carrick Avenue 500 yds; left Carricklee Road; 1st on right.

James & Penny Herdman

tel	+44 (0)2871 882205
fax	+44 (0)2871 884081
email	reservations@carricklee.com
web	www.carricklee.com

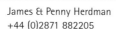

Country house

Map 1 Entry 31

Johnny's Cottage
Dunowen, Culdaff, Co. Donegal

The name is modest but there's nowhere in Ireland with more inventive style in so stunning a position. Standing on a hill in six acres of glorious country-house gardens, the cottage is a shining gem in the glittering crown of Donegal. After years of renovating for others, Chris seized the irresistible chance to convert a derelict 1820s stone cottage near his childhood home. He left the thickset cottage exterior, squat against the elements, deliberately low-key to make the inside all the more of an unexpected treat. Space, colour, tradition and contemporary design blend deliciously. A wall of windows frames the spectacular view of the sandy arc of Culdaff Bay. The kitchen is an ultra-modern mix of Muji and stainless steel, with sign-rolls from old buses for local history. The 'old kitchen' is totally authentic with turf fire, flagstones, an old Irish settle bed. Hear the sea in summer through open doors, or the blatter of rain in winter snug by a wood stove. There are fine woven fabrics, books, prints and paintings, a tiled open-plan shower, and… Book early to discover the rest yourself.

rooms	Cottage for 8 (1 double with bath, 1 double, 2 twins, family bathroom).
price	€1,400-€2,000 per week, plus heating & electricity.
meals	Self-catering.
closed	Rarely.
directions	Directions given on booking.

Self-catering

Chris Tinne
tel	+353 (0)7493 79510
email	christinne@dunowen.net
web	www.dunowen.net

Map 2 Entry 32

The Mill Restaurant

Figart, Dunfanaghy, Co. Donegal

Exposed to the mercurial Atlantic and enclosed by the Derryveagh Mountains and Mount Errigal, the hostile beauty of north-west Donegal is manna to the artist. Susan's grandfather, acclaimed watercolourist Frank Egginton, bought this 19th-century mill on the shores of New Lake in 1949. She and Derek have breathed new life into it, creating the B&B and a well-loved restaurant, aided and abetted by Frank's antiques and paintings that all flow beautifully from room to room. Derek cut his teeth on the prestige of Gleneagles in Scotland then returned happily to his native Donegal to cook with the fabulous local ingredients. Donegal lamb, oysters, duck, salmon, mussels – everything he uses is fresh. Susan, young, modest and wise, makes sure that guests and diners are well looked after. Pleasant bedrooms, some with sleigh beds or tapestries or Egginton paintings on the walls, have pretty tiled bathroom floors and lake views. By day, walk up Muckish Mountain or take a ferry to Tory Island where fishermen artists produce well-reputed works – or get your own paintbox out.

rooms	6: 4 doubles, 2 twins.
price	€90-€95.
meals	Dinner from €39. Restaurant closed on Mondays.
closed	Mid-December to mid-March. Weekdays in November, December & March-Easter.
directions	From Dunfanaghy N56 for Falcarragh past gallery on right, down small hill; entrance on right; house overlooks lake.

	Susan & Derek Alcorn
tel	+353 (0)7491 36985/6983
fax	+353 (0)7491 36985
email	info@themillrestaurant.com
web	www.themillrestaurant.com

Restaurant with rooms

Map 1 Entry 33

Ardroe Cottage
Portsalon, Fanad, Co. Donegal

Not only does it look like beloved great-granny's storybook cottage, it actually is Michael's 300-year-old ancestral home, and its renovation shows how much he and Margaret love it. The deep-country approach, the cobbled yard, half door and thatch outside, the amazing flagged floor inside, the open fire with its old cooking utensils (for you to use…) will transport you to never-neverland. Both living rooms are properly furnished with rustic antiques and old pottery pieces, red and white gingham giving the final cottagey flourish. It's a lesson in conservation: even light switches are hidden in old shelves in old walls. Upstairs, the enchantment is contained beneath pine-clad attic ceilings. One bedroom, on a raised wooden floor, has tiny eyes to the outside world, little windows dug deep in the gable ends, and soft cotton fabrics. The other has an old iron bedstead and larger windows. Through their arched doors, they are simple and inviting. Add a lovely tree-sheltered garden, Portsalon's fine beach, endless wonderful walks and Rathmullan House for an evening treat and you have perfect seclusion and rest.

rooms	Cottage for 4 (2 doubles, 1 shower).
price	€350–€580 per week.
meals	Self-catering.
	Restaurants in Portsalon, 3km.
closed	Rarely.
directions	Directions given on booking.

Self-catering

Michael & Margaret McElwee
tel	+353 (0)7491 22267
mobile	+353 (0)87 292 2499
email	enquiries@donegalholiday.com
web	www.donegalholiday.com

Map 1 Entry 34

Rathmullan House

Rathmullan (Lough Swilly), Co. Donegal

What a place! Always a step ahead: one bedroom has its own dog room. Despite expansion the four younger Wheelers, producing their own next generation, work to maintain the homely, family feel that their parents created and there are so many elegant sitting rooms inside, such lovely grounds to roam outside, that numbers may only be evident at breakfast. Rathmullan already had its fine Georgian looks, the same lively, friendly welcome, gardens that roll gently down to the spectacular shores of Lough Swilly and comforting fires. All different shapes, the richly-furnished new rooms overlook the garden through superb tall windows onto balconies or little terraces and have big panelled bathrooms. The tent-like canopied restaurant is well reputed and readers say the local salmon and lamb are superb. Work up an appetite at tennis or croquet, in the indoor heated swimming pool or the steamroom, stroll across the lawn and through the dunes to a long empty beach, or sally forth to explore the rocky coves of the Fanad Peninsula or Rathmullan village: it has bags of seaside charm. *Tennis on site.*

rooms	32 twins/doubles.
price	€170–€270. Singles €85–€135.
meals	Dinner €45–€50.
closed	Christmas; mid-January to mid-February.
directions	From Letterkenny R245 through Ra(th)melton to Rathmullan. Left in village at sign to hotel; gates on right, through holiday park to house.

The Wheeler Family

tel	+353 (0)7491 58188
fax	+353 (0)7491 58200
email	info@rathmullanhouse.com
web	www.rathmullanhouse.com

Hotel

Map 1 Entry 35

Frewin
Ramelton, Co. Donegal

Friendly and amusing, Thomas and Regina have taken Irish hospitality to a new level in their relaxed, book-glorious, historic home. The Victorian part was a rectory but the fortified annexe dates from 1698 when landowners needed protection from the odd bloody uprising. Thomas, a keen antiques collector and restorer of historic buildings, uncovered a curious family link: his great-aunt Susan, a servant girl here before the Great War, had carved her name on the back of a bedroom cupboard; he has made a small museum in her honour next to the antique shop in the courtyard. Hear his boxing gloves tale over a nightcap by the fire in the library, among antique lithographs and old *Vanity Fair* cartoons. The bedrooms, elegant and uncluttered with big bathrooms and woodland views, are the kind you never want to leave; the small green suite has its own library, a perfect writer's retreat. Regina will cook dinner for groups, served in the elegant buxom dining room – old crockery and silver beneath a chandelier of real candles. Ramelton, gateway to the lovely Fanad Peninsula, is a timeless place.

rooms	4 + 1: 3 suites; 1 double with separate bath. Cottage for 2.
price	€120-€180. Singles €70-€90. Cottage €450-€550 per week.
meals	Dinner €40, by arrangement. Restaurant within walking distance.
closed	Christmas week.
directions	From Letterkenny R245 to Ramelton 13km. Approaching Ramelton, right at speed limits; 300m on right.

B&B & Self-catering

Thomas & Regina Coyle

tel	+353 (0)7491 51246
fax	+353 (0)7491 51246
email	flaxmill@indigo.ie
web	www.accommodationdonegal.net

Map 1 Entry 36

Termon House, Dungloe, Co. Donegal

Contact: 25 Eustace Street, Temple Bar, Dublin 2

Down on the wild spectacular coast, far from modern mores (no telephone, no telly), where only water, wind and birds live, sea storms have accompanied Termon's human storms for centuries, there are rumours of a ghost. Built for a 19th-century rent collector with the stones of eviction victims' cottages, it has been faithfully renovated by Irish Landmark — limed walls, old quarry-tile or plank floors, open fireplaces — and wonderfully furnished with the right country antiques, lovely rugs on wood, strong-toned fabrics, painted tongue-and-groove bathrooms, one with a delightful free-standing tub, and proper old iron bedsteads (with modern mattresses, of course). The kitchen has the same timeless feel: a Belfast sink, a Stanley range, a dresser with blue-and-white china. The house is sheltered by a Famine Relief Wall built of beach pebbles in 1840-1850 by the stricken population in return for a shilling and a bag of meal. The sombre past is recognised but this restoration brings new life, colour and light to a remarkable spot on the Donegal shore. Fabulous walks beckon from the front door.

rooms	House for 7 (1 suite for 5, 1 double, 1 bath, 1 shower).
price	€1,379-€1,820 per week. Weekend & mid-week terms possible.
meals	Self-catering.
closed	Never.
directions	Directions given on booking.

	The Irish Landmark Trust
tel	+353 (0)1 670 4733
fax	+353 (0)1 670 4887
email	bookings@irishlandmark.com
web	www.irishlandmark.com

Self-catering

Map 1 Entry 37

Ardbeg House
14 Church Lane, Letterkenny, Co. Donegal

What could be better for a town and country holiday than this neat little Victorian terraced house in a quiet street in bustling Letterkenny? The wild and watery secrets of glorious Donegal start just down the road. Shops, pubs, restaurants and entertainments are here at your doorstep when you return from your day's exploring. Or you can do your own barbecue in the privacy of the patio. The delightful old house has been lovingly renovated with deep respect for its origins – admire the stained-glass door panels and the turned timber staircase – and is now in impeccable, freshly furnished condition: pine, leather, wicker and sheepskin marry well. Modern life does not lose out: you will find a fully equipped kitchen and utility room and gleaming new bathrooms. Crisp white sheets, soft towels and thoughtful extras such as homemade jams and fuel for the fire are provided by the owners who live conveniently next door. Letterkenny, Donegal's largest town, is growing in sophistication as well as size and its Erngal Arts festival in July is becoming quite an attraction. And there's space for the car.

Self-catering

rooms	House for 4 (2 doubles; 2 showers, 1 bath).
price	€700-€750 per week.
meals	Self-catering. Restaurants & pubs within walking distance.
closed	Rarely.
directions	From N13 or N56 turn for town centre; up main street; right into Church Lane. No 14 has blue door.

	Michael & Margaret McElwee
tel	+353 (0)7491 22267
mobile	+353 (0)87 292 2499
email	enquiries@donegalholiday.com
web	www.donegalholiday.com

Map 1 Entry 38

Mount Royd Country House

Carrigans, Co. Donegal

Jo's is an open, comfortable and friendly house. She will gather you in, pour you refreshing tea by the fire and entertain you with all you might want to know about the village, the area (Agatha Christie wrote thrillers on the hill opposite), the country past and present: she has won acres of awards for her landladying talents. Her cluttered living room juggles mementoes of the many visitors and every available space has a knick or a knack. The house was built as a farmhouse by one man in the 1940s, it took him four years. Today, creeper softens the edges and curious garden ornaments decorate the front. Don't be alarmed when you enter your boudoir bedroom: the teddy bears will not rush out to hug you nor the porcelain dolls seize you in a crazy waltz; they are simply part of the homely atmosphere, along with Jo's personal mixture of warm bright wallpapers, the fresh flowers she puts in all the rooms and the Jacob sheep grazing happily in the field. The village is proud of Monaragh Presbyterian Church, one of the oldest in Ireland. Jo is unusual in particularly welcoming single guests. Excellent value.

rooms	4: 2 doubles, 1 twin, 1 triple; extra bath.
price	From €65. Singles €35.
meals	Roadside diner 1 mile; restaurants 5 miles.
closed	Rarely.
directions	From Letterkenny N13/N14 16km; left R236 to Carrigans then A40 for Londonderry. House signposted on right on leaving village.

	Josephine Martin
tel	+353 (0)7491 40163
fax	+353 (0)7491 40400
email	jmartin@mountroyd.com
web	www.mountroyd.com

Country house

Map 1 Entry 39

Gorm Wagon
Bally-by-the-Waye, Co. Donegal

Wispie's old blue wagon ('gorm' means blue in Gaelic) is the perfect holiday home for green-minded urbanites, so simple you'd call it basic, so genuine you'll wonder why on earth you went to the rainforest for authenticity. It will carry you to a purer life. But to be carried you must first catch your fuel, Capall Meidhreach, one of the renowned Irish Mountain Ponies. He is strong and spirited, it's just a question of harnessing that strength and spirit for your purposes – not his. At night, let him out to graze in a sheltered spot as the wild mountain wind tends to make him frisky and he leaps around (his second name means frolicsome), taking your pursuit for a Great Game. Then the roaming sheep of Ireland dash down the hillside to join in and you are stuck for the day watching the herding demonstration of these 'domestic' animals; not quite the Folies Bergères, despite the name. Sleep under old-Irish horse blankets – there's nothing warmer or more aromatic, any sinus problems will be cleared in one night – and breakfast on fresh ewe's milk, if you can hold her down long enough.

Hovel

rooms	Just one double. Open-air washing & wc to be re-invented each day.
price	1 bale per 10 miles.
meals	Gather-your-own (ingredients and cooking fuel).
closed	In deeper-than-axle mud.
directions	Round the next bend.

Wispie Hayseed
tel   +353 (0)1234 56789
email hayseed@wisp.ie
web   www.ruttenwheel.bog

Map 0 Entry 40

The Green Gate
Ardvally, Ardara, Co. Donegal

Rabbits mow the lawn, birds vacuum the stone table, the sea pounds at the cliffs below and Paul revels in his windswept eyrie, the light of the sky, the wild life. He is the most un-Parisian of exiles, the most unlikely of adopted Irishmen, but his bookish leanings and many travels are revealed by his fireside when he tells the journey of a city intellectual into deepest Donegal. The compact cottage is big enough for Paul, his few treasures, his many friends and his all-ears guests – as well as an incredible number of homemade preserves and the lampshades made from mother-of-pearl that his son dived for off Corsica. Bedrooms are in low-slung converted cowsheds clustered round the cottage: stone, thatch and slate keep the elements out, beams and pine slatting, warm rugs and new tweed curtains, woven bedcovers, the odd country antique or unexpected French piece, brown water in the taps, hangers on hooks for a few clothes all create a simple, no-frills effect, a million miles from the American way of life. Dutch guests love his 'Swiss' coffee: go with an open mind, not a Bentley. *Smokers welcome.*

rooms	4 doubles.
price	€90–€110. Singles from €70.
meals	Pubs & restaurants in Ardara, 5-minute drive.
closed	Never.
directions	From Ardara for Donegal 200m; right up winding lane for about 1.5km following Green Gate signs.

	Paul Chatenoud	
tel	+353 (0)7495 41546	B&B
mobile	+353 (0)87 05 75748	
web	www.thegreengate-ireland.com	

Map 1 Entry 41

Cranny Manor
Inver, Co. Donegal

In this good old house with its graceful garden running down to the River Eany, you will be treated to tea, homemade cakes and wonderful chat. Emily and Dennis, who is American, 'came home' seven years ago to take over her mother's B&B (at 95, Mother still holds court) in her 150-year-old land steward's house. They completely refurbished the manor and bring a certain American shine to their hospitality: enormous care and attention, lots of floral bits, every treat possible in the traditional country-house bathrooms (lotions, potions, candles and matches and… rennies, in case you'd forgotten them, too). One double room has a jacuzzi bath, all have a lacey look and masses of homely touches against soft colours. They invite you to let go and sink in. Guests have the use of a large comfortable sitting area, newly done in old style, the breakfast room with big windows down to the river – the views alone are worth the trip – and, rather amazingly, a drinks room. All spick, span and gleaming. Emily's friendly presence and remarkable attention to detail will make your stay unforgettable.

rooms	4: 2 doubles, 2 suites for 3.
price	€80–€100. Singles €40–€65.
meals	Pub 1.5km; Castle Murray Hotel 5km; Donegal 17km.
closed	November–March.
directions	From Donegal N56 for Killybegs to Inver Bridge; left before bridge 0.5km; right at sign.

Country house

	Dennis & Emily Dolan
tel	+353 (0)7497 36010
mobile	+353 (0)86 151 3803
email	crannymanor@eircom.net
web	www.crannymanor.com

Map 1 Entry 42

Castle Murray House Hotel & Restaurant
St John's Point, Dunkineely, Co. Donegal

As far as castles go, there's the ruin of MacSwyne's castle down on the shore… but this house is simply the Murrays' old farmhouse – a warren with a big modern face on the front. Professionally, Marguerite grew up here: at 16 she was training under the previous French chef, went away to learn more and came back to buy it. Young, dynamic and unpretentious, she still works with current chef Rémy in the kitchen, to superb effect on your taste buds; does all the interior design; and welcomes house and restaurant guests with equal warmth. Three dining areas slalom through the long stone-floored conservatory and you eat virtually out of doors in billows of light. Upstairs, where nearly all rooms have a view of the scintillating bay, Marguerite has let loose her decorating versatility. Rooms are light, colourful and all different: Celtic (bits from the Book of Kells), Fairies (Victorian storybook illustrations), African (atmospherically soft brown, ivory and white), Laura Ashley (thick cream and charcoal), the honeymoon bed in rich warm purple and gold,… But leave plenty of time for their renowned food.

rooms	10: 6 doubles, 3 twins, 1 family.
price	€120-€150. Singles €79-€85.
meals	Lunch €27. Dinner €48.
closed	Mid-January to mid-February; Mondays & Tuesdays in winter.
directions	From Donegal N56 for Killybegs 25.5km; just past Dunkineely, left at sign, hotel 1.5km on left.

Martin & Marguerite Howley
tel   +353 (0)7497 37022
fax   +353 (0)7497 37330
email info@castlemurray.com
web   www.castlemurray.com

Hotel

Map 1 Entry 43

Co. Donegal

Bruckless House

Bruckless, Dunkineely, Co. Donegal

Bruckless revels in peace and the subtlest sea light, the gardens bordering the estuary add charm and a sense of freedom: life is exceedingly mellow in this handsome old 'grange' farmhouse. It has a faded, lived-in Georgian elegance and Joan and Clive are a delightful couple to spend time with. They are the leading breeders of Connemara ponies in the north-west with 20 acres of stud farm. On good days, they harness a pony to their 1890 Limerick gig and trot off down to St John's Point. The tall graceful reception rooms are filled with lovely things from their years in the East: brush-stroke paintings from China, beautiful rugs, a gorgeous rosewood table. Some finds are more local, such as the Irish oak sideboard, deeply carved with fish and gargoyles, that Joan restored after discovering it in a peat store. Comparatively unadorned family-feel bedrooms overlook the original cobbled courtyard. Joan's pride is the garden, a neat-wild mixture of lawn, flower bed, rockery and woodland where paths meander through mossy glades past bluebells and montbretia to the quayside by a tiny sea inlet.

B&B & Self-catering

rooms	4 + 1: 1 double, 1 twin, both en suite; 2 singles, sharing bathroom. Cottage for 4.
price	€100-€120. Cottage €230-€500 per week.
meals	Restaurant 1 mile.
closed	October-March.
directions	From Donegal N56 for Killybegs 19km & through Dunkineely. House signposted on left after 3km.

	Joan & Clive Evans
tel	+353 (0)7497 37071
fax	+353 (0)7497 37070
email	bruc@bruckless.com
web	www.bruckless.com

Map 1 Entry 44

Coxtown Manor
Laghey, Co. Donegal

Relaxed and amiable, a food and decorating enthusiast, Eduard came from Belgium to turn a drab Georgian manor into a popular and highly original Donegal getaway. Owned by Hamiltons from 1750 until 'Miss Sheila' died in 1992, it oozes history. To avoid any intimidations of grandeur, Eduard combines original wallpaper with continental antiques, minimalist Belgian art with tapestries and a sleek black piano. Also, lots of corners for chilling out in the main sitting room and a fine stone fireplace in the cosy bar. Bedrooms come in two styles: grand in the main house with old furniture, lots of space and open fires; contemporary in the coach house, also very generous, with power showers and more modern Belgian art. Luxury soaps for all and DVDs for the top rooms. But the restaurant is Coxtown's heart. A great chef, Eduard uses the freshest produce in a few beautifully cooked and presented dishes followed, for example, by mousse made with real Belgian chocolate or his own ice cream. Genuine free-range hens fed on gourmet scraps give the most wonderful eggs: Belgian breakfast is a must.

rooms	9: 3 doubles, 1 single. Coach House: 5 doubles.
price	€130; €170 Saturdays. Singles €70-€125.
meals	Dinner à la carte, €20-€45 (not Mondays).
closed	November to mid-February except Christmas & New Year.
directions	From Donegal N15 for Ballyshannon 11km; left on old Ballintra road 3km; house on right.

	Eduard Dewael
tel	+353 (0)7497 34575
fax	+353 (0)7497 34576
email	coxtownmanor@oddpost.com
web	www.coxtownmanor.com

Country house

Map 1 Entry 45

Portnason House

Portnason, Ballyshannon, Co. Donegal

Irish Georgian Portnason is Madge's striking re-creation, her flair aided by excellent proportions. The sense of history is enchanting and clever use of pin-striped wallpaper and soft colours, as well as Georgian furniture, sink-into sofas, a fine piano and elegant crockery, give the house a curiously pleasant colonial club feel. The big bedroom was the ballroom, shades of twirling uniforms and gowns will lull you; ponies graze on the old parade ground; the ghostly outline of a century-old tennis court fits well. Up the mulberry staircase, bedrooms have pitch-pine floors, fireplaces, wicker furniture, dhurries and big cotton-quilted brass beds. The Georgian appetite for space and light is evident, windows reveal the Erne estuary, where the Portnason heronry flourishes, the sunset over Horseshoe Mountain and miles of sandy beaches at Tullan Strand, accessible on foot or on horseback, the choice is yours. Guests' steeds are welcome and you all muck in with Madge's ubiquitous dogs. Or you can launch a dinghy from the private jetty and sail off to picnic in the sand dunes. The options are endless.

rooms	5: 3 doubles, 2 twins.
price	€150-€160. Singles from €90.
meals	Restaurants within 2 miles. Packed lunches for walkers.
closed	Rarely. Advance booking essential October-March.
directions	From Donegal N15 to Ballyshannon; through town, over bridge, right at r'bout for Sligo. Entrance on right down tree-lined avenue by stone gate lodge.

Country house

	Madge Sharkey
tel	+353 (0)7198 52016
fax	+353 (0)7198 52016
email	portnasonhouse@gmail.com
web	www.portnasonhouse.com

Map 1 & 4 Entry 46

Castle Leslie
Glaslough, Monaghan, Co. Monaghan

Ah! Castle Leslie, the crazy stories, the serenity, the inimitable rooms, the heart-lifting humour. Strong and fearless with a huge sense of fun like all the artistic, eccentric Leslies, Sammy now runs the family home, its theatrical dining hall, its living museum of a drawing room where a million cameos, fine antiques, heaps of Churchilliana (they are related) and ramshackle mementoes live in fading grandeur with yards of well-talked sofas and the vast lake view. And as she only employs humorous, intelligent staff, a sense of purposeful joy hovers over all. Up the great stairs, past the Leslie busts, bedrooms big and small burst with flair and individuality. Food is vital: top-class gastronomy by Noel McMeel (yes) on the Castle's fine white linen, good country fare at the Lodge. The simpler family-friendly Lodge has been smartened up: bring children, horses, rods and discover the wonderful Leslie estate. Informal-grand, funky, enchanting – an unforgettable experience. Riding centre and cookery school, too. *Castle unsuitable for children. Exclusive bookings possible.*

rooms	50 + 12: Castle: 19 doubles, 1 twin. Lodge: 10 doubles, 20 family. 12 cottages for 8-10.
price	€210-€390. Singles €160-€250. Lodge from €190. Singles from €140. Cottages €800-€1200 p.w.
meals	Dinner: Castle €52, Lodge from €45. Lunch: Lodge €22, Long Gallery à la carte.
closed	Rarely.
directions	From Monaghan for Armagh onto N12; left R185 to end of Glaslough.

Samantha Leslie
tel   +353 (0)47 88100
fax   +353 (0)47 88256
email info@castleleslie.com
web   www.castleleslie.com

Hotel & **Self-catering**

Map 2 & 5 Entry 47

Hilton Park
Clones, Co. Monaghan

Hilton Park is a stunning one-off, a majestic building in beautiful grounds that has been in the same family since it was built in 1734. The setting has something of an 18th-century Gainsborough and since this most imposing country house lies in a less-visited part of Ireland its original spirit remains intact. Johnny deserves much of the credit for this, steadfastly refusing to turn the family pile into a theme park and taking huge care of wildlife habitats and woodland (pine martens have even returned, a triumph). Walk the estate and see why he's holding on. Explore the biodynamic kitchen garden where Lucy grows for the table – and maybe for her next book. She already has *Potatoes* and *Squashes* on the shelves. They are a strong intelligent couple. Dine before an incomparable view that stretches across formal gardens and mature parkland to a lake where the evening sun glints. The two master bedrooms are fabulous; faded grandeur and the odd heirloom lend charm to the others. Lounge in splendid decadence and let Hilton Park cast its spell. There's nowhere quite like it. *Children over eight welcome.*

rooms	6: 3 doubles, 1 twin, 2 family.
price	€220–€300. Singles €150–€190.
meals	Dinner €55 (Friday & Saturday only). Wine from €20.
closed	October–March, except to groups.
directions	From Clones for Scotshouse 3 miles: gates on right.

Country house

Johnny & Lucy Madden

tel	+353 (0)47 56007
fax	+353 (0)47 56033
email	mail@hiltonpark.ie
web	www.hiltonpark.ie

Map 1 & 4 Entry 48

Rockwood House

Cloverhill, Belturbet, Co. Cavan

Its myriad lakes make County Cavan one of Ireland's best kept 'secrets', a mecca for fishermen and a place of limpid peace for all. Two enthusiastic Westies greet your arrival at Rockwood, with Susan and Jim not far behind. If the weather's good, you will be drinking tea on a sunlit patio before long, chatting away, surrounded by peaceful woodland. A gate leads from the garden to a wood where red squirrel and pine marten can be seen, and often lots of other wildlife. Susan and Jim, a quiet, friendly and unassuming couple, enjoy their home comforts, such as fires in the cosy sitting room on chilly, winter days. They designed the house themselves, knocking down an old building and using the stone to make raised terraces in the garden. The bedrooms are a touch spartan but everything looks sparkling brand new, with carpeted floors, matching pastel blue and yellow interiors and smellies in the bathrooms. The attractive conservatory-style breakfast room, decorated with Jim's Japanese carved animals, looks onto the garden. Very much a B&B, Rockwood is really good value in a friendly home.

rooms	4: 2 doubles, 2 twins.
price	€64. Singles €40.
meals	Restaurant 300m, pub 3km.
closed	Mid-December to end January.
directions	From Cavan N3 for Monaghan 6.5km; bear right at sign for Monaghan & Butlersbridge onto N54; house 3km on left.

Susan & Jim McCauley

tel	+353 (0)47 55351
fax	+353 (0)47 55373
email	jbmac@eircom.net

B&B

Map 1 & 4 Entry 49

Connacht

Ardtarmon House
Ballinfull, Co. Sligo

Sunset can bring those unusual 19th-century forms to glowing life and, beyond them, the magical mountains of four counties. The views are magnetic, on a clear day the eye travels 60 miles out to sea, sand and crashing surf are a short walk. Amazingly, Ardtarmon started as a thatched cottage. The Henry family's home since an ancestor bought it in 1852, it grew to country house stature a century ago, the 'cloud-shrouded' top being familiarly known as the cosmos, and you sense venerability as you walk through the door. Family oils and antiques, each with its story, lend warmth and personality to the main rooms; bedrooms, big and country-housey, give onto gardens, a labyrinth of walls, tangled orchards, Lady Pig and Jersey Cow grazing, and a giant cedar with a treehouse. Charles and Christa, a delightful, genuine couple, are bringing up their young family in this place of peace and environmental friendship. Charles's hearty cooking is served in the dining room as it ripples with more glorious sunset gold. Really good value – and Yeats all around you. *The simpler cottages are family comfortable.*

rooms	4 + 5: 3 doubles, 1 family. 5 cottages for 2-6.
price	€74-€100. Singles €52-€65. Cottages €145-€550 per week.
meals	Dinner €28.
closed	Christmas & New Year.
directions	From Sligo N15 for Donegal 8km to Drumcliffe; left for Carney 1.5km. In village, follow signs to Raghley 7km; left at Dunleavy's shop 2.5km; gate lodge & drive on left.

Country house & Self-catering

Charles & Christa Henry
tel +353 (0)71 916 3156
fax +353 (0)71 916 3156
email enquiries@ardtarmon.com
web www.ardtarmon.com

Map 1 & 4 Entry 50

The Old Rectory
Easkey, Co. Sligo

Though Robert and Lorely would call themselves designers, the Old Rectory is somehow a 'work of art'. There's nothing flash about this 1790s house, they have simply brought its warm comforting shapes to life with their vibrant colour sense and family furniture – plus heaps of drawings, paintings, books and china. The courtyard has tangled climbing roses and hurricane lamps – an ideal sun trap for tea and talk. The magical walled garden shelters fuchsias, exotic palms, vast fruit trees, a young orchard, a family-laid cobbled path and a formal kitchen garden. Starry ceilings twinkle over Lorely's imaginative and lovely rooms, their gold curtains, painted shutters and stencilled walls. Views of the River Easkey and the village church are memorable and the beach is world-renowned for surfing. It's a down-to-earth family home with dozy cats and friendly dogs at breakfast in the Aga-warm kitchen, strutting hens, munching sheep and two mellow donkeys outside. Lorely and Robert are easy folk to be with, friendly, creative and devoted to the little paradise they've built together.

rooms	3: 2 doubles, 1 family, sharing bathroom & shower room.
price	From €80–€90. Singles from €55.
meals	Restaurants in Easkey & Enniscrone.
closed	Christmas & New Year.
directions	From Dublin for Sligo; leave N4 dual carriageway at Coloomey to Ballisadare; before bridge left N59 for Ballina to Dromore West; right for Easkey 6km; house next to church.

Robert & Lorely Forrester
tel   +353 (0)96 49181
email   easkey14@eircom.net

B&B

Map 3 Entry 51

Temple House
Ballinacarrow, Ballymote, Co. Sligo

The gardens rolling down to the lake past some very special trees and the ruins of three earlier Temple Houses – medieval, Tudor, Jacobean – announce rich history. The looming bulk of the present house, built in 1864 by the 'Chinaman' ancestor (he made fortunes out east), reveals grandeurs galore in the most welcoming family atmosphere you can imagine, aristocratic relations gazing down on plastic tricycles in the monumental hall, tall morning-room windows sporting gorgeous pink velvet against cream furnishings. The very light is warmly gracious. After that echoing hall where a hundred could waltz, the 'Half-Acre' bedroom confirms the scale: fifty more could shimmy among the antique beds. Other rooms, though less vast, all bask in this old-fashioned ease, ideally partnered by revamped bathrooms. Roderick and Helena really enjoy their guests, their young children fill the house with youthful laughter and enthusiasm; these natural, unpretentious people wear their treasures lightly, farm carefully and organise winter shoots in this Special Conservation Area. An exceptional experience.

rooms	6: 2 doubles, 1 twin, 2 family suites; 1 family with separate shower.
price	€160-€190. Singles from €105.
meals	Dinner €42. High tea for under 5s at 6pm.
closed	December-March.
directions	From Sligo N4 for Dublin then N17 for Galway. House signposted left 0.5km south of Ballinacarrow.

Country house

	Roderick & Helena Perceval
tel	+353 (0)71 918 3329
fax	+353 (0)71 918 3808
email	enquiry@templehouse.ie
web	www.templehouse.ie

Map 1 & 4 Entry 52

Coopershill House
Riverstown, Co. Sligo

Coopershill is out of this world. The long drive winds through beautiful parkland to formal gardens where a muster of peacocks roams resplendent and you may glimpse Brian mowing in baggy corduroys. The house is one of the most handsome and distinguished examples of Irish Georgian. Despite these fine looks, the welcome couldn't be warmer: this is a well-loved home buzzing with activity, not a grand hotel. Brian and Lindy greet you with friendly smiles before inviting you into the awesome stone-floored hall. Pause a moment and look up at the flags, the stags, the marble figurines, the old parchment map of Ireland. That's just the hall! There are ancestors, antlers and antiques everywhere, fresh flowers and a chaise longue in every room, amazing high old beds with oh-so-fitting sheets, blankets and eiderdowns. Top-floor bedrooms look over copper beech and croquet lawn to the River Unsin and the four-poster room with huge corner windows is stunning. Great bathrooms, too: the 1900s canopied bath in its green-tiled grotto will knock your socks off. Penny Parrott roams around but only talks when alone. *Tennis on site.*

rooms	8: 4 doubles, 1 twin, 2 four-posters; 1 double with separate bathroom.
price	€208–€258. Singles €134–€159. Whole house €6,000 per week.
meals	Dinner, 5 courses, €55.
closed	November–March.
directions	From Sligo N4 for Dublin 17km to Drumfin x-roads. Left for Coopershill; entrance on left after 2km, before sharp turn.

	Brian, Lindy & Simon O'Hara
tel	+353 (0)71 916 5108
fax	+353 (0)71 916 5466
email	ohara@coopershill.com
web	www.coopershill.com

Country house

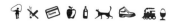

Map 1 & 4 Entry 53

Ross House

Ross, Riverstown, Co. Sligo

Genuine working farmers who finally decided to retire, Nicholas and Oriel are as natural and relaxed as their surroundings of cow pastures and the mellifluous sounds of nature. Both are infectious smilers who rejoice in life, obviously fascinated by the people with whom they travel the world from their plain snug little sitting room. "One day we had a Tongan, a St Lucian and two Indians," said Nicholas with amazement. They were made for B&B, it's hard to believe they only planned to do one year when they started… over 30 years ago. Their 1890s farmhouse has always been in Oriel's family, it feels warm, lived-in, loved-in. Enter through the flower-decked porch to discover a thoroughly down-to-earth, unpretentious family house. Bedrooms are light and palely decorated, nothing superfluous but the occasional fine old piece: the Gravett and Taylor armchair in the family room is enchanting, another has a stylish curvy daybed. Nearby lie the unsung archæological site of Carrowkeel with its elaborate passage tombs and the history of farm life in Sligo Folk Park. Unaffected peace on a proper Irish farm.

rooms	5: 1 twin, 3 family; 1 double with separate bathroom.
price	€80-€90. Singles from €40.
meals	Dinner €27. BYO wine. Packed lunch on request.
closed	Rarely.
directions	From Sligo N4 for Dublin to Drumfin 17km; left to Riverstown; follow signs in village for about 1.5km; house on left.

B&B

Oriel & Nicholas Hill-Wilkinson

tel	+353 (0)71 916 5787/5140
fax	+353 (0)71 916 5140
web	www.rossfarmhouse.com

Map 1 & 4 Entry 54

Cromleach Lodge
Castlebaldwin (via Boyle), Co. Sligo

Nothing is restrained here: the welcome is fulsome, the décor plusher than plush, the views spectacular and the food unforgettably epicurean. You have stylish uniformed staff at the marble counter, stitched quilts as thick as your thumbs, brocades and acres of carpet and, Nature's gift, views of Lough Arrow and beyond to Carrowkeel that can only be described as knock-out, framed by lavish ruched pelmets over huge windows. Better to be on the inside looking out. Bedrooms are pretty big and have some stunning decorative elements: loads of pictures (Victorian girls with velvet puppies…), bits of brass, glass and china, and plump frilly hearts on the doors. But let's not forget that people come a long way just for Moira's cooking. Locally-born and bred, easy, friendly and highly professional, she and Christy are turning Cromleach Lodge into a serious eating and meeting centre. A huge new restaurant with a keen new chef is under way, plus bars for all-day service and a vast reception room. There's a woodland walk, the lakeside is beautiful and don't miss the megalithic cairn tombs at Carrowkeel.

rooms	10 family rooms.
price	€252-€332.
meals	Dinner, à la carte, about €50. Tasting menu (8 dishes) €65.
closed	2 weeks in November.
directions	From Sligo N4 27km to Castlebaldwin; left at sign & follow signs 6km.

	Christy & Moira Tighe
tel	+353 (0)71 916 5155
fax	+353 (0)71 916 5455
email	info@cromleach.com
web	www.cromleach.com

Hotel

Map 1 & 4 Entry 55

Kingsfort Country House
Ballintogher, Co. Sligo

You can imagine the clergyman-magistrate who built Kingsfort in 1800, stoutly ensconced in his courtroom at the heart of village life. It is solid, quiet, deeply attractive and its eager new French owners, a partnership of three, have renovated the whole place with a gentle, harmonious, French touch. Bedrooms are lovely in soft cream and buff with accents of colour, good plain fabrics, wooden furniture and spanking modern bathrooms. The two in the main house are reminiscent of childhood holidays at Great-Aunt Maud's: low windows under eaves, ceilings high into the roof space, timber floors, cossetting. Across the yard in the outbuildings are six more pale and comfortable rooms: three give onto the outdoor sitting area, three outside staircases have their own tiny balconies. The same fresh smart look graces the reception areas where clever use of small spaces has magicked a conservatory-like hall/salon, a cosy sitting room round the fireplace, a tiny telly room and a light airy dining room. French chef Laurent's cooking should be worth the detour and the charming owners organise visits and tours.

rooms	8: 1 double, 6 twins/doubles, 1 family.
price	€90–€160. Discounts for 2 nights or more.
meals	Dinner, 4 courses, €40.
closed	Rarely.
directions	From Sligo N4 south 3km to Carrowmore r'bout; R287 for Dromahair 10km then to Ballintogher. House in village centre.

Country house hotel

Corine Ledanois

tel	+353 (0)71 911 5111
fax	+353 (0)71 911 5979
email	info@kingsfortcountryhouse.com
web	www.kingsfortcountryhouse.com

Map 1 & 4 Entry 56

Roosky Cottage, Rossinver, Co. Leitrim

Contact: 3310 North Bell Avenue, Chicago, Illinois 60618, USA

The prettiest Irish cottage in thoroughly rural surroundings: low stone walls to hug you in, rustling thatch to soothe, birdsung moorlands all around, the neighbour's cattle crossing the lane (so look before you leap). And Lough Melvin, peaceful yet exciting for nature-lovers and sportsmen: rent a boat and try your luck. Just inside Co. Leitrim, Roosky Cottage is a stone's throw from Donegal and 15 minutes from lovely seaside Bundoran. The interior is *au naturel*: the Bradleys have left the bare stone walls to tell the memories of the farmers who lived here for 100 years. Rooms are cosy, mildly colourful and rustic: simple holiday furniture sits peacefully, there are three open turf fireplaces – yes, each bedroom has a fire and a bathroom. To rub shoulders with so much ancientness is precious indeed yet the kitchen has all the necessary modernities as well as a fine old Irish dresser. The area is stuffed with things to do and see: the stunning Donegal coast, prehistoric sites, medieval monuments, mind-stretching walks, golf, riding, marvellous food. *Linen, heating, electricity included.*

rooms	Cottage for 4-5 (1 double, 1 twin, single sofabed, 2 bathrooms).
price	€420-€580 per week.
meals	Self-catering. Restaurants 15-minute drive.
closed	Rarely.
directions	Directions given on booking.

	Mary & Paul Bradley
tel	+1 773 528 1192 (USA)
email	mbradboo@aol.com
web	www.irishcottagerental.com

Self-catering

Map 1 & 4 Entry 57

Hollywell

Liberty Hill, Carrick-on-Shannon, Co. Leitrim

It's such a gorgeous surprise to leave the busy road and the town's tumult and two seconds later be driving quietly up to elegant country-house life. Gracious Georgian with 1850s add-ons, Hollywell is decorated with impeccable taste that never overpowers. Although Tom and Rosaleen live in the annexe, it has the feel of a real house. Former hoteliers, charming, helpful and easy to get on with (*maher* means hospitable in Gaelic), they know what guests like. No helter-skelter of children or dogs here, all is peace, the creeper peeks in at the windows, you may watch the ever-changing Shannon scene for hours from the front rooms, lounge in a living room stuffed with pictures, portraits and antiques, glory in the sofas and the view on the landing, retire to deeply welcoming bedrooms. For lunch or dinner, sons Conor and Ronan run the excellent Oarsmen pub and restaurant in Carrick, which is a pretty town, popular with Dubliners at the weekend, offering boat trips, megaliths, arts and crafts. Then retire to seclusion: soon breakfast will arrive on the beautiful burr walnut table. *Children over 12 welcome.*

rooms	4: 3 doubles, 1 twin/double.
price	€105–€140. Singles €55–€75.
meals	Restaurants in Carrick-on-Shannon.
closed	Mid-November to late February.
directions	From Dublin N4 to Carrick; over River Shannon; keep left at Ging's Pub up lane. Entrance 1st left, signposted.

Guest house

Rosaleen & Tom Maher

tel	+353 (0)71 962 1124
fax	+353 (0)71 962 1124
email	hollywell@esatbiz.com

Map 1 & 4 Entry 58

Clonalis House
Castlerea, Co. Roscommon

Standing in 700 acres, aloof up a mile-long drive, Clonalis is definitely a special place, a précis of Irish history. The O'Conor clan has been connected to this land for 2,000-odd years, O'Conors once sat on the High King's throne, Charles Owen O'Conor Don built this house in 1878 as a proud 45-room fanfare in the Victorian Italianate style and Pyers, your engaging, down-to-earth host, is the expert on its all-Irish history – a rarity in itself. Turn from the fine park where gardens, woods and trout rivers call, and enter the wonderful library, lined with ancient tomes full of the family and other tales; portraits observe you from the staircase, hall and dining room walls. Relaxed and informative, Marguerite will show you your impressive bedroom, a four-poster here, a half-tester there, gilt-framed mirrors, elegant fireplaces, massive bathrooms, family antiques, all looking over the formal gardens. Breakfast with the palm-tree silver in the superb dining room is fit for a lord – use your imagination, revel in it. Many great evenings are spent here, join one. *House open to the public.*

rooms	4: 1 double, 1 twin, 2 four-posters.
price	€190–€220. Singles €115. Discount for 3 nights or more. Booking essential.
meals	Dinner €44 (Tuesday-Saturday). 24 hours' notice required.
closed	October to mid-April. Groups by arrangement in winter.
directions	From Athlone N61 to Roscommon; bypass to N60 & Castlerea. House well signposted; long drive through fields & woodland.

Country house

Pyers & Marguerite O'Conor Nash

tel	+353 (0)94 962 0014
fax	+353 (0)94 962 0014
email	clonalis@iol.ie
web	www.clonalis.com

Map 4 Entry 59

Castlecoote House

Castlecoote, Co. Roscommon

In ten pastoral acres, Kevin welcomes you with easy affability to his Palladian mansion and stunning gardens. Built in the 1700s with medieval castle ruins dotted around like Victorian follies and the lovely River Suck flowing past the old ice house, it has been brilliantly restored by Ireland's best: panelling, moulding, stucco and hand-crafted sash windows. Duchesses grew up here: loved by George II, set in oils by Sir Joshua Reynolds. they hang in the hall. Underfloor heating and deluxe bathrooms are modern bonuses. Imagine browsing through rare tomes in the library before sitting down to a succulent dinner in the elegant dining room and then warming your toes before the drawing-room fire beneath a shimmering chandelier or playing a full-size game of snooker before bed. Bedrooms are magnificent: antiques, rich rugs, bucolic views; the master bathroom is a… masterpiece to delight a sybarite. Lower-ground-floor bedrooms are less spectacular but supremely comfortable. And Kevin is ever a friendly, attentive and interesting host. A romantic slice of real old Ireland. *Minimum stay two nights.*

rooms	4 doubles.
price	€180.
meals	Dinner €49.
closed	October–January.
directions	From Athlone N61 to Roscommon; there, take R366 to Castlecoote & follow signs to house.

Country house

	Kevin Finnerty & Sarah Lane
tel	+353 (0)90 666 3794
fax	+353 (0)1 833 0666
email	info@castlecootehouse.com
web	www.castlecootehouse.com

Map 4 Entry 60

Drom Caoin

Church Road, Belmullet, Co. Mayo

Máirín is passionate about Ireland ancient and modern, the Irish language, her tribe of nine (grown) children, the courses she takes and gives (rural tourism, cookery), her B&B guests,... How does she do it? You could listen to her for weeks. Gerry is the perfect foil, a quiet crinkly man with a tender smile who speaks little and well. They both teach Irish, delightedly. Way out at the end of a bleak bogside road, only just attached to the mainland, Belmullet, hunkered down before the elements, bustles on market day, welcoming eager anglers, twitchers, golfers (Carne Golf Links are ranked 28th in the world), sculpture vultures. You can come by bus! Drom Caoin, a modern, practical house on a rise, brims with light from the sea and family photographs, lots of pine, pale colours and simplicity: no clutter, no frills. Bedrooms are neatly tucked under the sloping roof, all whiteness and wood with excellent king-size beds and showers. Breakfast is superb, as is this natural, intelligent family who can take you to the heart of Ireland. Don't miss the astonishing 5,500-year-old settlement at Céide Fields. *Vegetarian meals available.*

rooms	4 + 1: 2 twins/doubles, 1 family, 1 single. Apartment for 4.
price	€70. Singles €42. Apartment available.
meals	Dinner €22. BYO wine.
closed	Mid-December-mid-January.
directions	In Belmullet, at central roundabout with granite pillars, take Church Road; up hill, past church, rich blue house on left.

Máirín Maguire-Murphy
tel   +353 (0)97 81195
fax   +353 (0)97 81195
email stay@dromcaoin.ie
web   www.belmullet-accommodation.com

B&B & Self-catering

Map 3 Entry 61

The Bervie
Keel, Achill Island, Co. Mayo

Elizabeth runs the Bervie wearing a contented smile. Who wouldn't? It's a superbly atmospheric place. Achill Island feels like the end of the world and is a favourite haunt of poets and painters. Right down by the sea, the Bervie fits its environment to a tee. Once a coastguard station, it became a salmon centre, then a guest house, a third-generation tradition that Elizabeth and John keep alive with love and gusto. More like a terrace of interconnected cottages than a guest house, the place looks so welcoming after a long journey: a fire burns in the hearth and the smell of real home cooking raises expectations. All is homely, simple and comfortable in here, bedrooms have big beds piled with fluffy blankets, those at the back give directly onto the Atlantic – it comes to within 30 metres of your window at high tide. The garden is that endless, fabulous beach and the breathtaking scenery all the way to the Cathedral Cliffs. Elizabeth takes pride in making all her visitors happy, from families and surfers to artists and writers. An unhurried place where humanity and delicious food nourish soul and body.

rooms	14: 7 doubles, 1 suite. Outbuildings: 6 doubles.
price	€100-€120.
meals	Dinner from €35. Afternoon tea.
closed	November-March.
directions	From Westport N59 to Achill Island then R319 across island to Keel. Bervie well signposted in village.

Guest house

Elizabeth & John Barrett
tel +353 (0)98 43114
fax +353 (0)98 43407
email bervie@esatclear.ie
web www.bervieachill.com

Map 3 Entry 62

Rosturk Woods

Rosturk, Mulranny, Westport, Co. Mayo

Only at the end of the wooded drive do you realise how close the sea is. The magical bay will steal your heart away. Along the headland, castle turrets peer over trees: Alan's birthplace. At high tide, the sea laps the garden; take the boat, see a seal? At low tide, walk to an island, see an otter? The Stoneys are a warm, humorous, fun young family. The Wing, one end of their superb modern house, has space, light, old fireplaces, a fine green and yellow kitchen with matching china and, upstairs, a deeply comfortable master bedroom. The Waterfall House stands alone, spreading its generous windows before a south-facing terrace, all in spanking new quality and, again, decorated for comfort and æsthetics with modern sofas and country antiques, thick rugs and good pictures. Another splendid kitchen, of course. In the garden you will discover a little stream and an extraordinarily rare Chinese Fern Tree. The games room is for all, so is the tennis gear. Turf for fires provided within reason; hot water is solar. An exceptional place for fishing, boating, birding or just being. *Occasional B&B for six in main house.*

rooms	The Wing for 6 (3 twins/doubles, 3 bathrooms). Waterfall House for 8 (1 double, 2 twins/doubles, 1 twin, 4 bathrooms).
price	€700–€1,200 per week plus heating, electricity & cleaning.
meals	Dinner €32 (24 hours' notice). Restaurant 4km, pub 1km.
closed	Never.
directions	From Newport N59 for Mulranny & Achill 11km; blue sign on left.

Louisa & Alan Stoney

tel	+353 (0)98 36264
fax	+353 (0)98 36264
email	stoney@iol.ie
web	www.rosturk-woods.com

Self–catering

Map 3 Entry 63

Enniscoe House
Castlehill, Crossmolina, Ballina, Co. Mayo

History and good taste are the pillars of Enniscoe, a splendid Heritage House set beneath the towering presence of Mount Nephin in parkland surrounding Lough Conn. If the sitting room's superbly restored ceiling and cornices make you gasp, the rarer, grander drawing room will bowl you over: 1790s marble fireplace, 1850s wallpaper, masses of antiques. Susan is a descendant of the original family who arrived here in the 1660s and family portraits grace the walls. An oval landing and stairs in all directions lead to grand, tall-windowed rooms with plush-draped beds, paintings by Susan's mother and the spectacular lake view, or to lower, cosier farmhouse rooms with spriggy florals and super garden views. And great bathrooms to go with them. The grounds are a must: five acres of superb restored Victorian gardens, trails through woodland, boats to fish the lake and a Heritage Centre that traces family trees. Food here is excellent, too. How does Susan manage to run all this and remain such good company? Energy, brains and a genuine love of the place, is the answer. Very special indeed.

rooms	6 + 4: 1 double, 1 twin, 2 triples, 2 family suites. 4 apartments for 4-6.
price	€180-€224. Singles €90-€112. Apts €450-€700 per week.
meals	Dinner €48. Packed lunch from €10.
closed	November-March. Groups in January by arrangement.
directions	From Ballina N59 to Crossmolina; left R315 for Castlebar 3km. House entrance 1st of two on left.

Country house & Self-catering

Susan Kellett
tel +353 (0)96 31112
fax +353 (0)96 31773
email mail@enniscoe.com
web www.enniscoe.com

Map 3 Entry 64

The Crooked Cottage
Terrybawn, Pontoon, Co. Mayo

Could this be the perfect retreat? Once here, you are alone in a rural idyll, a little huddle of buildings in 10 acres, surrounded by trees, old walls and gorgeous views to lovely Lough Conn. The cottage is furiously ancient, not a right-angle in sight, the windows furiously modern, the interior appealingly personal with books and painted floorboards, old stones and white walls, old-fashioned bedcovers on pine beds and a comforting lived-in feel. The main bedroom under the rafters has space and a huge bed. Along the passage where the friendly wellies are kept you find the simple white bathroom and the smaller bedroom. The galley-like kitchen has all you need to prepare a good spread for the big old table in the easy, open living room. 100 years ago, the then owner did a roaring trade in poteen, an illegal potato alcohol. The fierce brew was made on an island in the lake then stored in a secret place in the thatch — never discovered. Stock up before you arrive, the nearest village is five miles away, but a nearby hotel serves good dinners. *Noel also owns Dublin hotel Number 31, entry 222.*

rooms	Cottage for 4 (1 twin/double, 1 double, 1 shower).
price	€500-€750 per week.
meals	Self-catering.
closed	Rarely.
directions	Directions given on booking.

	Noel Comer
tel	+353 (0)1 676 5011
fax	+353 (0)1 676 2929
email	info@number31.ie
web	www.number31.ie

Self-catering

Map 3 Entry 65

Delphi Lodge
Sherwood, Leenane, Co. Galway

That picture tells Delphi more graphically than any words: the estate's 1,000 acres of mountain, water and bog, all kept alive by buckets of lovely Irish rain: no money can buy such bleak and mighty beauty. The Marquis of Sligo built the house in the mid-1830s as his fishing lodge in the wilds of Connemara. Fly-fishing is still popular with guests – they run courses for all levels – but there's far more to Delphi than fishing. Long walks in unspoilt country; friendly outgoing company and a warming whiskey in front of a roaring fire on your return; delicious dinner with the other guests at one long table with gentle, kind Peter often at the helm: the lively conversation, local ingredients and superb house-party atmosphere make these occasions hard to beat and just as hard to leave. Simple, uncluttered bedrooms have good pine beds, plain ticking-type fabrics, proper bathrooms, the odd stuffed trout; front rooms have a heart-stopping view of Fin Lough. A home not an hotel, Delphi does it well whatever the season, whatever the reason, and most guests know it's only a matter of time before they return.

rooms	12 + 5: 12 doubles. 5 cottages for 4-6.
price	€200-€260. Singles €130-€160. Cottages €500-€1,200 per week.
meals	Lunch €16. Dinner €50.
closed	Mid-December to mid-January.
directions	From Westport N59 for Leenane & Clifden. 3km before Leenane, right onto Louisburgh/Delphi road for 9km; lodge on left in woods 1km after Delphi Spa.

Country house & Self-catering

Peter Mantle

tel	+353 (0)95 42222
fax	+353 (0)95 42296
email	info@delphilodge.ie
web	www.delphilodge.ie

Map 3 Entry 66

Crocnaraw Country House
Moyard (Connemara), Co. Galway

Prepare to leave this century, detach from material cares, and join Lucy on the 'hill of the fairy fort' (Crocnaraw means just that). Both place and owner have an untroubled, almost ethereal quality so you may sit talking to Lucy for hours in the comforting Aga country kitchen. She took over her mother's Georgian country-house B&B here in 1985 and has left most things religiously as they were: rooms like eclectic period pieces, fossilized somewhere between the '60s and the '80s, are a lot of fun with bizarre '60s lampshades, a motley array of pieces before the log fire in the big airy drawing room, a unique bamboo wardrobe made by a local craftsman, unusual mixtures of colours and finishes. Take your time, ask Lucy to walk you round the wonderful garden and explain its history and development. Planted unbelievably from scratch by her mother in 1960, it has won award upon award. Lucy looks after it now, decorating the house with fresh flowers. She also cares for four special donkeys in a field next door. Here in the heart of Connemara the magic of Ireland is alive and well. *Non-smoking rooms available.*

rooms	4: 2 doubles, 2 twins.
price	€100–€150. Singles from €50.
meals	Dinner €35. By arrangement. BYO wine.
closed	November–February.
directions	From Clifden N59 for Westport 9.5km; small sign on left 200m before entrance on left; drive slowly or you'll miss it.

Country house

	Lucy Fretwell
tel	+353 (0)95 41068
fax	+353 (0)95 41068
email	rooms@crocnaraw.co.uk
web	www.crocnaraw.co.uk

Map 3 Entry 67

Rosleague Manor Hotel

Letterfrack (Connemara), Co. Galway

From the moment you see the Twelve Pins of Connemara National Park across the front lawn and over Bearnaderg Bay, you know you've made a good choice. This delightful 200-year-old Regency manor looks, feels, even smells just as a country-house hotel should: where others fall short of expectations, Rosleague delivers. It doesn't feel impersonal, either. Snug drawing rooms have unstuffy elegance: open fires, comfortable seats, private cubbyholes. The grand dining room draws in the view – ideal for a leisurely breakfast by the window. In the evening, it has the buzz of a dinner party despite the separate tables. Friendly staff orchestrate each course with little fuss, serving much-lauded dishes, and the bar overlooking the courtyard feels friendly and somehow colonial. Front bedrooms with the view are the best but the other few compensate by being absolutely enormous. A double room may have a giant bed and a palatial bathroom that make it feel more like a suite. If you can pull yourself away from all this laid-back luxury, visit Inishboffin Island, play tennis, take a sauna, or climb a Pin. *Pets by arrangement. Tennis on site.*

rooms	22: 15 twins/doubles & triples, 4 suites, 3 four-posters.
price	€140-€240. Singles from €85.
meals	Dinner from €45. Lunch from €15.
closed	Mid-November-mid-March.
directions	From Clifden N59 for Westport 11km; through Moyard. Hotel entrance sign on left as road dips into Letterfrack.

Hotel

Mark & Edmund Foyle

tel	+353 (0)95 41101
fax	+353 (0)95 41168
email	info@rosleague.com
web	www.rosleague.com

Map 3 Entry 68

Dolphin Beach House

Lower Sky Road, Clifden, Co. Galway

Imagine lying in a mahogany sleigh bed watching dolphins play in the bay (if you're lucky), then walking to a private cove for a swim. Youthful and vibrant, Dolphin Beach is no ordinary place. Extended and modernised, the 200-year-old farmhouse lies at the windswept edge of Europe among wild fuchsia and the light of the Atlantic. Big bedrooms are full of luxurious fun and eccentric detail: mosaic tiles, wooden ceilings, portholes, underfloor heating and patio doors that open with smooth precision onto quiet courtyards or staggering views. With enthusiasm and lightness of heart, Clodagh and Sinead have taken over from their lovely parents Billy and Barbara. They will organise just about any activity you want – riding, deep-sea fishing, hikes, bikes – and Sinead cooks with inspiration and fresh produce from the farm and the local area – Connemara lamb, organic veg, wild salmon, fresh lobster. Savour it in the raised dining room overlooking Clifden Bay. After dinner, visit bustling Clifden by taxi or lounge in leather in the dark sitting room. Finally, let the sea lull you to sleep.

rooms	8: 4 doubles, 3 twins/doubles, 1 single.
price	€130–€185. Singles €80–€100.
meals	Dinner €40.
closed	December & January.
directions	From Clifden, Sky Rd for 3km to Y-junction; left on Lower Sky Rd. House on left after 2.5km, overlooking bay.

	Clodagh & Sinead Foyle
tel	+353 (0)95 21204
fax	+353 (0)95 22935
email	stay@dolphinbeachhouse.com
web	www.dolphinbeachhouse.com

Guest house

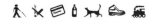

Map 3 Entry 69

Sea Mist House

Seaview, Clifden (Connemara), Co. Galway

Ah, the flowers! Sheila is new to gardening but she's clearly a natural and the garden that leans up the hill behind her house, past the old stables and the suntrap terrace, is a flurry of berries, flowers and scented herbs – they all come into the house for your greater pleasure – with the prettiest little church peering over the wall. Sheila loves having guests in her old family home, you can feel it has always been a happy house. Her auctioneer grandfather furnished it well: a fine sideboard is set with cut-glass wine glasses and a corkscrew for your use in the sitting room, the dining-room paintings hover proudly over a huge old dresser, bought from the Maharajah of Ballinahinch, and some gleaming silver. The effect is welcoming, country, not at all pretentious. There are more paintings, each with a story of its own, in the 'gothic' conservatory which frames the garden so lovingly and keeps the geraniums and ferns warm. Husband Rod gardens at weekends, too. Comfortable bedrooms are generous, simple and fresh, breakfast is delicious, you are in a quiet street bang in the town centre.

rooms	4: 3 doubles, 1 twin; 2 overflow rooms for 4.
price	€70–€120. Singles €50–€80.
meals	Restaurants within walking distance.
closed	Christmas; midweek in winter.
directions	Follow one-way system round town to square; turn left at square: house down on right.

B&B

	Sheila Griffin
tel	+353 (0)95 21441
email	sgriffin@eircom.net
web	www.seamisthouse.com

Map 3 Entry 70

The Quay House
Beach Road, Clifden, Co. Galway

You too should visit the Quay House once in your life, even if animal skins and hunting trophies are not always your thing – it defies description. Imagine the best bits of the nicest houses you've ever seen under one roof and you begin to get the picture. Paddy has a magician's touch for mixing the remarkable and the elegant with casual style. The tiger skin draped over the sofa in the drawing room is unforgettable. Built in 1820 for the harbour master, the house overlooks Clifden Bay and the fishing boats moored at the quayside. Rooms have fantastic mirrors, white-shuttered windows and painted wooden walls; some have views, others four-posters. Next door, six themed studio rooms, four with open fires, have little balconies and the lovely view – *Safari* is zebra skins and African shields, *French Regency* rejoices in ornate furniture. Long breakfasts are taken in a leafy conservatory where birds chirp cheerily with amazing regularity. Julia is English, Paddy Irish, both are full of natural *bonhomie* – they make a charismatic couple. Clifden is ever lively and nearby Connemara ever inspiring. Hard to beat.

rooms	14: 9 twins/doubles, 2 triples, 3 four-posters.
price	€140-€170. Singles from €95.
meals	Restaurants within walking distance.
closed	November to mid-March.
directions	In Clifden, Beach Road down hill from centre of town. House 500m on right, on quayside.

Julia & Patrick Foyle
tel	+353 (0)95 21369
fax	+353 (0)95 21608
email	thequay@iol.ie
web	www.thequayhouse.com

Guest house

Map 3 Entry 71

Ballynahinch Castle Hotel

Recess (Connemara), Co. Galway

Ballynahinch, 'the household of the island', with several thousand acres of fishing and shooting rights, once claimed the longest drive in the world (28 miles from the castle to Oughterard). Today, after a mere 700-year absence, O'Flahertys are back in the house. Patrick's predecessors were labelled ferocious but he is a friendly dapper presence in Irish tweed who looks after people with genuine warmth while his staff make you feel you are guest rather than client. A maze of rooms, the castle was expanded from a modest inn in 1813 by famous duellist and MP Richard Martin, nicknamed 'Humanity Dick' after proposing a bill to set up the Irish RSPCA. In 1924, a Maharajah cricketer known fondly as Ranji bought the castle, landscaped the gardens and kept elephants and bears on the island. Guitarist Eric Clapton caught his first salmon here and probably paraded it in the timeworn bar where fishermen come to weigh their catch and relax after a long hard day. Panelling was made with estate timber, bedroom furniture is locally crafted, there is elegance, comfort and variety. Not bad for an hotel. *Tennis on site.*

rooms	40: 14 doubles, 11 twins/doubles, 3 suites, 12 four-posters.
price	€200-€400.
meals	Dinner from €49. Lunch €3.50-€20.
closed	Christmas week & February.
directions	From Galway N59 for Clifden through Recess & continue 5km; left R341 at sign to hotel & Roundstone.

Hotel

	Patrick O'Flaherty
tel	+353 (0)95 31006
fax	+353 (0)95 31085
email	bhinch@iol.ie
web	www.ballynahinch-castle.com

Map 3 Entry 72

The Anglers Return

Toombeola, Roundstone (Connemara), Co. Galway

Warm, funny, self-deprecating, Lynn adores her gorgeous garden and her guests equally, giving you her undivided attention. In her highly personal house, lavender-blue woodwork sets off a stunning runner carpet by Millar's of Clifden, odd chairs full of personality stand on the red sitting-room tiles, the whole effect is fresh, simple, thoroughly country. She is an artist, has lived here all her life, knows the best fishing and walking spots. She sings, too, and listens to classical music while making her bread and scones to go with the organic cereals and homemade jams next morning. In the peace of whitewashed walls, the house breathes through wooden floors, old maps, antiques, fresh wild flowers, log fires. Lynn's pretty mixed-size bedrooms have enchanting river views and robes for the corridor run to the bathroom, the walls of the huge dining room carry musical instruments, seascapes, boats and baskets. An impossibly cute courtyard leads to three acres of natural garden; paths wind past azaleas, an organic veg patch, wild rocky outcrops to bluebell woods and a well-earned hammock.

rooms	5: 1 double en suite; 2 doubles, 1 twin, 1 family, sharing 2 bathrooms.
price	From €95.
meals	Dinner for groups by arrangement. Restaurants 3-7km.
closed	December-January.
directions	From Galway N59 for Clifden through Recess & continue 7km; left R341 for Roundstone; house on left.

Lynn Hill

tel	+353 (0)95 31091
mobile	+353 (0)87 126 2667
web	www.anglersreturn.com

B&B

Map 3 Entry 73

Emlaghmore Lodge
Ballyconneely (Connemara), Co. Galway

The Tinne family's holiday house for over 80 years, now Nick's permanent home, Emlaghmore still has the air of an 1860's fishing lodge. Near the wild Atlantic coast, surrounded by the only trees for miles, it looks across its own little river and oceans of lake-strewn moorland to the Connemara mountains. Otters, badgers, birds of prey and unusual plants abound in a nature-lover's paradise. In simple country-house style, gilt-framed ancestors look down from faded pink walls in the elegant dining room and uncluttered bedrooms have that old-world charm of rooms just waiting for the family to arrive. Climb the nearby mountain to see as far as County Kerry, fish on private lakes, walk on sandy beaches where seals may be sprawling on the rocks and fishermen bring in their lobster catch (it sometimes finds its way to the kitchen). Don't miss the chance to dine in candlelit style with Nick, who once owned Snaffles Restaurant in Dublin where the rich and famous dined, and his partner Janet, who now does a lot of the cooking. A deeply peaceful and secluded house, an exceptional welcome.

rooms	4 + 1: 1 double, 1 twin, both en suite; 1 double, 1 single, with separate bathrooms. Cottage for 8.
price	€120-€160. Singles €60. Cottage €350-€850 per week.
meals	Dinner €50. Book 24 hrs ahead.
closed	November-Easter.
directions	On R341 9.5km from Roundstone, 4km from Ballyconneely. 100m on Roundstone side of Callow bridge, take narrow lane inland (no sign) 100m; sign on gate.

B&B & Self-catering

Nick Tinne

tel	+353 (0)95 23529
fax	+353 (0)95 23860
email	info@emlaghmore.com
web	www.emlaghmore.com

Map 3 Entry 74

Cashel House Hotel
Cashel (Connemara), Co. Galway

If you believe that luxury is service not things, that a superior establishment can also be a cosy 1840s house, come to Cashel House. Kay and Dermot combed the auction rooms for fine furniture and ornaments, their loyal staff attend to every detail with ready smiles and not a jot of intrusiveness, Kay will cook for special needs then visit your table to make sure all's well. The panorama of fascinatingly lovely gardens – with masses of special plants – and the bay beyond may try to invade your table but the food, from fresh sea fish to Connemara lamb, deserves all your attention. Beneath swags and ruches, deep armchairs invite you to relax by the library fire or engage in talk of fish or horseflesh, mice or men in the drawing room. There's a Connemara pony and Irish sport horse stud right here. Bedrooms in the main house, with the original furniture, have a powerful sense of country-house living at its best, all have big beds, fine deep carpets, huge windows to the bay or the vast garden. Despite the 30 rooms, you are an important individual here. *There are two Cashels: this is the Galway one.*

rooms	32: 7 doubles, 3 twins, 13 suites, 5 family, 4 singles.
price	€170-€310. Singles from €160.
meals	Lunch from €10. Dinner €52-€54.
closed	January.
directions	From Galway N59 to Recess (61km); left for Cashel & follow signs to hotel.

	Kay & Dermot McEvilly
tel	+353 (0)95 31001
fax	+353 (0)95 31077
email	res@cashel-house-hotel.com
web	www.cashel-house-hotel.com

Hotel

Map 3 Entry 75

Zetland Country House Hotel

Cashel Bay (Connemara), Co. Galway

Ruaidhri ('Rory') runs Zetland with warm professionalism and friendly staff, many of them French, who clearly enjoy working here. It is one of those rare hotels that oozes old-style luxury yet feels like a family home, albeit a smart one. Built as a sporting lodge in the early 1800s, it certainly looks more house than hotel, with rambling creeper giving lots of seasoned character at the front. Fresh lilies welcome you inside, turf fires glow in lovely fireplaces, oil paintings and antique plates cover the walls, some life-worn fabrics endear. There's a quiet library corner, huge dining-room windows look onto fine gardens and Cashel Bay, a snug bar and snooker room add a less formal option. The food here has won several awards and menus change daily. Help yourself to breakfast from warmed silverware in true country-house tradition. Bedrooms have antiques, warm colours, old-fashioned style and the view, with a bit less character in the new wing, though the four newest are coolly contemporary in their fawn, coffee and taupe garb. But it all has timeless style – in the wilds of Connemara. *Tennis on site.*

rooms	22: 12 twins/doubles, 9 twins, 1 four-poster.
price	€150–€240. Singles €110–€125.
meals	Dinner, 5 courses, €56. Packed lunch €15.
closed	Week before Christmas.
directions	From Oughterard N59 for Clifden. 2.5km after Recess (Srath Salach) left at sign to hotel 5km; right at next sign; entrance 1km on right.

Hotel

	Ruaidhri Prendergast
tel	+353 (0)95 31111
fax	+353 (0)95 31117
email	zetland@iol.ie
web	www.zetland.com

Map 3 Entry 76

Currarevagh House
Oughterard (Connemara), Co. Galway

The consecrated ritual at this graceful early-Victorian manor is English afternoon tea in the drawing room or, in clement weather, on the lawn. Cucumber sandwiches, scones, homemade cake, delicate bone china cups. On the banks of vast Lough Corrib, Currarevagh (pronounced 'Currareeva') is surrounded by 150 acres of woodland with rhododendrons brought back from India by the generation of Hodgsons who built the house in 1842. You may feel you have gone back to the pace and seclusion of that time, such is the bucolic quiet of the place. Harry, June or son Henry will meet you and suggest croquet, tennis, fishing... and explain that there are no rules except turning up for dinner at 8 o'clock sharp. Bright, welcoming bedrooms, three with great lake views, have big Victorian beds, old-style décor, space and excellent bathrooms. June cooks beautifully and has won many accolades for her creative flair. After dinner beneath the Old Masters, guests come together for coffee by the drawing room fire. You can boat and fish from their private jetty — but no drifting off, the lake is 30 miles long.

rooms	15: 14 twins/doubles, 1 single.
price	€160-€210. Singles from €85. Half-board (min. 3 nights) €125 p.p.
meals	Dinner, 5 courses, €42.50, 8pm. Afternoon tea included.
closed	Mid-October to March.
directions	From Oughterard, Glann Lakeshore road for 6.5km; entrance on right.

Harry & June Hodgson
tel	+353 (0)91 552312
fax	+353 (0)91 552731
email	mail@currarevagh.com
web	www.currarevagh.com

Country house

Map 3 Entry 77

Railway Lodge

Canrower, Oughterard (Connemara), Co. Galway

A brave and lively woman, Carmel, to have painted her house red — and it works. She travelled afar before starting B&B on the family farm in a new young house built beside a railway line that's been closed since 1936: a new silhouette blending with ancient surroundings, the magnificent Cloosh Hills in the distance, new trees growing on ancestral land, old-fashioned shutters in modern gables. Carmel has done a wonderful job inside. Cottage-style bedrooms under sloping ceilings are pristine and cosy with polished floors, old Irish pine furniture, stitched bedcovers, big Oxford pillowcases, and bathrooms alive with indoor plants. The log fire and comfy armchairs make the snug living room feel old and settled; the conservatory, with wicker chairs and writing tables, gives onto a garden full of vigorous young trees. Carmel's family have long roots in Connemara and she can tell hours of local history; her father breeds Connemara ponies and is the inspiration behind much of the railway memorabilia dotted about. Walks and rides into stunning scenery start from the door. Real, warm, Irish B&B.

rooms	4 + 1: 3 doubles, 1 twin. Cottage for 2.
price	€100–€110. Singles €70. Cottage €550 per week.
meals	Restaurants within walking distance.
closed	Rarely.
directions	From Galway N59 for Clifden to Oughterard; through town; left after Corrib House Hotel and immed'ly right; follow signs to house.

B&B & Self-catering

	Carmel Geoghegan
tel	+353 (0)91 552945
email	railwaylodge@eircom.net
web	www.railwaylodge.net

Map 3 Entry 78

Camillaun

Oughterard (Connemara), Co. Galway

It was the river and the river life that made Greg and Deirdre choose this spot to build their cosy new family house down by the River Owenriff. They had real open fires built and created a fisherman's dream. Camillaun means 'hidden island': to know its secret, walk past the tennis court to Greg's pontoons where seven boats are moored in season. A mile or so down river and you're out on Lough Corrib to fish for brown trout, salmon, perch and pike; a ghillie can be arranged, a hot tub shelters in a gazebo (yes!) for your return, then those crackling fires. A more leisurely alternative is a boat trip to Inchagoill Island; take a picnic and explore its two monasteries. Upstairs, bedrooms look over the azaleas and rhododendrons to the burbling river – you can hear its soothing sounds with the windows open. Rooms are attractively, simply done with polished wooden floors and plain-coloured rugs, bright colours, the odd antique; nothing is overwrought. This is a lively, cheerful, involving household who care greatly about your comfort. The village is just a short stroll down the leafy lane. *Tennis on site.*

rooms	4: 1 twin, 3 family.
price	€70-€90. Singles €48-€55.
meals	Dinner from €35. BYO wine. Packed lunch from €8.
closed	November-February.
directions	From Galway N59 to Oughterard; in centre of village right into Glann Rd, 1st right after bridge; house signposted 200m on right down side road.

	Deirdre & Greg Forde	
tel	+353 (0)91 552678	
fax	+353 (0)91 552439	B&B
email	camillaun@eircom.net	
web	www.camillaun.com	

Map 3 Entry 79

Souladio Cottage
The Glann Road, Oughterard, Co. Galway

The grandeur of the landscape may be enough soul food in itself – Amelia built this incredibly romantic old-style retreat on top of a hill where the land slopes down to world-famous (to anglers) Lough Corrib – but there are masses of other things to seduce you: golf and pony-trekking as always in Ireland, exhilarating bike rides and, should country indigestion set in, the wild delights of Galway city only 20 miles away. With her fine flair for interior design Amelia has done her cottage with warmth, taste and a passion for all things Italian. Oriental carpets soften wooden floors, the big sitting room has sink-in armchairs before the lovely turf fire, soft attractive watercolours, light streaming in through mint-green French windows. In the generous bedroom, Italian plates glow in alcoves, the bedlinen is luxuriously Italian, too. The little bathroom and kitchen are neatly perfect for two. Amelia is a cosmopolitan gem: she has lived in California and Italy, is privileged to be a Joyce from Joyce country and her knowledge alone is worth the trip – all the secrets of her beloved Connemara.

rooms	Cottage for 2 (1 twin/double, 1 bathroom).
price	€600 per week, including linen & electricity; heating extra.
meals	Self-catering.
closed	Rarely.
directions	Directions given on booking.

Self-catering

	Amelia Joyce-Lynch
tel	+353 (0)91 552872
mobile	+353 (0)87 274 6733
email	ameliajoyce@hotmail.com
web	www.connemaracottage.com

Map 3 Entry 80

Killeen House
Killeen, Bushypark, Co. Galway

Like many of the best Galway houses, Killeen House overlooks a lake. This one is fishing-famous Lough Corrib and the water's edge is a short walk from Catherine's garden. Guests come for the Galway races, too. The 1840s house was recently extended, the new rooms overlooking colourful shrubs and a baize-smooth lawn all fit perfectly. In a clever mix of old style and modern service, each bedroom is themed – English Victorian, Edwardian, Regency. The plasma telly screens are a surprise in Connemara, the retro antique radio sets a quirky bonus. Thick, locally-made hand-woven rugs stretch luxuriously over wooden floors while huge, comfortable beds – some are strapping seven-footers – may tempt you to a siesta as well. Catherine has a magpie's love of shiny objects and the house sparkles with antique silver. She cares hugely about your contentment and relaxation so expect proper tea on arrival, served in the finest china, as you sink into regal high-backed armchairs in the formal drawing room. A wonderful setting and ideal for exploring Connemara by day and the buzz of Galway city by night.

rooms	6: 5 doubles, 1 triple.
price	€150-€190. Singles from €100.
meals	Restaurants nearby, or in Galway city.
closed	Christmas.
directions	From Galway N59 for Clifden 6.5km; house signposted on right.

Catherine Doyle

tel	+353 (0)91 524179
fax	+353 (0)91 528065
email	killeenhouse@ireland.com
web	www.killeenhousegalway.com

Guest house

Map 3 Entry 81

Castlegar Stables

Castlegar House, Ahascragh, Ballinasloe, Co. Galway

Just out of the village, a mile down its private drive, Castlegar stands in fifty acres of beautiful grounds with two lovely wooded paths looping the house. The conversion of the stables and the pretty stable yard is smart and luxurious and the American and French owners have taken great care over every detail: bathrooms have the latest fittings and you will want for nothing in the way of furnishings, linen or cutlery. Both houses are the same, only the number of bedrooms changes. The front door opens onto an attractively furnished kitchen/diner where you will be happy to cook and eat. Upstairs is the enormous sitting room with pretty little windows looking out. Douglas has helped the air flow over the heavy, dark, sink-or-swim sofas with big black ceiling fans. Bedrooms are in the same vein of luxurious modern comfort. This strong masculine atmosphere is deeply restful. Moreover, guests are welcome to use the gym, hot tub, sauna, table tennis, boules set, internet and lots of other toys in the main basement. And the walking here is rich. *The two houses can connect.*

rooms	Stables I for 6 (3 doubles, 2 baths). Stables II for 4 (2 doubles, 2 baths). Communal laundry.
price	Stables I €2,000. Stables II €1,300. Together €3,000. Prices per week.
meals	Self-catering.
closed	Rarely.
directions	Provided on booking.

Self-catering

	Douglas Woessner
tel	+353 (0)9096 88653
mobile	+353 (0)87 981 4773
fax	+353 (0)9096 88689
email	castlegarhouse@eircom.net

Map 4 Entry 82

Iverna Cottage

Salahoona, Spiddal, Co. Galway

Come to Iverna to linger in good company among tempting books and be utterly spoilt: Patricia puts duvets under mattresses, reading lights on beds and her breakfasts are works of art. Evenings drift by in a log-fire atmosphere of chat, wine and possibly song. Patricia and Willy built the house after giving up London careers to return home. Overlooking Galway Bay, it is a welcome sight along the coast road, a gem on a string of banal white bungalows; the distinctive stone façade sits between huge oak posts salvaged from Canary Wharf in London; the pretty garden gives onto a lane leading to three miles of sandy beach for head-clearing strolls. Inside, slate floors and wooden beams create a homely atmosphere and pretty cottage-style bedrooms have wrought-iron beds and patchwork quilts. Patricia loves to exercise her mind with good literature in between rustling up mushroom and potato cakes and making you feel at home with tea and rock buns or a big glass of wine. If Willy is "a lot of people's idea of a leprechaun", their happy home is a crock of gold – and Patricia is brilliant with children.

rooms	4: 2 doubles, 2 family; extra bathroom.
price	€85-€90. Singles €50-€60.
meals	Restaurants in Spiddal.
closed	October-May.
directions	From Galway R336 coast road to Spiddal 19km. Through village; house 1.5km on left.

	Patricia & Willy Farrell
tel	+353 (0)91 553762
email	ivernacottage@eircom.net
web	www.ivernacottage.8m.com

B&B

Map 3 Entry 83

Man of Aran Cottage
Inishmor, Aran Islands, Co. Galway

People visibly unwind as they stoop through the door into Maura and Joe's immediate warmth. They have been regaling their guests with gripping tales of island life for decades. Built right by the ocean in the 1930s for Robert Flaherty's documentary on the islands, *Man of Aran*, the house is surrounded by wild roses, gentian, maidenhair fern, saxifrage and Joe's splendid hydroponic garden that he would gladly talk about all day: they are almost self-sufficient. He's not afraid to use what nature provides and his salad was a riot of colour with nasturtium flowers, pansies and young leaves: "It's the only artistic inclination I have," he says, "getting better by the year". So is Maura's brilliantly home-spun cooking: delicious soups, stews, omelettes and cakes. Thick, white-painted stone walls enclose three quaint little rooms with lots of simple character and the restaurant. The Aran Islands get very popular in summer so it's best to visit in spring or autumn – or even a wild winter's day. This is the perfect little hideaway – go there and write your first novel. *They let the whole place out in winter.*

rooms	3: 1 double with separate bathroom; 1 double, 1 twin, sharing bathroom. Overflow rooms outside cottage.
price	€74-€80. Singles €45-€47.
meals	Dinner €35. Lunch from €5. Packed lunch on request.
closed	November-February.
directions	From Galway R336 through Spiddal 36km; left to Roseaveal Ferry. On island, hire a minibus or bike.

Restaurant with rooms

	Maura & Joe Wolfe
tel	+353 (0)99 61301
fax	+353 (0)99 61324
email	manofaran@eircom.net
web	www.manofarancottage.com

Map 3 Entry 84

Irish place names

Irish place names are often compilations of Gaelic words which tell us something about the colour, geography or history of the place.

Gaelic	Meaning	Example	Translation
abhainn (owen)	river	Avonbeg	small river
agh, augh	field	Aghamore	big field
ard	hill, height	Ardmore	big hill
ath(a)	ford	Athlone	Luain's ford
baile (bally)	town,settlement	Ballynamuck	town of the pigs
ban	white	Bantry	white beach
beag (beg)	small	Ballybegs	small town
beann (ben)	mountain	Bengorm	blue mountain
boy	yellow	Gortboy	yellow garden/field
caher	circular stone fort	Caherlough	fort of the lake
carraig (carrig)	rock	Carrickfergus	rock of Fergus
carn, cairn	heap of stones	Glencairn	valley of the cairn
caislean (cashel)	castle, fort	Cashel Murnhan	fort of Munster
ceann, ken	headland	Kenmare	head of the sea (where it comes to)
cill (kill)	church	Kildare	church of the oak
cloch	stone	Clogheen	little stone
clun, cluain (clon)	meadow	Clonmel	meadow/vale of honey
		Clonturk	boars meadow
cnoc (knock)	hill	Knockanean	hill of the birds
coill (kyle)	wood	Kyleglass	green wood
coreach (cork)	marsh	Cork	(the town was built on a marsh)
cruagh	(croagh)	rounded hill	Croaghross, wooded hill
dair, doire (dar)	oak tree	Kildare	church of the oak
daire (derry)	oak wood/grove	Derrybeg	small oak grove

continued on page preceeding entry 85

Munster

Irish placenames continued

derg, dearg	red	Lough Derg	red lake
dubh	black	Dublin	black pool*
drom (drum)	small hill, ridge	Druncondra	Condra's ridge
dun (doon)	fortress, palace	Donegal	fort of the Galls
ennis (inish)	island	Inishowen	island of the rivers
fionn	clear, white	Finglas	clear green
glas	green	glaise	small river
		Glasagh	field of the stream
gleann(glen)	valley	Glendalough	valley of the lake
gort	field, garden	Gortboy	yellow tilled field/garden
lios (lis)	(earthen) fort	Lismore	big earthen fort
loch (lough)	lake, sea inlet	Loughrea	grey lake
ma, maigh, moy	plain	Mayo	plain of the yews
		Mallow	plain of the River Allo
móna, mone	bog, turf	Knockmona	hill of the bog
mór	big, great	Oranmore	big/great cold spring
muc (muck)	pig	Muckross	peninsula of the pigs
poul (poll)	hole	Poulaphaca	hole of the demon
rath (raw)	ring-fort	Rathdrum	the fort on the ridge
rinn	point	Rinkyle	wooded point
ros, ross	headland	Rossnaree	headland of the king
sean (shan)	old	Shandangan	old stronghold
sidh(e), (shee)	fairy hill	Ard na Sidhe	hill of the fairies
sliabh (slieve)	mountain	Slieveanamon	mountain of the women
tober (tubber)	well	Toberaheeny	Friday's well
tor	tower	Toormore	big tower
trá	beach, strand	Bantry	white beach
tuaim (toom)	burial ground	Tuam	burial mound
torc (turk)	boar	Inishturk	island of the boar
uaran (ooran)	cold spring	Oranmore	big/great cold spring

*Dublin's traditional name is Baile atha Cliath, the town of the ford of hurdles
Consultant: Maírin Maguire-Murphy, Drom Caoin, entry 61

Drumcreehy House
Ballyvaughan, Co. Clare

Eyes front to the shimmer of Galway Bay, eyes back to the Burren strangeness: this fabulous spot was what Armin and Bernadette really wanted. She used to come here as a child, he fell under the spell when they moved from Germany with their dream of running an old country guest house in Ireland. They looked and looked. In the end they built a new one – in solid old style. Its lemony façade and white dormers blend well into the surroundings, whitethorn and fuchsia hedges now make a colourful border and, beyond the reception desk, they have indeed created a handsome guest house. Wooden floors, old walnut furniture and an ever-lit open fire make for a homely atmosphere, while the two breakfast rooms vie for custom: choose Yellow for morning sun, Red for the exceptional view at any hour. Breakfast is a mouth-watering spread of stewed and fresh fruits, local meats, cheeses and fish, home-baked breads, pastries,... Generous bedrooms, each with a hand-painted local wild flower nameplate, are spick and span in their mixture of old and new pine furniture; bathrobes, too. Great value.

rooms	12: 5 doubles, 7 twins/doubles.
price	€80-€100. Singles €50-€80.
meals	Choice in village.
closed	Rarely.
directions	From Ennis R476 to Corofin; through village, right R480 to Ballyvaughan; right in village at Hylands Hotel. House 1.5km on right past blue cottage.

	Bernadette & Armin Moloney-Grefkes
tel	+353 (0)65 707 7377
fax	+353 (0)65 707 7379
email	info@drumcreehyhouse.com
web	www.drumcreehyhouse.com

Guest house

Map 3 Entry 85

Gregans Castle Hotel
Ballyvaughan, Co. Clare

In overwhelming scenery, Gregans' darkly imposing look belies the gentle open-doored open-armed welcome of the aromatic turf fire, the quirky antiques and the jug of unpretentious country flowers on the hall mantelpiece. Simon and Frederieke, a particularly charming, outgoing, no-nonsense couple with buckets of energy, have taken over from his parents and are bringing Gregans into the 21st century – slowly. So there's a bit of everything in this rabbit warren at present, an endearing confusion of country house traditional and clean-limbed 1930s elegance: old botanical prints and modern art in the drawing room, horse brasses on the hefty beams and super soft Bennison bird fabric at the windows in the bar, dated florals falling from pelmets to the superb new pale green carpet in the huge Galway Bay suite (stunning great Victorian antiques set off its fine bones), new tiles on bathroom floors, old on walls. A fascinating work in progress complemented by lovingly-made 50% organic food, a beautiful garden and an annual Burren rubbish removal commando. *Vegetarian meals available. Bikes for hire.*

rooms	21: 15 doubles & twins, 6 suites.
price	€180–€225. Singles €120–€180.
meals	Lunch €10–€30. Dinner €30–€55.
closed	Late October to late March.
directions	From Ballyvaughan N67 south 5km then follow signs.

Hotel

	Simon & Frederieke Haden
tel	+353 (0)65 707 7005
fax	+353 (0)65 707 7111
email	stay@gregans.ie
web	www.gregans.ie

Map 3 Entry 86

Mount Vernon
New Quay (Burren), Co. Clare

Gazing across cornflowers and poppies to the dancing bay, the house flows, airy and gentle, like one of the Impressionist paintings famously collected by Hugh Lane when he lived here. Then came Lady Augusta Gregory, bringing Yeats, Synge, Shaw and the Celtic literary revival in her wake. There are three Augustus John fireplaces – and more. The place oozes artistic temperament. Ally, the bright Mercury, and Mark, the laid-back Epicurus, both talented and interesting, fit it perfectly. They have added some astounding and exotic travel mementoes to the lovely pieces left by Mark's mother – Kalahari bushmen's baskets, vast green birds from Bali, great kites in the kitchen, elephants everywhere (their 'thing'). It's not a shrine to the past, rather a vibrant evolving home where dining and drawing rooms are stunning in their mix of soft colours, antiques and quirky modern pieces and bedrooms are a delight. They work as a team in the kitchen, Mark creating imaginative wonders with whatever he finds, straight from the sea, Ally baking breads and making puddings. An exceptional place.

rooms	5: 4 doubles, 1 single.
price	€99. Singles €99.
meals	Dinner €49. By arrangement.
closed	January-March.
directions	From Dublin N6 then N18 south 19km to Kilcolgan; right N67 through Kinvarra 7km; right to New Quay; 1st right after Linnanes Lobster Bar: 3rd house on shore.

	Mark Helmore & Ally Raftery
tel	+353 (0)65 707 8126
fax	+353 (0)65 707 8118
email	mtvernon@eircom.net
web	www.hiddenireland.com/mountvernon

Country house

Map 3 Entry 87

Vaughan Lodge Hotel

Ennistymon Road, Lahinch, Co. Clare

Michael can't help himself: a fourth-generation hotelier, he wants things to be perfect for his guests and is putting his heart and soul into his new hotel. He has a charming, twinkling presence, clever ideas (big drying room, extendable bedside reading lights), an eye for detail and is an interesting photographer. Lovely people, he and Maria chose a modern-classic interior designer and are still adding their essential personal touches to the low-key high-luxury result. Everything that comes to them has a story attached. The family's 1850s mahogany sideboard presides over the hexagonal dining room, an eclectic collection of old china smiles out of an antique cabinet on the way to the bedrooms, generous friends leave great paintings, a piano, a plant,… The Vaughans and chef Philippe Farineau care hugely about local produce and traceability, their butcher and fishmonger are named, their food is of the highest quality. You will lounge in leather to read Michael's invaluable local guides or Golfing Ireland, dine excellently under his convivial guidance, sleep in smooth/crisp white and plum comfort.

rooms	22: 21 doubles, 1 suite.
price	€140–€300.
meals	Dinner €42–€55.
closed	November–March.
directions	From Ennis N67 to Lahinch. Hotel just inside 50km zone.

Hotel

Michael & Maria Vaughan

tel	+353 (0)65 708 1111
fax	+353 (0)65 708 1011
email	michael@vaughanlodge.ie
web	www.vaughanlodge.ie

Map 3 Entry 88

Moy House
Lahinch, Co. Clare

Moy House is different: it looks not landwards but out to sea, to the mercurial Atlantic whose raging grey tempests and deliriously pink sunsets can hold you, recharging your soul, for hours. There's a sandy beach at the bottom of the garden and the awesome Cliffs of Moher rise from the sea in the distance. Built on 9,000 acres in the 1820s as a summer house for Augustine Fitzgerald, Moy now stands on just 15 well-kept acres that include an ever-developing organic vegetable garden and orchard: good news for dinner. The incomparable O'Looney family, funny, intelligent, imaginative, have restored it into unintimidating formal splendour. In clear good taste, the feel is friendly and welcoming: exquisite antiques, original art, sumptuous bedrooms, even pop-up TVs in wooden cabinets. A glass-panelled floor in one of the stunning bathrooms looks down into the old well; a spiral wooden staircase leads up the tower for quiet contemplation at the summit. Dinner is superb and you will retire to find chocolates and slippers waiting for you: Brid O'Meara sees to that. Wonderful, worth every cent.

rooms	10: 4 doubles, 3 twins/doubles, 2 singles, 1 suite.	
price	€220-€260. Singles €135-€165. Suite €250-€295.	
meals	Dinner, 4 courses, €55.	
closed	January to mid-February.	
directions	From Lahinch, N67 south for Milltown Malbay 1.5km. Entrance on right in wooded dip.	

The O'Looney Family

tel	+353 (0)65 708 2800
fax	+353 (0)65 708 2500
email	moyhouse@eircom.net
web	www.moyhouse.com

Country house

Map 3 Entry 89

Berry Lodge & Cookery School
Annagh, Milltown Malbay, Co. Clare

An amazing cook, Rita sources the best of what is locally available on the basis that "it would be a crime not to use all the lovely fish we have on our doorstep". She used to have a popular radio show on cookery and still teaches here, with verve, including a course for Men in the Kitchen. The whole team are smiley, helpful, efficient and flexible, the place has a relaxed feel, dinner in the rustic cottage-style restaurant or the big light conservatory is fun and pleasurable (sizzling garlicky tiger prawns with pilpil then lavender crème brulée, for example). The locals love it. The modernised Victorian house, sheltered from the Atlantic blasts by its walled garden where patio chairs await you on balmier evenings (or there's the breakfast/sitting room), has been sweetly furnished with solid pine and thick rugs on wooden floors. Pretty bedrooms have window-seats, firm beds, warm colours, patchwork quilts, tied-back curtains, original fireplaces and, on generous days, views of the sea. Ask for an upstairs room. Breakfast absorbs the taste buds and seaside walks are ideal for rebuilding the appetite.

rooms	5: 2 doubles, 3 triples.
price	From €84. Singles from €50.
meals	Dinner, 4 courses, €35. By arrangement.
closed	January to mid-February.
directions	From Ennis N85 to Inagh; left R460 for Milltown Malbay. In village, N67 for Killimer car ferry road, past Bellbridge Hotel, over bridge, 2nd left; house 1st on right.

Restaurant with rooms

Rita Meade
tel   +353 (0)65 708 7022
fax   +353 (0)65 708 7011
email   info@berrylodge.com
web   www.berrylodge.com

Map 3 Entry 90

Fergus View

Kilnaboy, Corofin, Co. Clare

Declan, a school principal, is the latest in a long line of country teachers: this house was built 100 years ago and his great-grandfather was the first occupant, out here on the edge of the moon. A short walk through the Burren wilderness, with its weathered limestone, prehistoric dolmens and rare flowers, is said to be great therapy for mind and body. Declan can guide you to the best parts. Everything is done well here, both owners are eager to make you welcome and communicate their love of the Irish language and music, with original readers on phonetics displayed by the fire in the living room. Mary's breakfasts, with her own sodabread, are acclaimed by guests from all over the world. The small vibrantly-coloured bedrooms are compact and cosy with orthopædic beds, elegant bedcovers and timber windows that keep the cold out. The garden stretches down towards the River Fergus which disappears behind a welter of colour in summer. You can walk to the ruins of an Elizabethan fortress or a medieval churchyard, then out into the moonscape. Genuine Irish hospitality in a lovely family home.

rooms	6 + 1: 3 doubles, 1 twin/double, 1 family, all en suite; 1 double with separate bathroom. Cottage for 5.
price	€74-€76. Singles €52-€54. Cottage €400-€640 per week.
meals	Restaurants 3km.
closed	Mid-October to February.
directions	From Shannon N18 through Ennis to r'bout for Ennistymon 3km; right R476 to Corofin then Kilnaboy. House on left after ruined church.

Mary & Declan Kelleher

tel	+353 (0)65 6837606
fax	+353 (0)65 6837192
email	deckell@indigo.ie
web	www.fergusview.com

B&B & Self-catering

Map 3 Entry 91

Ballyportry Castle
Corofin, Co. Clare

Walk into this Gaelic tower house and step back in time. It was built in the late 15th century, occupied for 200 years, left to decline, saved at last in the 1960s by an American; its history vibrates beneath your feet. The present owners, architect and archæologist, let the original dynamic of Ballyportry guide them in their brilliant conservation project: its ancient fabric demands deep respect (hence the damages deposit). Four floors pile room upon room – vaulted ceilings, massive fireplaces – up to the roof where hammocks are slung between battlements for sunbathing, stargazing, Burren poetry; come at full moon. First you encounter the kitchen: giant fireplace, of course, range and pans, Liscannor stone coffee table – and mod cons neatly hidden away, plus a bathroom. Next, two great bedrooms, one with a huge waterbed and a stone bath in an alcove, the other a four-poster. The much smaller twins and their bathroom are off the tall winding stone stairs and the top floor explodes in atmosphere with its double-height living room and another smaller kitchen. Ballyportry is a unique experience.

rooms	Castle for 8-10 (2 doubles, 2 twins, 2 singles, 2 bathrooms, extra wc).
price	€2,300-€2,900 per week. 2-4 day break €1,900. Prices for 4-8 people. Electricity & heating extra.
meals	Dinner & breakfast can be arranged in advance. Otherwise self-catering.
closed	Never.
directions	Directions given on booking.

Self-catering

	Siobhán Cuffe & Patrick Wallace
tel	+353 (0)1 660 9038
fax	+353 (0)1 663 0011
email	info@ballyportry.ie
web	www.ballyportry.ie

Map 3 Entry 92

Mount Cashel Lodge
Kilmurry, Sixmilebridge, Co. Clare

First, the remoteness squeezes your mind, then the setting grabs your eyes, then your hosts will seize your heart. They so love this place that you cannot conceivably leave unconverted. Some say it's the best self-catering in the west. The two pretty 18th-century stone lodges stand creeper-clung round a courtyard, the stables stand apart. Renovated with a light, sensitive hand, they feel unassuming and genuine, the interiors done in a straightforward modern country style for comfort and practicality: good pine kitchens with all the bits, iron beds with excellent bedding, proper armchairs before open fires, French doors to private terraces stretching out to the limpid lake and moorland. Barbecues are there for guests to use, even baby-sitting (book ahead). The beautiful lakeside position, its paths, boats and rich fishing, are yours for the duration. Pat has built a jetty, provides safety equipment and is ever willing to guide and advise. You are 20 minutes from Limerick and Ennis; famous Dromoland Castle is just down the road; a perfect base for day trips to Clare, Kerry, Connemara and Cork.

rooms	2 lodges for 5 (1 twin, 1 triple , 1 bathroom). Stables for 9 (3 doubles, 1 triple, 4 bathrooms).
price	€600–€1,600 per week.
meals	Self-catering.
closed	Never.
directions	From Limerick N18 for Ennis 15km; exit Cratloe onto R462 through Sixmilebridge 2.5km; right after castle, follow signs for Mt Cashel Lodge: lane 1km by stone wall on left, long drive through black gates.

	Pat & Annette Shanahan
tel	+353 (0)61 369142
fax	+353 (0)61 369142
email	pat@mtcashel.com
web	www.mtcashel.com

Self-catering

Map 3 Entry 93

Old Parochial House Cottages

Old Parochial House, Cooraclare, Kilrush, Co. Clare

West Clare is steeped in culture, has pubs that swing to traditional music, fabulous countryside, beautiful deserted beaches, cliff walks – and friendly easy-going people. None more so than Alyson and Seán in their 1872 former parish priest's house. The main house stands on four acres overlooking the sleepy village of Cooraclare. The old stables, coach house and shibeen have been converted and two stone cottages built in traditional Irish style. All the O'Neills' work, it's a labour of love expressed in turf fires, stone floors, exposed beams, old artefacts and bags of character. It would be hard to pick a favourite but the open-plan living room in the stables is beautiful, with views over rolling countryside. Lean on your half-door, breathe the heavy gorse-scented air, chat to whomever goes by – and take your time. Goats and a pony graze the front field and there are three pubs in the village with good beer and music, five minutes' walk away. The Cliffs of Moher and the magical Burren are not that far. Come and let the world go by: just being here will do you a power of good. *50km from Shannon airport.*

rooms	6 cottages: 1 for 5 (2 doubles, 1 single, 1 shower); 4 for 2-3 (1 double, 1 single, 1 shower); 1 for 3-4 (2 doubles, 1 shower).
price	€310–€600 per week.
meals	Self-catering.
closed	Rarely.
directions	From Ennis N68 for Kilrush 29km; right to Cooraclare, following signs. In village, right at petrol station R483 for coast; 3rd house on left.

Self-catering

	Alyson & Seán O'Neill
tel	+353 (0)65 905 9059
fax	+353 (0)65 905 9059
email	oldparochialhouse@eircom.net
web	www.oldparochialhouse.com

Map 6 Entry 94

Glin Castle
Glin, Co. Limerick

The FitzGeralds have lived by the Shannon since 1200: Desmond FitzGerald is the 29th Knight of Glin. Drive through cow-grazed parkland to find the river flowing sublimely past, 400 yards from the front door. Enter to fanfares of aristocratic splendour: Corinthian columns, swords fanned on the walls, staggeringly beautiful ceilings, incredible Irish antiques. Open fires leap in the deep blue library, the sinful red smoking room, the fine drawing room that floods with river light. Not an hotel, something grander, rarer: a castle home. Downstairs, a square piano, pedimented mahogany doors and an old stringless harp. Climb the flying staircase to glorious rooms and find chaises-longues, old dressers, gilt mirrors, armchairs in waiting by claw-footed baths. Garden flowers grace the rooms. Tumble back down the stairs and a huge window frames the formal garden. You are free to roam the 400 acres and their woodland walks. There are probably other things to do locally but you may wish to spurn them for the grandeur of Glin, one of Ireland's treasures. *Minimum stay two nights. Children over ten welcome. Tennis on site.*

rooms	15: 4 doubles, 10 twins/doubles, 1 four-poster.
price	€310–€495. Whole property €5,900 per day.
meals	Dinner, 4 courses, €53.
closed	November–March. Off-season by arrangement.
directions	From Limerick N69 west 51km to Glin; left up main street; right at top of square; entrance straight ahead. Tabert car ferry 6.5km.

Desmond & Olda FitzGerald
tel +353 (0)68 34173
fax +353 (0)68 34364
email knight@iol.ie
web www.glincastle.com

Country house

Map 6 Entry 95

Fitzgerald's Farmhouse & Riding Centre

Mount Marian, Abbeyfeale Hill, Abbeyfeale, Co. Limerick

Riding centre, animal sanctuary and B&B (self-catering coming soon), this place has a cheerful, youthful, happening atmosphere. There are poultry, rabbits and, of course, horses and ponies galore. Tim, former athlete and gentle giant, has built special pens so children can wander safely. A two-mile walk leads past the stream to a gazebo with lovely views, then to an exhibition of antique farm machinery. Comfortable, jolly bedrooms have bright yellow walls and wooden floors. The ever-bubbly Kathleen serves meals in the dining room, among the family snaps but you're always welcome in the kitchen or the guest sitting room with its open fire and the family's riding and athletics trophies. They own 30 horses and specialise in riding and riding holidays: anything from a couple of days to children's summer camps or riding-and-English for young foreigners. Tackle the cross-country course, trek through stunning countryside, gallop on Beale beach… Non-riders can go golfing or walking in the Stack Mountains, knowing the young are in safe hands. Fun and welcoming for parents and children alike.

rooms	7: 2 doubles, 3 twins, 2 family rooms.
price	€70–€105. Singles €50.
meals	Dinner €30.
closed	Rarely.
directions	From Limerick N21 for Tralee 64km to Abbeyfeale; left in square, between O'Rourke's Bar & Cellar Bar. House up hill on left 1.5km, signposted.

B&B

	Kathleen & Tim Fitzgerald
tel	+353 (0)68 31217
fax	+353 (0)68 31558
email	fitzfarmhouse@eircom.net
web	www.fitzgeraldsfarmhouse.com

Map 6 Entry 96

Flemingstown House
Kilmallock, Co. Limerick

Soft towels and sweet-clove apple tart: "Imelda is a lovely lovely lady," says one reader, and a fine cook who grows her own fruit. The square old farmhouse has been in the family for generations. Inside its thick walls, there's not a right-angle to be seen and it is stuffed with fascinating antiques. Clean, comfortable bedrooms have king-size beds, all differently attractive – embossed Regency, inlaid French – with sweetly embroidered sheets, lovely quilts, roomy showers and baths, views over fields and a lush orchard. There are lots of peaceful walks around the farm with more in the surrounding Golden Vale and the Ballyhoura Mountains. What really sets this place apart is Imelda and her fabulous cooking; she studied in Cork – and must have been a good student. You eat round one big dining table in a pretty conservatory that sparkles with Waterford crystal; the stained-glass windows were designed by the late Bill Malone, a church glass maker; aromatherapy sessions can be arranged. Imelda runs the house with the help of her daughter and daughter-in-law; you are in safe hands.

rooms	5: 4 doubles, 1 family; extra bath.
price	€120-€140. Singles €65.
meals	Dinner €40.
	Packed lunch on request.
closed	November-February.
directions	From Limerick R512 to Kilmallock; leave Kilmallock on small road to Tipperary for Fermoy (don't take left bend to by-pass) 3km; house on left, set back from road.

Imelda Sheedy-King

tel	+353 (0)63 98093
fax	+353 (0)63 98546
email	info@flemingstown.com
web	www.flemingstown.com

B&B

Map 7 Entry 97

The Mustard Seed at Echo Lodge

Ballingarry, Co. Limerick

The Mustard Seed (a biblical quote) gets top marks on all counts. Dan's cheerful energy makes the whole place sparkle: nothing seems beyond his creative grasp and his presence will bring a smile to the stoniest face. Step over the sleeping cat into a sumptuous world of understated excess, a shrine to colour and good taste. Dan's many backpacking journeys have fathered all this far-flung exotica: hangings, silk prints, maps and other worldly goods to delight the senses, yet nothing is overdone. Some exciting new recipes arrived on that camel, too. Authentic luxury washes over you: deep sofas and carved marble fireplaces, elephants and a few thrones, crackling fires and bedrooms full of lovelinesses – big armoires, lacquered screens, more exotic wall hangings, rugs on warm wooden floors. There are ten rooms in the main house and six in the old schoolhouse where ground-floor suites have windows onto terraces. Then there's the restaurant with its superb atmosphere of candles and opulent flowers on every table. We haven't even scratched the surface, so come and dig deeper yourself. *Pets by arrangement.*

The staggering two-acre organic kitchen garden, a work of art, a labour of love, produces artichokes and alpine strawberries, pumpkins and exotic cucumbers, even grapes - they make wine, so there's a statue of Bacchus, naturally. The weeds are plucked daily and not a drop of chemistry is spread. Meet the chefs picking dinner right here. They have their own bakery, make whatever they can with their own hands, pour fresh fruit juices into fine glasses every morning and serve exceptional food in their renowned restaurant.

rooms	16: 6 doubles, 2 twins, 1 family, 3 singles, 1 four-poster, 3 suites.
price	€180-€320. Singles from €120.
meals	Dinner, 2-4 courses, €37-€56. Light lunch for residents. Restaurant closed on Mondays November to spring.
closed	Rarely.
directions	From Limerick N21 to Rathkeale; left R518 to Ballingarry; in village follow signs.

	Daniel Mullane
tel	+353 (0)69 68508
fax	+353 (0)69 68511
email	mustard@indigo.ie
web	www.mustardseed.ie

SPECIAL GREEN ENTRY
see page 16

Hotel

Map 7 Entry 98

Allo's Townhouse
41 Church Street, Listowel, Co. Kerry

Listowel, a pretty little market town above the River Feale with none of the gaudy gaiety of some Kerry places, was is home to Writers' Week, Ireland's top literary event. Thanks to Helen's loyalty to local artists, Allo's has a clear artistic bent too, and the restaurant is hung with big and interesting pictures. Armel and Helen are both chefs with a talent for spoiling the most temperate souls: they offer generous helpings of good bistro food in the lively atmosphere of the traditional bar with its wooden booths, or superb fish and game in the smarter foodie restaurant next door. And for added romance, you can now dine al fresco. Armel is proud of his collection of Irish whiskeys — one vintage malt costs a whopping €60 a shot - but he's prouder of his happy young staff and his care for ingredient sourcing. The stylish bedrooms upstairs are full of panache: baroque mirrors, designer lampshades, maybe a four-poster bed, an oil painting, a cherub pedestal. Bathrooms have claw-footed baths and green Connemara marble. No breakfast here but several super coffee shops, one opposite, open by 9am.

rooms	3: 2 doubles, 1 twin.
price	€90-€100. Singles €55. Breakfast not served.
meals	Lunch from €9. Dinner, 2 courses, €35.
closed	Sundays & Mondays. Christmas Day, New Year's Day, Good Friday.
directions	From Limerick N69 to Tarbert then to Listowel. House on left in High St, with bay trees outside.

Inn

	Armel Whyte & Helen Mullane
tel	+353 (0)68 22880
fax	+353 (0)68 22803
email	allosbar@eircom.net

Map 6 Entry 99

Mount Rivers

Listowel, Co. Kerry

Friendly Mount Rivers has been in the family since 1869 and Liz keeps it the simple, comfy, warmly welcoming home it has always been, with tea and delicious cakes on arrival, communal breakfasts at a smart mahogany table (homemade scones, full Irish extravaganza), and books to read by an ever-smouldering fire. Bedrooms come in different shapes and sizes, the same homely décor covering all. One has wooden Bavarian beds (grandmother's dowry), there are stripped floors, country dressers, floral duvets and flowers from the garden. The big room, flooded with light from its double-aspect windows, comes with a nursery and is ideal for families. Shower rooms are adequate. You're wrapped in 35 acres (watch out for the bull), so a good night's sleep is assured, and you can follow the river Feale into town passing the Garden of Europe and the recently-renovated castle. Liz, fount of knowledge for all things Listowel, will point you in the right direction. Ballybunion (golfer's heaven) is up the road and golfing stars have slept in these very rooms. Then hunker down with one of those books.

rooms	3: 1 double, 1 family; 1 twin with separate bath.
price	€60-€70.
meals	Choice of restaurants within 1.5km.
closed	Rarely.
directions	From Listowel, south over bridge & straight ahead (not right for Tralee); right after 100 yds; house immediately right.

	Robbie Robitzki & Liz O'Reilly	
tel	+353 (0)68 21494	
fax	+353 (0)68 23366	B&B
email	robbie@iol.ie	
web	www.mountriverslistowel.com	

Map 6 Entry 100

Gorman's Clifftop House & Restaurant

Glaise Bheag, Ballydavid (Dingle Peninsula), Co. Kerry

Vincent and Sile (Sheila in Gaelic) have done amazing things here, turning their modest café and B&B into a luxurious restaurant with rooms. Their philosophy is simple and reassuring, they provide everything you need: a genuine welcome, good food, an excellent bed. You find wooden furniture crafted in Tralee, Louis Mulcahy pottery, arty sea-shell prints in rooms with warm colours where you feel you're almost walking into an Atlantic sunset ("a happy coincidence", says Sile) and organic fair-trade coffee at breakfast. The restaurant looks across Smerwick Harbour to the Three Sisters and the giant ocean beyond – stunning at all times. Vincent's robust and flavoursome Irish cooking uses local and organic ingredients where possible: Dingle Bay prawns, Irish Hereford beef, farmhouse cheeses. The Gorman family has lived on the land since the 1700s and this is one of the few areas left in Ireland where Gaelic is the first language. Hire bikes for the Slea Head Drive, explore the many archæological sites, or just curl up next to the turf fire. This is place of high standards, lots of space, great people.

rooms	9: 6 doubles, 3 triples.
price	€120-€190. Singles €85-€125.
meals	Dinner €37.50.
closed	Christmas; 5 January-12 February.
directions	From Dingle take R559 with harbour on left to r'bout; go straight across for An Fheothanach 6.5km; fork left. House 6.5km on left beside round house.

Restaurant with rooms

	Sile & Vincent Gorman
tel	+353 (0)66 915 5162
fax	+353 (0)66 915 5003
email	info@gormans-clifftophouse.com
web	www.gormans-clifftophouse.com

Map 6 Entry 101

Greenmount House

Gortonora, Dingle, Co. Kerry

Greenmount may not be the most beautiful house in the world to look at but the interior was designed by a young local architect as his end-of-year project: he passed with flying colours. It is a place of great style, wall-to-wall carpets and easy living where sitting spaces with slow-burning fires flow into each other. There are a number of large, split-level suite-style bedrooms, each with simple décor, thick carpets, a sitting area and doors to a balcony; standard rooms have the same facilities but are smaller, of course. The long conservatory dining room is beautifully lit by natural light. The house stands on a hill overlooking Dingle Bay and its famous resident, Fungi the dolphin. Wonderfully friendly Mary likes to ensure every guest feels able to relax and unwind here. Not bad after 20 years in the business. The deliciously moist Citrus Cake is memorable and one reader wrote that "this must be best breakfast in the world". Come to Dingle for fabulous walking across dramatic cliff, hill and sea scenery studded with prehistory, but bear in mind that it gets very crowded in the middle of summer.

rooms	9: 3 doubles, 6 suites.
price	€100–€170. Singles from €70.
meals	Restaurants in Dingle.
closed	December & January.
directions	N86 into Dingle, right at r'bout; right at next junction; up hill; house on left.

Mary & John Curran
tel	+353 (0)66 915 1414
fax	+353 (0)66 915 1974
email	info@greenmount-house.com
web	www.greenmount-house.com

B&B

Map 6 Entry 102

The Captain's House
The Mall, Dingle, Co. Kerry

Jim was a captain in the Merchant Navy, he and Mary both sail, their house is full of pictures of boats, and you would think it appropriately named – only it was built in 1840 for a Captain of the Railway. Standing by a stream, it is reached across a romantic bridge and through the very pretty little garden. The warren-like interior has all its original personality behind the decorative florals and plushes, ornaments and carved antiques of the Milhenches' snug and welcoming sitting areas. Theirs is true old Irish style with inviting bedrooms that feel like ships' cabins: compact comfort and florals, antique dressers and good beds. The conservatory dining room is their creation, however – ideal for those superb breakfasts. Jim knows all there is to know about Dingle past and present and will tell you the tales, without mincing his words. Mary is a gentle, easy person whose house must be one of the cleanest ever. She loves her cat, her furry, friendly old dog and her garden, which was radically replanted in 2005. Their luxurious self-catering bungalow nearby has sea views.

rooms	9 + 1: 5 doubles, 1 twin, 2 singles, 1 suite. Bungalow for 8.
price	€90–€100. Suite €130. Singles €60. Bungalow €1,250-€1,750 p.w.
meals	Restaurants in Dingle.
closed	Mid-November to mid-March.
directions	N86 to Dingle; right at r'bout for Connor Pass and Town Centre. House 200m on left, with footbridge over stream.

B&B & Self-catering

	Mary & Jim Milhench
tel	+353 (0)66 915 1531
fax	+353 (0)66 915 1079
email	captigh@eircom.net
web	www.captainsdingle.com

Map 6 Entry 103

Emlagh Country House
Dingle, Co. Kerry

Big old country houses are an extinct breed in Dingle so the next best thing is Emlagh House, designed in 2000 as if it was an extension to an old Georgian house, beautifully done and apparently just as natural. The results are pretty awesome and a few seasons' growth in the landscaped garden have softened the surroundings. There are only ten bedrooms, a luxurious collection of vastnesses decorated with great style and panache. Each one is themed and painted in the colours of native Kerry flowers. All have wide beds, springy carpets, creative lighting, CD players, heated mirrors, creaky antique cupboards – and chocolates on the turned-down beds. There's a John Bronsmead piano in the drawing room, Irish art all over the house, history books and internet in the library and views across Dingle Bay from the breakfast conservatory. The attention to detail is extraordinary. The Kavanagh family give really friendly service and Gráinne, the hands-on 'head girl' here, knows what people want. Mount Brandon just asks to be climbed and Dingle has 53 pubs to celebrate in afterwards.

rooms	10: 8 doubles, 2 twins.
price	€190-€290. Singles €115-€185.
meals	Restaurants in Dingle.
closed	November to mid-March.
directions	Entering Dingle on N86, 1st left after Shell garage; house on corner.

Gráinne & Marion Kavanagh
tel	+353 (0)66 915 2345
fax	+353 (0)66 915 2369
email	info@emlaghhouse.com
web	www.emlaghhouse.com

Guest house

Map 6 Entry 104

The Old Anchor
Main Street, Annascaul Village, Dingle Peninsula, Co. Kerry

Tom Crean, a member of Shackleton's expedition, was born in Annascaul. Marie the hotelier and Maeve the walker, deeply into the Crean Society, tell endless fascinating stories collected from explorers' descendents, Shackleton's leather ration bag hangs on the wall and you feel Crean and his pipe could walk in any minute. The Old Anchor buzzes with life and encounters. Where other places have a view, a lovely garden or gorgeous antiques, here you meet the village: the resident magician, perhaps, or the keeper of folk tales and songs. You could continue over a glass at the South Pole Inn. Marie, the quiet considerate anchor in this social mælstrom, also runs painting courses with established artists from a studio behind the guest house. With the beautiful Dingle Peninsula on the doorstep, inspiration is guaranteed. Long sandy beaches, pebble coves and mountain ranges dotted with prehistory are close enough to walk to, the hiking is exceptional. Comfortable bedrooms are plain, simple, modern, a hearty breakfast sets you up for a day's exploration: this is the Ireland one hopes to discover.

rooms	7 twins/doubles.
price	€70. Singles €42.
meals	Dinner €30, by arrangement (min. 8 people). Pub within walking distance. Packed lunch €5.
closed	Mid-December to mid-March.
directions	From Killarney N72 to Castlemaine; left R561 for Dingle. Right N86 for Tralee. Annascaul 1km: house in middle of village, on right.

Guest house

	Marie Kennedy
tel	+353 (0)66 915 7382
fax	+353 (0)66 915 7382
email	dropanchor@eircom.net
web	www.walkingbootstours.com

Map 6 Entry 105

Fleur & Kizzie Cottages
Sunhill, Killorglin, Co. Kerry

These sweet hideaway cottages are ineffably romantic, the site is stunning, the views over to the Macgillycuddy Reeks, Ireland's highest mountains, will swallow your heart at any time of day. Set in a fine mature garden, the minute Kizzie for two and the larger Fleur for a family have been renovated, decorated and furnished with flair, loving care, well-chosen furniture on warm wooden floors, and delightful fabrics. The style is perfectly cottagey without ever being twee and the nostalgic aroma of an open turf fire is the best thing ever when you come in from a long day's fishing, walking or history-hunting. The two sofas in Fleur, the one in Kizzie just ask to be relaxed into. Their kitchens have the old-fashioned patina of slate floors and weathered pine – and all the modern bits you expect. Bedrooms rejoice in tempting quilted bedding on new old-style beds and good storage space. In Kizzie, you can lie in bed and gaze at those magic mountains. In Fleur, the sunroom draws them in. Each has its own patio or garden spot with barbecue and furniture. And pretty Killorglin is within walking distance.

rooms	2 cottages: Fleur for 5 (1 double, 1 family, 1 bath); Kizzie for 2-3 (1 double, 1 sofabed, 1 bath).
price	Fleur: €350-€650. Kizzie: €250-€450. Prices per week.
meals	Self-catering. Restaurants within walking distance.
closed	Rarely.
directions	From Killarney to Killorglin. Cross bridge, through town square, down narrow one-way ahead, over small r'bt; cont. 3km, cottages on left.

	Joanne McNicholl
tel	+44 (0)7919 982305
email	info@kerry-country-cottages.com
web	www.kerry-country-cottages.com

Self-catering

Map 6 Entry 106

Carrig House
Caragh Lake, Killorglin, Co. Kerry

At the end of a long wooded drive, this mid-19th-century country house looks out onto the timeless beauty of Caragh Lake, a supreme spot, discovered by Frank and Mary 25 years ago. They run their stylish house with a good-natured professional touch, he full of likeable charm and disarming patter, she ministering with sincere warmth and a big smile; she is also the interior designer. Dinner, by a multi-talented team of chefs, is memorable: Carrig's reputation as "possibly the best restaurant in Kerry" is well deserved. Ponder the menu with an aperitif by the fire in the snug drawing room then move into the intimate atmosphere of the lake-view dining room. Comfortable bedrooms mix old and modern. The suite with its lushly-draped arch and lake views and the double with wisteria creeping round the windows both have a lovely old-fashioned grace befitting a house of this period. 1,000 different plant species deck the garden. There are walks through woods with secluded seating areas, a path down to the lake and the small jetty. Fishing, golf and hill walking can be arranged. *Children over 10 welcome.*

rooms	16: 12 doubles, 3 twins, 1 single.
price	€130-€350. Singles €110-€180.
meals	Dinner, 4 courses, €38.
closed	December-February.
directions	From Killorglin N70 for Glenbeigh 5km; left for Caragh Lake 2.5km; right at village shop, entrance on left.

Hotel

	Frank & Mary Slattery
tel	+353 (0)66 976 9100
fax	+353 (0)66 976 9166
email	info@carrighouse.com
web	www.carrighouse.com

Map 6 Entry 107

Ard Na Sidhe

Caragh Lake, Killorglin, Co. Kerry

Great gardens are a hallmark of western Ireland and Ard Na Sidhe ('fairy hill', pronounced 'she') has a garden to rival most. Beside the lake you find 40 exhilarating acres of mature woodland, tiered beds, stone-flagged paths and trim lawns – a tranquil Irish Eden. Paths lead to the water and you can row across to Robert's Island for absolute stillness. The house, a sporting lodge built in 1913 by the Gordons, as in gin, looks much older than it is (another Irish trait), while the mullioned windows that you find all over the house **are** old – 1713 to be precise, swiped from an Edinburgh mansion. In good weather you can breakfast on the terrace or take afternoon tea in the garden but two fires in the huge sitting room guard against the odd spot of rain and there's a grand piano on which to practise your Shostakovich. Old radiators, thick walls, grand furniture – that says it all. Bedrooms, five with lake views, are split between the main house and the garden rooms, the décor is 'smart floral', thin-legged period chairs and not a TV in sight. Expect wooden beds, dressing tables, draped crowns and fluffy bath towels.

rooms	18 twins/doubles.
price	€160–€290. Singles from €150.
meals	Dinner à la carte from €50.
closed	October–April.
directions	From Killorglin N70 for Cahersiveen; 1st left for Caragh Lake; straight over x-roads for 1.6km; house sign on right.

Nuala Brunner

tel	+353 (0)66 976 9105
fax	+353 (0)64 32118
email	hotelsales@liebherr.com
web	www.killarneyhotels.ie

Hotel

Map 6 Entry 108

Arbutus Hotel

College Street, Killarney, Co. Kerry

A fabulous place. A star in today's hotel sky, the Arbutus sings of an Ireland past – smart, solid, quietly prosperous, the stalking ground of wealthy farmers who gathered here on market days to chew the Killarney cud. It has its own history. In 1909, Tim Buckley decided, at 24, to buy the place. Penniless, he sought his fortune (and a wealthy wife) in New York, returned 16 years later, bought his dream and ran it until he died at 93. His daughter-in-law Norrie, grandson Sean and Sean's wife Carol keep the place shining brightly: they are wonderful. The feel is crackling fires, polished floors, leather benches in the oak-panelled bar and a chandelier in the ladies loo. Original woodwork throughout the hotel has Celtic motifs carved into it. Bedrooms are impeccable and excellent value: plush fabrics, big old beds, crisp sheets and blankets, well-upholstered armchairs. There's Gaelic music in the bar, great food in the restaurant, peace and quiet in the drawing room. Delightful staff stop for a chat; they are part of an extended family and make sure you get what you want. Very special indeed, don't miss it.

Hotel

rooms	37: 33 twins/doubles, 2 family suites, 2 four-posters.
price	€130-€180. Singles €70-€120. Suites from €170.
meals	Lunch €8-€16. Dinner, 3 courses, €35; also à la carte. Restaurant closed Sun or Mon low season.
closed	Mid-December to mid-January.
directions	N22 into Killarney from north: left at r'bout for Cork 500m; 1st right to T-junc.; hotel directly opposite.

Sean & Carol Buckley

tel	+353 (0)64 31037
fax	+353 (0)64 34033
email	stay@arbutuskillarney.com
web	www.arbutuskillarney.com

Map 6 Entry 109

Killarney Royal
College Street, Killarney, Co. Kerry

Here is a luxury hotel that breathes an atmosphere of friendly splendour. No self-righteous snobbery, just genuine attention. Rooms have hotel class yet friendly, helpful staff, most of whom have been here a decade or more, work together to give you that personal dedication you expect from smaller places. Margaret and Joe are justly proud of this great team spirit. The pair were nurses before Margaret inherited the Royal. Her family has a long pedigree in hotel management so they could easily have sat back and tapped the voracious Killarney market. Instead, she scoured Europe for new ideas and then became her own interior designer with remarkable, occasionally stunning, results. Luxurious rooms are all different, doffing their cap to the restrained elegance of French and Italian styles; many of the curtains were made by an old school friend. Margaret's tour de force is the split-level dining room, its centrepiece a chandelier hanging from a beautiful circular moulded ceiling. The Royal is a cut above the rest of the hotel troop. Plus broadband, massage, receptions... *Amex cards accepted.*

rooms	29: 10 twins, 14 twins/doubles, 5 suites.
price	€140–€360. Singles €120–€205.
meals	Dinner, 4 courses, €35.
closed	Christmas.
directions	College Street in Killarney town centre. Hotel opposite Arbutus Hotel.

	Joe & Margaret Scally
tel	+353 (0)64 31853
fax	+353 (0)64 34001
email	info@killarneyroyal.ie
web	www.killarneyroyal.ie

Hotel

Map 6 Entry 110

The Cahernane House Hotel

Muckross Road, Killarney, Co. Kerry

Killarney's only big, luxury, country-house hotel, Cahernane is the mixture you might expect of old Irish history and modern hotel comforts. The original neo-Gothic house, built in 1877 by the Herbert family, Earls of Pembroke, on the site of their previous mansion, rejoices in old marble fireplaces, heavy creaky doors, family portraits, exquisite wood-framed mullioned windows onto water meadows and an elegant sitting/music room. The fire always burns beneath the extraordinary carved ceiling in the splendid hall. History lingers in the air. The big new wing has larger rooms but all are sedately smart and softly comfortable in their high-class mahogany repro, crisp linen and padded headboards. There are balconies in some, garden doors in others. You can hear cathedral bells chiming across the fields. Bring your wellies, walk out of the gate, down to the lake and into miles of National Park. Or stroll ten minutes into the town centre. Then back for fine formal dinner, served with Cahernane graciousness in the smart well-reputed restaurant, or relaxed bar food in the old wine cellar. *Tennis on site.*

rooms	38: 36 twins/doubles, 2 suites.
price	€264-€420. Suites €320-€380.
meals	Dinner, 4 courses with coffee, €39; à la carte from €20. Lunch from €12.
closed	Christmas & New Year.
directions	From Killarney N71 for Kenmare, through traffic lights, over bridge, right at sign into long leafy drive.

Hotel

Sarah Brown

tel	+353 (0)64 31895
fax	+353 (0)64 34340
email	info@cahernane.com
web	www.cahernane.com

Map 6 Entry 111

Rockcrest

Killarney Road, Kenmare, Co. Kerry

After twisting in from Killarney through some of the craggiest, most desolate scenery in Ireland, you find yourself on the road into Kenmare – and there is the house, perched above the road like a beacon: you can't miss it. It was the first bungalow ever built in Kenmare (that was 50 years ago) and is no ordinary bungalow inside. A large hallway leads to rooms with wooden floors, rugs, oak furniture, big and deeply comfortable new beds and fresh modern bathrooms. The warm-hued sitting room has the bliss of an open fire, the cupboards in the bright, welcoming kitchen contain everything you need, patio doors lead onto a paved sun terrace and there's a lovely private garden, too. The house feels comfortable without being cluttered and is a two-minute walk from the centre of handsome Kenmare with its busy restaurants and colourful pubs. And your host Gráinne, a local livewire, owns and runs the Purple Heather gastropub: not to be missed, particularly with your privileged introduction. Rockcrest is the perfect base for touring or just relaxing in peace.

rooms	Cottage for 6 (3 doubles, 1 bath, 1 shower).
price	€450–€950 per week.
meals	Self-catering. Choice in Kenmare, 1km.
closed	Christmas.
directions	In Kenmare, N71 Killarney road from town centre for 1km, then left up lane. Entrance immediately left.

Gráinne O'Connell

tel	+353 (0)64 41016 /41132
fax	+353 (0)64 42135
email	oconnellgrainne@eircom.net

Self-catering

Map 6 Entry 112

Virginia's Guesthouse
Henry Street, Kenmare, Co. Kerry

Neil was born in Room 23, has lived here all his life and has wonderful tales to tell. His father was a cobbler whose past customers included Fred Astaire (a couple of belts) and Prince Rainier of Monaco (shoes). Noreen is an intelligent, energetic and inventive host. Marvellously unposh, Virginia's is a great find — friendly, relaxing, full of its own good ideas. The marathon breakfast, much of it Noreen's own work, brings homemade breads and muesli, fresh orange juice, banana pancakes, blue cheese pears, the full Irish works (and champagne on New Year's Day). The sitting room has books and games, a kettle, loads of different teas and coffees: help yourself. Bedrooms are simple-perfect with beds of varnished wood, pretty linen, fluffy towels and power showers. Those at the front look onto Henry Street, those at the back are less light but get no passing noise; all are spotless. Kenmare is one of the prettiest small towns in Ireland, a real treat. You can tour its streets in ten minutes, choose your restaurant, stop in a pub, chat with the locals. Great hospitality, great people, great fun.

rooms	8: 5 doubles, 1 twin, 1 single, 1 triple.
price	€80-€120. Singles €55-€75.
meals	Mulcahy's Restaurant below.
closed	Rarely.
directions	Kenmare has 3 main streets, all one-way. From post office on Henry Street, house 50 metres down hill (above Mulcahy's Restaurant).

Guest house

	Noreen Harrington
tel	+353 (0)64 41021
fax	+353 (0)64 42415
email	virginias@eircom.net
web	www.virginias-kenmare.com

Map 6 Entry 113

Shelburne Lodge
Cork Road, Kenmare, Co. Kerry

People in Kenmare say Maura has the Midas touch, excelling at everything she does: Shelburne Lodge certainly glows. Maura's colourful personality is stamped all over the house: lovely yellow bedrooms with huge mirrors, beautiful lime-washed furniture, antiques galore, modern art, thick rugs on wooden floors – it all shows a keen eye for elegant, unstuffy interior design. The rooms are divided between the 1740s lodge and the secluded coach house which overlooks a cottage garden and grass tennis court. All are gorgeously different, full of flair and modern country-house style. The house vibrates: Maura creates the buzz. She or a daughter will settle you in with other guests by the ever-burning log fire for a cup of tea that appears to arrive by magic. The atmosphere is relaxed, the family helpful and easy-going. Tom's encyclopædic knowledge of the area, and especially Lord Shelburne, is remarkable: a lovely, sincere man, he'll inspire you to explore at length. Steep country lanes lead to sweeping views of the river and surrounding hills, and their restaurant Packies serves seasonal and organic food. Outstanding.

rooms	9: 6 doubles, 2 twins, 1 family.
price	€120-€170. Singles from €80.
meals	Restaurants within walking distance in Kenmare.
closed	December-February.
directions	From Killarney N22 for 15km; right R569 to Kilgarven; continue for Kenmare. House signposted on right just before town.

Maura & Tom O'Connell-Foley

tel	+353 (0)64 41013
fax	+353 (0)64 42135
email	shelburnekenmare@eircom.net
web	www.shelburnelodge.com

Guest house

Map 6 Entry 114

Sallyport House
Kenmare, Co. Kerry

An enterprising grandfather who exported railway sleepers to England is to be thanked for the lovely antiques here: rather than use conventional ballast for the return boat journey, he brought back beautiful furniture. The Arthurs, a warm and attentive family, are justifiably proud of his collection and put it to full use in every room – even the bedroom tea cups are antique. This extraordinary man also bought the local workhouse, knocked it down and used the stone to build Sallyport in 1932 – you can see the worn stepping stone in the hall. You will find yet more interest in the excellent Irish art on the walls. Bedrooms lead off a central landing and have silk bedspreads, thick carpets, big baths, lots of light and views over the orchard to Muxnaw Mountain and the Caha Mountains. Walk from the house through the park or stroll along the River Kenmare in the evening. Breakfast is wonderful, with smoked salmon on the menu, staff are delightful and Kenmare is a pretty town with lots of life. It is also a good base from which to explore the Ring of Kerry and, better still, Beara.

rooms	5: 2 doubles, 1 twin/double, 1 four-poster, 1 family.
price	€150–€180. Singles from €100.
meals	Restaurants within walking distance.
closed	November–March.
directions	From Killarney N71 to Kenmare. Follow Bantry signs through town. On left before suspension bridge.

Country house

	The Arthur Family
tel	+353 (0)64 42066
fax	+353 (0)64 42067
email	port@iol.ie
web	www.sallyporthouse.com

Map 6 Entry 115

Somerton

Killaha East, Kenmare, Co. Kerry

Yes, a new house on the shores of Kenmare Bay with those devastatingly beautiful views. No, not another beastly bung but a superb architect-designed house set against the hillside, living sensitively in the landscape. Every room has vast sky-filled windows, the Mackintosh-style dining area opens onto a sheltered terrace, the outside rushes in to grab you: walk straight out into the Kerry wilderness. With matching sensitivity, the owners have furnished their well-loved house in natural materials, subdued tones and quiet opulence. You will love the sleek fitted kitchen – a cook's dream of steel and maple with all the gadgets – and revel in the rainy-day delights of the little library, the eye-catching art, the DVDs and the wraparound music system before the ultra-modern gas fire. Plus bathrobes and a welcome basketful of organic goodies. These are the comforts that real people have chosen for themselves and there is a sense of family here – personal photographs here and there, soft fabrics on hand-crafted beds. Somerton is a wow, worlds away from the anonymity of a standard rental.

rooms	House for 8 (1 double, 2 twins/doubles, 1 twin, 2 bathrooms, extra wc).	
price	€1,950-€2,900 per week. Check for special offers.	
meals	Self-catering. Wide choice of restaurants 2km.	
closed	Rarely.	
directions	From Kenmare post office turn away from town; cross bridge; right for Beara 1.5km; house on left. More details on booking.	

	Colette Hamel	
tel	+353 (0)21 487 0820	
mobile	+353 (0)87 272 4240	**Self-catering**
email	info@somertonkenmare.com	
web	www.somertonkenmare.com	

Map 6 Entry 116

The Lake House
Cloonee Lakes, Tousist, Kenmare, Co. Kerry

Mary is the warmest, most gracious south-Kerry soul, deeply committed to proper hospitality and the local community, working her apron off from dawn to dusk to cook the superb pub food that the Lake House is renowned for. The setting is gorgeous, peace wafts up from the surface of the lake and the silent hills around. Indoors, the atmosphere is alive with wild fishermen's tales of battllng brownies and rare grisles. Bring your rods, hire a boat and by the evening you too can tell a tale over delicious food and drink. Then you won't notice too much that your bedroom is a totally basic, hostel-style room. Rooms will be refurbished – when funds permit: Mary is doing all she can to keep her family place up and running. Her grandfather opened the pub in 1926 and also built the dance hall here which she turns over to the community for exhibitions and... the annual dance. She is thinking of setting up a cookery school there, quite rightly. Come for the food, come for the fishing, come for the marvellous *craíc* and the Wednesday night traditional music session, and close your eyes to the rooms.

rooms	5 doubles sharing 3 bathrooms.
price	€70.
meals	Lunch €4-€10. Dinner €15-€25.
closed	Rarely.
directions	From Kenmare N71 for Glengariff over bridge; right R571 for Castletownbere. Inn on this road; signposted. (15km from Kenmare.)

Restaurant with rooms

Mary O'Shea
tel +353 (0)64 84205
fax +353 (0)64 84205
email mary@clooneelakehouse.com
web www.clooneelakehouse.com

Map 6 Entry 117

Tahilla Cove Country House
Tahilla Cove, Tahilla, Sneem, Co. Kerry

If Tahilla Cove rings of the south seas it's because there is a whiff of paradise in this part of 'Ireland's Riviera', with its lush semi-tropical vegetation and balmy micro-climate. James's father built the house on its 14 landscaped, wooded acres by the secluded cove; James now runs it with his wife Deirdre, the local GP. His mother Dolly, a great character, will happily relate the whole history of this unique place and son Charles may take you out in his boat to see the estuary. They are a wonderful, welcoming bunch of people. As are the two springer spaniels who do so love a walk. Big unpretentious bedrooms have modern comforts and most have a private balcony or terrace and views of the legendary Beara Peninsula. Walk through oak groves to idyllic viewpoints where seals can be seen basking on rocks, swim off the private pier or mess about in a rowing boat before coming back for afternoon tea on the sun terrace. Dinner is a relaxed affair – more house party than stuffy restaurant. The best possible therapy for speeded-up urbanites – you should stay at least three nights to get a proper taste of heaven.

rooms	9: 2 doubles, 1 twin, 6 twins/doubles.
price	€120-€150. Singles €100.
meals	Dinner €30 (not Tues/Weds). Restaurant in Sneem, 10-minute drive.
closed	Mid-October to Easter.
directions	From Kenmare N70 for Sneem 16km; house left down drive at sign.

	James, Deirdre & Dolly Waterhouse
tel	+353 (0)64 45204
fax	+353 (0)64 45104
email	tahillacove@eircom.net
web	www.tahillacove.com

Country house

Map 6 Entry 118

Westcove House & Stables

Castlecove, Co. Kerry

The history of beautiful Westcove House is as full of movement, human quirks and fine things as the house, which has looked proudly across Kenmare Estuary for 350 years. From the imposing hall, dominated by an ancestral portrait, move into the soft informality and open fires of the sunken sitting room and the bar – wonderfully relaxing. The views from the more ceremonious dining room will grab your eyes and the kitchen is superb: suffice to say it has two dishwashers. Katherine, the charming housekeeper, knows Westcove inside out and, for a total holiday, will cook some or all of your meals – deliciously, and as organically as possible. Bedrooms are full of personality too, there's a reading gallery, a sauna, a terrific games room in the Stables, shared by all, where local musicians may come to dance Irish reels with you. Also, a fine north-lit artist's studio. What more could you want? The more simply furnished Stables are warm and comfortable, with pretty, soft bedrooms ('nanny's' room is a bit smaller) and loads of storage. The Atlantic lies below, there are forts and lakes to be explored in the hills.

rooms	House for 8-10 (2 doubles, 1 twin, 2 singles, 4 bathrooms). Stables for 9-10 (2 doubles, 1 twin, 1 single/ twin, 1 bunk room, 3 bathrooms).
price	House £1,500-£2,205 p.w. Stables £650-£1,050 p.w. Including daily cleaning. Shorter stays possible.
meals	Self-catering. Cook at extra charge.
closed	Rarely.
directions	Directions given on booking.

Self-catering

	Mike & Susannah Adlington
tel	+44 (0)1420 23113
fax	+44 (0)1420 22063
email	info@westcovelettings.co.uk
web	www.westcovelettings.com

Map 6 Entry 119

Westcove Farmhouse

Castlecove, Co. Kerry

Up here above the harbour, Jane runs a small bakery making delicious additive-free goodies: enjoy the brown sodabread from your welcome pack or pop down for hot scones. Her shop sells the range plus Jane-painted picture frames, lavender candles, unusual crafts. She has created this delightful first-floor sea-view apartment in her new whitewashed wing. You are quite private, with your own small enclosed courtyard where you can pick your herbs, and steps to the front door into a little pot-hung kitchen/dining room with views of fields from the sink. The bathroom: corner bath, luxurious power shower, sea pebbles embedded in a slate and timber floor; the bedroom: a padded window seat for ocean-gazing. Perfect simplicity and peacefulness – beams, creamy whites, a sofa, an old Mexican chest of drawers. The downstairs room is just as charming. It's five minutes to the water's edge: go deep-sea fishing, walk the Kerry Way or swim from sandy beaches. But Jane is the star of this much-loved place and can be persuaded (in low season) to cook the odd meal, with notice.

rooms	Flat for 2-3 (1 twin/double, 1 single futon). Additional double in private part of main house.
price	€330–€500 per week. 3-night break from €220 (not July/August). 2nd room (same group only) €150 p.w.
meals	Restaurants in Caherdaniel & Castlecove, 3km.
closed	Rarely.
directions	From Kenmare N70 for Waterville 25km. House signposted on left 3km beyond Castlecove.

	Jane Urquhart
tel	+353 (0)66 947 5479
mobile	+353 (0)87 294 2138
email	westcovefarmhouse@oceanfree.net
web	www.westcove.net

Self-catering

Map 6 Entry 120

Iskeroon

Bunavalla, Caherdaniel, Co. Kerry

This is the place where the road runs out. The house is cradled by ridge and rock; huge windows frame views of land and sea. David knew the house as a child: his grandfather lived nearby and he used to sneak up for a glimpse. He and Geraldine, an easy-going couple with a young family, have renovated marvellously, filling the house with light and colour (one room is Dragon's Blood Red), stone floors, coir matting and a sitting room where you can pick any book from an impressive collection. Bedrooms delight: a smart cottage feel of timber floors, high ceilings, arts-and-crafts furniture and Fired Earth colours. Across the corridor is your private panelled bathroom with sea-shell mirrors. Spellbound by the view, you can breakfast while watching the locals pass by: seals, seagulls, the odd boat. And there's more magic outside: Derrynane Bay, Abbey Island, Hog's Head. Walk through the semi-tropical gardens (rare Kerry lilies) to the private pier, swim in clear water, follow the path to the pub, or take the boat to the enchanting Skellig Rocks. Come for a couple of days and forget your car. *Minimum stay two nights.*

A short stroll away is a magnificent mile of pure sand, bursting with invigoration and shells: Ireland's finest beaches. Aware of the fragility of even this lands-end piece of our planet, the Hares heat water with solar panels and their house with the latest low-energy system (20% of traditional energy consumption). You may notice that they only use eco-friendly cleaning products and they will ask you to be as conscientious about recycling as they are. The building materials, the textures and the delicious breakfast feel clean, organic, nourishing – all in an incomparable position.

rooms	3 + 1: 2 doubles, 1 twin, each with separate bathroom. Apartment for 2-4.
price	€150. Apartment €450-€500 p.w.
meals	Pub 20-minute walk, restaurants 8km & 11km.
closed	October-April.
directions	Between Caherdaniel & Waterville on N70. At Scarriff Inn take road for Bunavalla Pier; at pier, left on unpaved private road along beach & through white gateposts.

	David & Geraldine Hare
tel	+353 (0)66 947 5119
fax	+353 (0)66 947 5488
email	info@iskeroon.com
web	www.iskeroon.com

SPECIAL GREEN ENTRY
see page 16

B&B & Self-cateri

Map 6 Entry

Picín

Brackaragh, Caherdaniel, Co. Kerry

The loveliest hideaway for two where you may both decide to live in the bathroom, more opulent and original than most drawing rooms. A cast-iron roll-top bath stands on herring-bone boards, a wood-burning stove creates heart-warming cosiness, a velvet antique sofa embraces the non-bathing conversationalist and a Tudor wardrobe just looks benign. Amelia and Nick – young, artistic, warm and so happy to have brought their two children from London to grow up in Kerry – have stroked every little stone alcove back to life. You arrive via your own garden and terrace into a big light space rich in oriental rugs, a bold red sofa, a wall of books and an antique rocking horse. Through that amazing bathroom, steep stairs bring you to the softly muted bedroom in greys, blues and creams where touches of pure luxury finish the seduction: Egyptian cotton bedlinen, a silk bedspread, a painted chest, stone walls hung with a fascinating choice of paintings. All done with such loving care, this is no run-of-the-mill B&B and exceptional value. Their first guests kept saying "it's like the Waldorf Astoria."

rooms	1 double.
price	€90–€120. Singles €60–€80.
meals	Restaurants & pubs in Caherdaniel, 4km.
closed	Rarely.
directions	From Kenmare N70 for Waterville 45km; through Castlecove, continue 4km; sign on right.

B&B

	Nick & Amelia Etherton
tel	+353 (0)66 947 5894
email	netherton@eircom.net
web	www.picincottage.com

Map 6 Entry 122

Ulusker House & Mossie's Restaurant

Adrigole, Beara, Co. Cork

Billy the lovable ugly bulldog reigns over a beautifully crafted interior, magical views over Bantry Bay, warm artistic owners and a charming little restaurant. David and Lorna's is a tale of hard work and talent. They came from Bath, found a ruin, rebuilt every bit with extraordinary skill and heaps of reclaimed materials – David is an architectural salvage expert, Lorna has a love of texture, perfection and food – and summoned the world to eat and sleep in it. Communal rooms lead off one another like an open invitation; a cosy terracotta sitting room is alive with fresh flowers and candles; opulent bedrooms are like poems where unusual antiques rhyme with soft colours, perfect details with luscious bathing. David created the garden from scratch, Lorna grows her own veg and herbs and does the cooking. Dinner happens in the elegant dining room or the flagstoned conservatory or on the summer terrace: in the flickering light of candles and three fantastic Victorian cast-iron gas lamps, you will want to linger for hours. Lovely people and tremendous value. *Vegetarian meals available.*

rooms	4: 3 doubles, 1 twin.
price	€90–€140. Singles €50–€85.
meals	Dinner, 3 courses, €35. Lunch on request.
closed	November & January.
directions	From Glengariff for Castletownbere to Adrigole. Entering Adrigole, left/right at sign; 1km down lane.

David & Lorna Ramshaw

tel	+353 (0)276 0606
fax	+353 (0)276 0606
email	mossies@eircom.net
web	mossiesrestaurant.com

Restaurant with rooms

Map 6 Entry

Hagal Healing Farm
Coomleigh, Bantry, Co. Cork

Hagal is different, marvellously different. It always was: the farmhouse was built 150 years ago by one man in 40 days. You can now seek yourself or the truth in a leafy labyrinth, take lemon balm tea under the huge old vine in the conservatory among candles, jingling buddha chimes and lots of harmony, retreat from the pressures of modern life into a secluded corner of the beautiful wild garden, left natural like everything here, eat subtly-spiced organic vegetarian food – or learn to cook it yourself. Seating is low, ethnic and tempting; the yoga room at the top has breathtaking views of Bantry Bay, as does the chill-out room with its white sofas and angel cards. This is a place for seekers, be it themselves, enlightenment, balanced health or peace that they seek, and the list of therapies, pamper menus, courses is a whole New-Age programme. All run by gentle Dutch folk – Fred the garden-lover, Janny the yoga teacher, both involved in Bantry farmers' market – among simple pine furniture, colourful bedcovers in neat unfrilly rooms, white walls, chunks of oak timber and the boundless natural energy of this land.

Ask about weekend courses & week-long healings.

Sound in body and mind is their goal. Janny and Fred have ever been eco-life crusaders, seeking harmony and respect in all the boxes. Love of the earth serves the human body which serves the human soul-mind which serves... the earth. They smile a lot, too. On top of their vegetarian ethic fed by the wild-alive organic garden, they are creating a reed bed sewage treatment system for the whole centre and a new treatment building that will be geothermally heated. You sit on, sleep in and dry with natural fabrics - and you imbibe buckets about living differently, more awarely, just by being here.

rooms	4 doubles.
price	€60. Singles €55. Full-board €130. Full-board €90 singles.
meals	Lunch €15. Dinner €25. BYO wine. Book ahead.
closed	Rarely.
directions	From Bantry for Glengariff; right after Casey's petrol station at Donamark; 12km of winding road; left at Hagal Farm sign.

	Janny & Fred Wieler
tel	+353 (0)27 66179
fax	+353 (0)27 66179
email	hagalhealingfarm@eircom.net
web	www.hagalhealingfarm.com

SPECIAL GREEN ENTRY
see page 16

Map 6 Entr

Ballylickey House
Ballylickey, Bantry Bay, Co. Cork

The lawns of Ballylickey roll down to Bantry Bay, Whiddy Island looms across the water, the Caha Mountains rise beyond: in this incomparable setting, four generations of the Graves family have nurtured their house and gardens into glory. Don't miss the lily pond and the two myrtle trees, indigenous to Bantry. The elegant old mansion houses the breakfast room, one suite with gorgeous sea views from its drawing room and a smaller double, both with real country-house vibes. Reached by a granite path curling through rhododendrons and azaleas, the cottages sprawl round the gardens down to the road. Paco has taken the B&B over from his parents and is gradually refurbishing. The cottages vary in size – the larger have their own drawing room and fireplace – and décor: old-fashioned florals or glamourous midnight blue and gold; bathrooms are adequate if not the latest design. The best big suite has a stupendous view. Come for the peace of the garden, the majesty of Bantry Bay, Bantry's excellent restaurants and bars, and Francine's friendly helpful welcome. *Pets by arrangement. Vegetarian meals available. Bikes for hire.*

rooms	8: Main house: 1 double, 1 suite. Cottages: 5 doubles, 1 suite.
price	€100-€150.
meals	Restaurant 50 yds. Choice in Bantry, 3-minute drive.
closed	November to mid-March.
directions	From Bantry N71 for Ballylickey; house signposted on right in village.

Guest house

	The Graves Family
tel	+353 (0)27 50071
fax	+353 (0)27 56725
email	ballymh@eircom.net
web	www.ballylickeymanorhouse.com

Map 6 Entry 125

Bantry House
Bantry, Co. Cork

Wreathed in history, basking in its famous Italianate gardens (the house stands on the third of seven grand terraces) and spectacular view over The Bay, this is one of Ireland's finest stately homes. Egerton, the earnest and knowledgeable trombone-player, will serve your breakfast kippers with fine old cutlery. His family are the ninth generation of Whites to live here since 1739. His staff are competent and charming, too. The vast drawing room, dining room, library and halls are open to the public. Go one better: after visiting hours sit by the blazing hearth, the 1st Earl's coronet and the grand piano in the incredible library. The racing-green billiard room has the hugest table, great family portraits hang everywhere, there are books, an honesty bar, sitting spaces, generosity. Refurbished east-wing bedrooms (two with bay view) now have super bathrooms. West-wing family-friendly rooms look over the wisteria-hung water feature of those fabulous restored gardens. A flight of 100 stone steps, the Stairway to the Sky, leads to awesome views of islands and distant mountains. Staying here is a rare treat. *Tennis on site.*

rooms	7: 4 doubles, 2 twins, 1 family.
price	€220–€240. Singles €130. Children under 10 free, 11s-15s half price.
meals	Snack lunch in tea room €5-€15. Restaurants within easy walking distance.
closed	November–February. End of June.
directions	From Cork, N71 to Bantry. Big entrance on right just before village.

	Egerton & Brigitte Shelswell-White
tel	+353 (0)27 50047
fax	+353 (0)27 50795
email	info@bantryhouse.com
web	www.bantryhouse.com

Country house

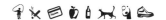

Map 6 Entry

Carbery Cottage Guest Lodge
Durrus, Nr. Bantry, Co. Cork

In a jaw-dropping setting, a happy house where people and dogs love to be. In fact Mike and Julia, with three super animals of their own, have made it something of a dog sanctuary. Both sought refuge in West Cork from top-speed England where she was at the Theatre Royal in Bath, he a chef, a Merchant Navyman and a lifeboatman: they have pictures of beached whales and royalty to prove it. Shyer than larger-than-life Julia, Mike is quietly friendly and spends lots of time in the kitchen with fresh local delights, conjuring up your dinner. She offers a formidable sense of humour and an open-hearted welcome. Their ten-year-old granite house looks down Dunmanus Bay to the Mizen Head: spectacular seas and sunsets from the wild shrubby garden. Pine-floored bedrooms are pale, warm and simply furnished in an easy relaxing style with good firm beds. All have those stirring views. Guests dine by the open fire at an elegant long dark table decked with candles and no clutter, the sitting room has soft sofas, garden doors and a fish tank. The famous Sheep's Head Way passes by the door, so walk your fill.

rooms	3 + 1: 1 double, 2 suites. Cottage for 2.
price	€80–€90. Singles €40–€45. Cottage from €300 per week.
meals	Dinner, 3 courses, €30. Packed lunch on request.
closed	Rarely.
directions	From Durrus for Ahakista 4.5km; right at sign for Carbery Cottage; house up hill on left.

B&B & Self-catering

	Mike & Julia Hegarty
tel	+353 (0)27 6138
mobile	+353 (0)87 757 743
email	carberycottage@eircom.net
web	www.carbery-cottage-guest-lodge.net

Map 6 Entry 127

Rock Cottage
Barnatonicane, Nr. Schull, Co. Cork

Barbara is clear: she enjoys having guests, especially animal-lovers, as "the animals are part of the place", so dogs, cats, sheep, horse and donkey must be introduced – they are all as friendly and down-to-earth as she is and her eco-credentials include protecting habitats on her left-to-the-wilds land. With great humour she tells, in a wonderful mix of German and Cork accents, how she fought to restore this property. An 1826 hunting lodge, it is built on a huge slab of rock, hence the split levels on the ground floor. It looks irresistible when you arrive – then Barbara's fine cooking, much of it organic, and her enticing bedrooms cast their spell. Her many talents include a wonderful sense of colour. Rooms, each with its own personality, are stylishly simple with timber floors, country-house beds and views over lightly-wooded paddocks. Behind the house, a path through gorse bushes leads up a small hill where you can sit and gaze at the spectacular view over Dunmanus Bay. A successful shoe designer, Barbara is now excelling at B&B in a region where she spent many a happy holiday as a child.

rooms	3 + 1: 1 double, 2 triples. Cottage for 2-3.
price	€110–€140. Singles €80–€100. Cottage €430–€550 p.w.
meals	Dinner from €45. Supper on request.
closed	Rarely.
directions	From Cork N71 west. Just before Bantry, left R591 to Durrus; left for Goleen 13km. Entrance on right after small cemetery.

	Barbara Klötzer
tel	+353 (0)28 35538
fax	+353 (0)28 35538
email	rockcottage@eircom.net
web	www.rockcottage.ie

B&B & Self-catering

Map 6 Entry

Ballyroon Mountain

Kilcrohane, Bantry, Co. Cork

Spectacularly remote, in one of the last inhabited spots before Europe sinks into the Atlantic, Ballyroon ('secret place' in Gaelic) lives in the drama of plunging ocean and mountainous peninsulas. Friendly and sophisticated, Roger and Sue – ex-cameraman and garden designer – came to this rugged hillside to farm and breathe a clearer air. The little stone bothy beyond the main house is your cosy mountain cabin: one large bed-sitting room, simply, thoughtfully furnished with stone, timber and a thick woolly rug, the bed raised to catch the view, and your own garden where stylish recliners invite you to contemplation as merlins and peregrines wheel above, or laze with a book from the well-stacked shelves in your room. Over breakfast in the conservatory next door Roger and Sue will talk about the lovely walks they have opened up, the waterfall, their conservation efforts, myriad other things. Take all day to explore their 36 varied acres, walk the Sheep's Head and Poet's Ways, feel how every minute counts. You will come to love this retreat from urban frazzle as much as they do.

As natural as the best, Ballyroon is organic in all but certificate (paperwork too heavy, fee too high). Pigs provide rashers and delicious sausages, Angus cattle give the beef, bees harvest the hillsides for your honey. Hard work produces fresh chemical-free veg and fruit, the conservatory gathers heat, renewable woods grow the fuel, delightful donkeys carry it. Indeed, wearing their tailor-made willow baskets they are Ballyroon's principal hauliers: the van is seldom used. Your hosts keep swathes of their land as safe habitats for wildlife to reproduce and prosper.

rooms	1 double.
price	€80–€100.
meals	Dinner €25. BYO wine.
closed	Rarely.
directions	Directions given on booking.

	Roger & Sue Goss
tel	+353 (0)27 67940
email	info@ballyroonmountain.com
web	www.ballyroonmountain.com

SPECIAL
GREEN ENTRY
see page 16

B8

Map 6 Entry

🗶 🐾 🐈 🚜 👞

Fortview House

Gurtyowen, Toormore, Goleen, Co. Cork

Set in a shrubby garden beside the little road, the house looks understated. Then Violet appears and the welcome begins. She is infectiously good-humoured and, with Richard's constant support and her imaginative way with country antiques, old pine and some decent paintings, she has turned a simple farmhouse into a sophisticated country B&B with harvest garlands over fireplaces but not a cutesy anything. The U-shaped sitting room and small conservatory are perfectly relaxing but the gem is the breakfast room: the big communal table dressed in gingham, Stephen Pearce pottery and myriad baskets of homemade sodabread, scones and jams is a unforgettable morning vision. Comfortable brass beds, old washstands and antique trunks bring the same country serenity to soft pastel bedrooms. Choose from the remarkable menu (pancakes, potato cakes, kippers, omelettes) and wait until morning to enjoy one of the freshest, tastiest breakfasts ever: "local food by local people used with pride". Then set out to explore one of Fortview's many walks. Family B&B at its best. *Also self-catering, see opposite.*

rooms	5: 3 doubles, 1 family, 1 single.
price	€90-€100. Singles €50-€55.
meals	Restaurants nearby.
closed	November-February.
directions	From Skibbereen N71/R592 to Toormore. There, R591 for Bantry & Durrus 2km.

		Violet & Richard Connell
B&B	tel	+353 (0)28 35324
	email	fortviewhousegoleen@eircom.net
	web	www.fortviewhousegoleen.com

Map 6 Entry 130

Fortview & Elacampane Cottages

Gurtyowen, Toormore, Goleen, Co. Cork

Welcome to Connell country. Richard has cattle and this land has been in his family for four generations. Wander around and you'll find reed beds, hedgerows and a small lake for wildlife, all of which are part of a rural environment protection scheme and have made his 70 hectares a Department of Agriculture demonstration farm for West Cork. He also built these imperious stone cottages – single-handedly. A couple of miles apart, they are pretty much identical and offer the very lap of countryside luxury: big country views, contemporary kitchens and every mod con. There are timber floors, heavy beams, quilted throws and high brass beds – stylish, cosy, uncluttered, elegant. Light floods onto the yellow rendered walls giving the place a smart rustic feel. Wood everywhere, slate patios outside, and Richard's Friesians for company in the fields. Alternatively, climb the ridge that leads up to Mount Gabriel for huge panoramic views, walk up to Dunmanus Bay to watch the seals or visit Mizen Head (the southernmost point of mainland Ireland) and search for whales. *B&B in Fortview House.*

rooms	2 cottages for 6: Fortview (1 double, 2 twins, 2 bathrooms); Elacampane (2 doubles, 1 twin, 2 bathrooms).
price	€320–€695 per week, plus electricity & heating.
meals	Self-catering.
closed	Never.
directions	From Skibbereen N71/R592 to Toormore. There, R591 for Bantry & Durrus 2km.

Violet & Richard Connell

tel	+353 (0)28 35324
email	fortviewhousegoleen@eircom.net
web	www.fortviewhousegoleen.com

Self-catering

Map 6 Entry 131

The Heron's Cove
The Harbour, Goleen (Mizen), Co. Cork

This is a spectacular part of Ireland with its deep inlets, steepling cliffs, scintillating or thundering seas; roads dip, twist, clamber round the hills, then peter out or land you at a beach or village – an explorer's heaven. Choose the Heron's Cove and belong here for a spell. Sue has been part of the village for 20 years, launched and still carries the Mizen Head Signal Station Visitors Centre (don't miss it), and knows all the lore – just ask. She is also deeply eco-aware (see opposite). Sitting on its own bay, the Heron's Cove has four main bedrooms with lots of window, lots of limpid views and a nautical feel. The balcony with wide-armed Adirondack chairs is a wonderful place to sit out on soft days. But the heart of the house is the airy restaurant with a fire at each end, wicker chairs and, miracle, a Slow Food ethos, that organic search for local, seasonal goodness that requires taking proper time to prepare, to cook – and to consume. "Breakfasts to die for" was one reader's report. A warm-hearted, no-nonsense woman, Sue enjoys having guests a while – and swears there are herons here.

As well as being a caring Slow Food restaurant, Heron's Cove is surely the most waste-conscious hotel in Cork, a green temple built upon pillars with names like Biotec and Fatstrippa (illustrated) – and old-fashioned shore protection. The Titanic treatment plant breaks down all the contents of all waste waters, including chemicals, though kitchen water has its fats removed first by good ole Fatstrippa. They shred all office, kitchen, bedroom and restaurant paper. They used to produce 80 bags of rubbish over 10 peak days, now it's never more than eight, even in high summer.

rooms	5: 3 family rooms for 3, 1 family room for 4-5, 1 single.
price	€80.
meals	Dinner from €30 à la carte. Restaurant closed November-April except for residents.
closed	Christmas & New Year.
directions	From Skibbereen N71 to Ballydehob; left R592 to Toormore; left R591 to Goleen; there, left opp. Green Kettle café to harbour. 75 miles from Cork.

	Sue Hill
tel	+353 (0)28 35225
fax	+353 (0)28 35422
email	suehill@eircom.net
web	www.heronscove.com

SPECIAL GREEN ENTRY
see page 16

Restaurant with rooms

Map 6 Entry 132

Blair's Cove House

Durrus, Co. Cork

The picture can tell the brilliant setting but not the charm and atmosphere on the ground, the embrace of the cobbled courtyard where modern sculpture stands by old lily pond. Stone outbuildings have been converted into one magnificent lofty restaurant and three deeply attractive suites, each with its own kitchen, all different: you could have country antiques and Victorian bedsteads or a superb contemporary look and modern art. Philippe (from Belgium) and Sabine (from Germany) are a cosmopolitan, art-loving couple who believe in fabulous food and sophisticated comfort. Breakfast is delivered to you in the morning: wake up to a healthy spread ordered the night before and relax into the bay view. The restaurant serves gorgeous seafood in season, laid out like sculpture in the middle of the room; meat is grilled over logs, a pianist plays on Saturdays: a feast for all five senses. Such style and atmosphere can only improve the food. On summer evenings, dinner is served in the conservatory overlooking the courtyard. The De Meys are thoroughly professional, good at detail and know how to spoil you.

rooms	2 apts for 2; 1 apt for 4; 1 cottage for 8; 1 coastal cottage for 4.
price	Apts €140–€220. Cottage for 8, €875–€1200. Cottage for 4, €585–€890. Prices per week.
meals	Dinner €55.
closed	November–March. Restaurant closed Sunday & Monday.
directions	From Cork N71 west; just before Bantry, left R591 to Durrus; left for Goleen 2.5km. Entrance on right before sharp right bend (caution).

Guest house & Self-catering

	Philippe & Sabine De Mey
tel	+353 (0)27 61127
fax	+353 (0)27 61487
email	blairscove@eircom.net
web	www.blairscove.ie

Map 6 Entry 133

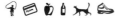

Grove House

Colla Road, Schull, Co. Cork

Katarina is Swedish and quite a woman. Not only talented — she teaches the piano, rides in events, cooks inventively — she is also full of zest and fun, loving her new life as B&B and restaurant owner. Looking across to the living picture that is Schull harbour, the charming old house, where Bernard Shaw once stayed, has kept its former riches of warm cranberry hall, racing green library/piano room and fudge-cream dining room, now an atmospheric restaurant. The food, prepared by Katarina and son Nico, served by son Max in candlelight, has already attracted attention. Guests may play the piano and impromptu sing-songs are frequent. Comfortably worn bedrooms have the odd quirk: a funny Edwardian fireplace, interesting oddments, an original Victorian loo with a square wooden seat. Excellent bathrooms have careful tile patterns. Katarina has planted trees and bushes to hide the new houses next door; her next project is to restore the garden. There are seats for admiring the superb harbour view, a croquet lawn and a great welcome for children to this friendliest of houses. *Pets by arrangement.*

rooms	5: 4 doubles, 1 twin.
price	€90–€120. Singles €60–€90.
meals	Dinner €30–€35.
	Lunch €10–€15.
closed	Never.
directions	From Cork N71 to Ballydehob; R592 to Schull; left opp. AIB bank. House 500m on right.

	Katarina Runske
tel	+353 (0)28 28067
fax	+353 (0)28 28069
email	katarinarunske@eircom.net

B&B

Map 6 Entry 134

Co. Cork

Horseshoe Cottage
Horseshoe Harbour, Sherkin Island, Co. Cork

Joe and Fiona, the happy new owners of little old Horseshoe, are wonderfully warm fun characters who have achieved much, including raising unnumbered goats and nine children. Joe, a retired commercial fishing skipper, has sailed the Atlantic, can take you whale or dolphin watching in the sailing schooner 'Anna M', show you his film on humpback whales near the Cap Verde Islands or his book of sea-faring yarns. Fiona, a registered homeopath and massage therapist, expends her exuberant energy re-vamping the garden, collecting eggs from her hens for your delicious breakfast, baking bread and flapjacks. Horseshoe is three cottages, built about 400 years ago, now rolled into one. The bedrooms are small and cosy, newly painted with colourful soft rugs on wooden floors, views are dizzying, the corridor is lined with books – but linger not, you are here to walk, swim, sail, discover. After breakfast sally forth to experience the peace and solitude of this beautiful little island (pop. 120): the Franciscans thoughtfully left a ruined friary to explore, the Jolly Roger has an excellent French chef. *Vegetarian meals available.*

rooms	3: 1 double, 1 twin/double, 1 single.
price	€65-€80. Singles €32-€40.
meals	Pubs within walking distance.
closed	Rarely.
directions	Ferry from Baltimore (all year) or Schull (summer only). Up hill past friary ruins; left at telephone box; cottage on right.

B&B

Fiona & Joe Aston
tel +353 (0)28 20598
mobile +353 (0)87 996 1557
email joe@gannetsway.com
web www.gannetsway.com

Map 6 Entry 135

Trag Retreat
Gokane, Tragumna, Skibbereen, Co. Cork

Be you indoors or out, you'll be kidnapped by the dramatic setting of sea, endless beautiful beach and rugged coastline: you are alone with the landscape in this unspoilt and aptly-named "retreat". The old farmhouse, faithfully restored in simple vernacular style, stands at ease with its architect-designed extension – opposites certainly attract here – where any cook would love to perform among the sleek modern fittings, gazing through the glass wall at a view to die for. Rooms are quietly modern and understated. In the snug sitting room, a modern hearth glows in a wall of old stone to reflect on the new wooden floor; the ground-floor master bedroom has a treat for the master couple: the old stone fireplace can be lit for your arrival. The bathrooms and other bedrooms show the same attentive hand: Owen and Sarah live nearby and take great care of it all. Last but possibly first, the stunning new timber-clad hot tub is placed just where you want to lie watching the sun set on a chilly winter's evening: supreme luxury. A place to slow down and renew yourself – there's nothing like it.

rooms	House for 6 (2 doubles, 1 twin, 2 bathrooms).
price	€580-€1,250 per week.
meals	Self-catering. Pub 1km, restaurants 8km.
closed	Never.
directions	From Skibbereen for Castletownshend 3.2km; after grotto on left, right for Tragumna 1.6km; left at old tower 4km (leaving Tragumna Beach on right); up hill, 2nd farmhouse on right.

	Owen & Sarah O'Driscoll
tel	+353 (0)28 40833
mobile	+353 (0)86 822 6404
email	info@tragretreat.com
web	www.tragretreat.com

Self-catering

Map 6 Entry 136

Riverbank Cottage & Barn
Skibbereen, Co. Cork

Real romantic retreats, both cottage and barn are ideal for two and their double jacuzzis, heart-themed linen and super beds (one four-poster, one super-king) make them fun, unpretentious hideaways for couples. Peter and Anna carefully restored the old-world faces of these friendly solid buildings, laboriously repointing the stonework, creating lofty interiors beneath old beams, making new timber windows for existing openings. Then they furnished them thoughtfully in a mix of bright modern and old country with all the comforts. Workmanship is excellent, lamps and rugs fit well, the atmosphere is cottagey with lots of pine, gingham and wrought iron. Each has a shower room as well as that jacuzzi; in the Cottage: a well-equipped kitchen, in the Barn: a handy, attractive kitchenette on one side of the open plan area, so while the Cottage has generous living space for two to four, the smaller Barn is just as quaint and perfect for two. But outside is endless space: walk your socks off or... down by the little river at the bottom of the meadow hangs a tempting hammock. *B&B available: see opposite.*

rooms	Barn for 2 (double with bath). Cottage for 2-4 (double with bath, double sofabed on gallery).
price	Per week: Barn €500; cottage €750; together €825-€1,150. 2-3 nights: Barn from €160, cottage from €225.
meals	Self-catering. Restaurants 3km
closed	Never.
directions	Directions given on booking.

Self-catering

	Peter & Anna Warburton
tel	+353 (0)28 23213
fax	+353 (0)28 22958
email	info@riverbankcottage.net
web	www.riverbankcottage.net

Map 6 Entry 137

Grove House
Skibbereen, Co. Cork

No-one could be more helpful than these two and, despite its formal chequered hall, Grove House is neither precious nor super-smart but the most relaxed place you could hope for. Peter, whose passion is old buildings, will point out the best local secrets, the beaches without ice-cream vans, the special walks; he also serves in the red, antique-furnished dining room, stopping to chat if you want. Anna does the cooking. She trained with a former chef at the Ritz but fear not, it won't be over-sophisticated: she decides what to cook when she goes shopping each day, just the freshest local ingredients done simply to reveal their innate goodness. Then she too will emerge to chat with her guests. Delightful rooms have fine canopied beds, the best ones have three windows to the front lawns, one is super-French in pink Jouy prints; much attention to detail has gone into refurbishing the big bathrooms. Should you stay in one of the cottages, you will relax in a clear modern interior that enhances the old stones and timbers. Remarkable value. *Self-catering available: see opposite.*

rooms	6: 4 four-posters. 2 self-catering suites also used for B&B.
price	€98–€138. Singles €60–€75.
meals	Dinner with wine, €27.
closed	Christmas.
directions	From Cork N71 to Skibbereen; at Skibbereen r'bout follow signs to Hospital. House 1km past Hospital on right.

Peter & Anna Warburton
tel	+353 (0)28 23213
fax	+353 (0)28 22958
email	relax@grovehouse.net
web	www.grovehouse.net

B&B

Map 6 Entry 138

Lis-ardagh Lodge
Union Hall, Co. Cork

Carol is utterly genuine and gentle, her lovely big smile just says "come on in" and you'd never guess she used to be in the police. Jim, a Cork man, gardens, professionally and passionately. He's also a keen road bowler... They left London with their two children to build this house in local stone, lay soft pine floors and live in peace. The children now help in the house, as does lovely labrador Megan. Carol's rich, generous breakfast, served in the bright and cheery dining room or on the flagstoned patio, includes her own brown sodabread and possibly kippers from the local smokery. The odd teddy bear fits easily into the big floral-friendly sitting room. Jim's garden meanders slowly, revealing quirks among its various levels: an old curragh boat turned into a sheltered seaview seat with creeper growing up the 'roof', a hot tub on the south-facing deck, a sauna, a stone stable (horses will come), fabulous birdlife. Two rooms look over this marvellous spread and out to sea (you can go whale watching here), all are pine-clad, homely, comfy and fresh blue in colour. Tremendous value.

rooms	3 + 2: 1 triple, 1 suite for 5, 1 family for 5. 2 apartments for 4.
price	€60-€70. Singles €45-€50. Apartments €300-€500 per week.
meals	Pubs 5-minute walk. Restaurants 3-6km.
closed	Christmas & New Year.
directions	From Cork N71 to Leap (75km); there, left at sign for Union Hall Fishing Village 2.5km; stone house on right.

B&B & Self-catering

	Carol & Jim Kearney
tel	+353 (0)28 34951
mobile	+353 (0)87 769 9583
email	info@lis-ardaghlodge.com
web	www.lis-ardaghlodge.com

Map 6 Entry 139

Glenlohane
Kanturk, Co. Cork

Desmond's ancestor built Glenlohane in 1741, the Sharp and Bolster families having settled nearby 150 years earlier. Desmond and his American wife Melanie returned to the fold about 12 years ago, after a stint in America, to take up the reins and turn Glenlohane into the most comfortable of country houses. The best of the old and new worlds meet in harmony and humour with this wonderful couple, Desmond's deep crackling tales, Melanie's intelligent humanity. One could spend a lot of time with them. 'Bird Sanctuary' at the gate simply means no shooting – there's nothing more exotic here than some guinea fowl – yet Desmond "lived for hunting" and still keeps several horses as well as myriad sheep on his 300 acres of parkland, paddocks and fields. Melanie, whose great interest is carriage-driving, takes in retired greyhounds – who are so grateful. Relax in the warm elegance of rooms filled with antiques and family memorabilia. Large, fresh bedrooms are done with consummate, easy taste, lots of windows and proper bathrooms. Sophisticated comfort and great fun. *Groups can reserve the whole house.*

rooms	4 + 1: 1 double, 2 twins, 1 single. Cottage for 6.
price	€200. Singles €85-€100. Cottage €750 per week.
meals	Restaurants within 2 miles.
closed	Rarely.
directions	From Kanturk R576 for Mallow; bear left R580 for Buttevant; 1st right for Ballyclough; entrance on left after about 3km, signposted 'Glenlohane Bird Sanctuary'.

Desmond & Melanie Sharp Bolster
tel +353 (0)29 50014
fax +353 (0)29 51100
email info@glenlohane.com
web www.glenlohane.com

Country house & Self-catering

Map 7 Entry 140

Longueville House
Mallow, Co. Cork

Cromwell seized these lands from clan O'Callaghan in 1650; Dromineen Castle, their long-lost ancestral seat, looms hauntingly across the fields, protected by ancient oak, a view as grand and timeless as any in Ireland. But wheels turn full circle. Wrapped in 500 fertile acres, Longueville is now back in O'Callaghan hands. Rebuilt in 1720 with a pillared porch, stone-flagged floors, a Robert Adam mantelpiece and, most staggering of all, hand-painted ceilings in green, red, yellow and gold – jaw-dropping stuff. Country-house comforts at every turn – open fires, deep sofas, gumboots by the back door for guests to use. Pull on a pair and discover the grounds: woodlands, 50 acres of orchard (for calvados), a small vineyard (they make their own wine), and a fabulous three-acre organic walled garden that provides almost everything for your plate. You eat in a Victorian conservatory, built by the man who built Kew, with voile drapes tumbling from the ceiling. Smartly quilted, padded and pelmeted bedrooms are as you'd expect: the best beds, the odd antique, softness. Ideal for that special celebration.

rooms	20: 11 twins/doubles, 7 junior suites, 2 singles.
price	€235-€340. Singles from €110. Whole house from €4,800 per night; sleeps up to 38.
meals	Lunch from €45. Dinner, 4 courses, €60-€95.
closed	Early January to mid-March. Sunday night & Monday in low season.
directions	From Mallow N72 for Killarney 5km; right at Ballyclough junction; entrance to house 100m.

Hotel & Self-catering

	William & Aisling O'Callaghan
tel	+353 (0)22 47156
fax	+353 (0)22 47459
email	info@longuevillehouse.ie
web	www.longuevillehouse.ie

Map 7 Entry 141

Ballyvolane House
Castlelyons, Co. Cork

A most excellent house. Set in an idyllic private estate, Ballyvolane is one of Ireland's great old houses – with owners to match: lovely Anglo-Irish aplomb, great enthusiasm, charm incarnate, from generation to generation. The house was built in 1728 then remodelled in the Italianate style. The pillared hall with its fine ceilings, crackling fire and wonderful furniture has a Blüthner baby grand – you are welcome to play. The new south-facing drawing room rejoices in a spectacular view of formal terraces and gardens. Egyptian lucifers stand attendant as guests dine at the baronial table, sparkling with the best silverware. It's a real feast – they even forage for wild foods. Bedrooms lie off a long narrow corridor: all are different with huge beds – turned down before bedtime – antique furniture, armchairs, thick carpets, maybe an early 19th-century bath and tall windows onto the gardens. Wander through woodland, sit by restored trout lakes, hone your croquet skills, or fish for salmon on their six-mile stretch of the River Blackwater. The Greens deserve their reputation, they do it marvellous well.

rooms	6: 3 doubles, 3 twins.
price	€160–€200. Singles €95–€115.
meals	Dinner, 4 courses, €50. Packed lunch for fisherfolk €15.
closed	Christmas & New Year.
directions	From Cork N8 for Fermoy about 24km. At River Bride right R628, before Rathcormac, for Tallow & follow signs.

Justin & Jenny Green

tel	+353 (0)25 36349
fax	+353 (0)25 36781
email	info@ballyvolanehouse.ie
web	www.ballyvolanehouse.ie

B&B

Map 7 Entry 142

Maranatha Country House
Tower, Blarney, Co. Cork

The wonderful fantasy world of Maranatha awaits you, up on a hill surrounded by rhododendron, monkey-puzzle and giant redwood. This late Victorian mansion has some of the most imaginative bedrooms in Ireland. Lounge in shimmering palatial luxury dreaming of Persia and the Orient as each room follows its own sumptuous theme, even unto the bathrooms. Gleaming fabrics flow across four-posters, pour from coronets and frame views of landscaped garden and secluded woodland. Walks lead in all directions. Olwen inherited the old house from her Scottish father in 1982 and, with no previous experience of interior design, she transformed the place utterly. She has a natural eye for lush, opulent colours — deep burgundy, claret red, forest green — and a love of inlaid French furniture. Olwen and Douglas have huge affection for the house and their enthusiasm rubs off on those who stay; many return year after year. Breakfasts, served in the floral-draped conservatory, are memorably good. A wonderful silk-flower place with real heart, it is exceptional value.

Country house

rooms	6: 1 double, 2 four-posters, 3 family.
price	€68–€120. Singles €45–€75.
meals	Choice in Blarney.
closed	Mid-December to February.
directions	From Cork N20 then R617 through Blarney 2.5km. House signposted just after Tower village sign; right up hill.

Olwen & Douglas Venn

tel	+353 (0)21 438 5102
fax	+353 (0)21 438 2978
email	info@maranathacountryhouse.com
web	www.maranathacountryhouse.com

Map 7 Entry 143

Allcorn's Country Home
Shournagh Road, Blarney, Co. Cork

Helen's wooden house is bright, jovial and open-hearted in warm yellows, fresh flowers, big skylights, bigger rooms and well-stocked bookshelves. Generous bathrooms, too: once extracted from your Egyptian cotton sheets, you can comfortably mambo on the mosaic among the spoiling smellies. Enchanted by the patient sounds of the River Shournagh on its way from hillside to ocean and the seclusion of the wooded valley, the Allcorns built the house themselves 30 years ago. It is still just as enchanting. Helen's simple philosophy is do-as-you-would-be-done-by. She loves animals and people in equal measure, her many pets are often strays in need of a good home – Betsey the black lab is a happy newcomer – and the dogbed is a pretty nice sofa. There are super pieces of family furniture everywhere, each room has real personality. On sunny days, or even drizzly ones, you can wander through the three acres of peace and garden, carefully landscaped with willow, dogwood and wildflower meadows down to the water's edge – and wait for the leap of a passing salmon. Breakfast is also a treat which should not be hurried.

rooms	4: 2 twins/doubles, 1 double; 1 single with separate bath.
price	€70-€75. Singles €45-€50.
meals	Restaurants in Blarney.
closed	November-February.
directions	From Blarney R617 for Killarney 1.5km; right at major turn by River Shournagh, sign to house; entrance 2nd on left.

	Helen Allcorn
tel	+353 (0)21 438 5577
email	info@allcorns.com
web	www.allcorns.com

B&B

Map 7 Entry 144

Co. Cork

Farran House
Farran, Cork, Co. Cork

Rather than paper over the cracks when restoring their grand 18th-century country house, these two young photographers stripped it back to a bare shell, removed the problems, then put it back together again. Their hard work is repaid in full, the house looks amazing, a model for Georgian houses in Ireland – and there's also the 19th-century stained glass. Rooms are elegantly done with pine floors, antiques, brilliant old shutters, kilim rugs from Afghanistan, the odd spear, paintings by Patricia's grandmother – but still space to swing a tiger. A sign of the friendly, relaxed atmosphere is the full-size snooker table and honesty bar combination on the ground floor. Bathrooms are a real treat, as big and luxurious as the stylish bedrooms. Nothing has been compromised in this lovely house. There's lots of room to relax in, books to read, the Bechstein to play in the drawing room, the patio with views over the Lee Valley to sit and wallow in the country peace. The twelve acres of grounds have gardens and woodland to explore and Cork is only a short drive for the odd lively excursion. Fabulous.

rooms	4: 2 doubles, 1 twin, 1 family.
price	€140-€200. Singles €100-€130.
meals	Dinner €40.
closed	November-March. Groups off season by arrangement.
directions	From Cork N22 for Killarney 16km; 2nd right after Dan Sheahan's pub, up steep lane; entrance 1st on left.

Country house

Patricia Wiese & John Kehely
tel +353 (0)21 733 1215
fax +353 (0)21 733 1450
email info@farranhouse.com
web www.farranhouse.com

Map 7 Entry 145

Farran Coach House

Farran House, Farran, Cork, Co. Cork

Perfect for anyone wanting it all – the bliss of deep country and the buzz of Cork just down the road – this beautifully restored Georgian coach house has few equals in Ireland. Sympathy for the original design, hard work and a gift for good taste are the secrets. Patricia and John based their conversion on original drawings of improvements made by the Penrose family in 1886. They tore down wallpaper and plaster, ripped up carpets and floor boards and went to it. The results are stunning. Walk into a big, bright open-plan living room and super kitchen area with long comfortable sofas on big terracotta tiles and the owners' excellent photographs alongside kilims on the walls. The bedrooms upstairs remain true to the Georgian spirit of uncluttered elegance, pleasing to the eye and immensely comfortable. The sunny patio has views of Bride Valley and Kilcrea Abbey and 12 lovely acres are at your door. Cork has, of course, the full choice of pubs and restaurants and nearby Midleton is the home of Jameson whiskey, also known as Uisce Beatha, the 'water of life', as perfected by 6th-century monks.

rooms	Coach house for 6 (1 double, 2 twins, 1 bath, 1 shower).
price	€500-€690 per week, plus heating & electricity.
meals	Self-catering.
closed	Rarely.
directions	Directions given on booking.

Patricia Wiese & John Kehely

tel	+353 (0)21 733 1215
fax	+353 (0)21 733 1450
email	info@farranhouse.com
web	www.farranhouse.com

Self-catering

Map 7 Entry 146

Lotamore House

Lower Glanmire Road, Tivoli, Cork, Co. Cork

A shipping merchant built this imposing mansion in a lush garden 200 years ago to overlook the docks and his industrial prosperity – now the main road and the gas works. Behind the house the old glory is being resuscitated: four acres of mature rhodendendrons and lawns are being carefully relandscaped. Always ask for a room over the garden. Lotamore is a splendid house and there are some magnificent antiques, ideally suited to the Georgian proportions and tall windows. Geri is eager to make her operation a success. Flowers, dried or fresh, burst from vases, logs crackle before soft deep sofas corseted in rich upholsteries. Bedrooms are sumptuous, each a skilful mix of lovely fabrics in the mauve to red spectrum, the best bedding and proper linen on beautiful antique beds – carved, inlaid, canopied – and sometimes even a sofa. Under Edyta's kindly efficient eye, service is in keeping with the ethos: careful, friendly, impeccable. A most comfortable place to stay, on the garden side, so close to this vibrant historic city and the joys of the countryside. *15-minute drive from airport & ferry. Vegetarian meals available.*

rooms	20: 14 twins/doubles, 6 suites.
price	€120-€130. Singles €75-€90.
meals	Snack menu from restaurant next door. Cork 10-minute drive.
closed	Christmas & New Year.
directions	From Cork N8 for Waterford & Dublin. Hotel on left just past Flemings Restaurant; big sign.

Hotel

Geraldine & Sidney McElhinney

tel	+353 (0)21 482 2344
fax	+353 (0)21 482 2219
email	lotamore@iol.ie
web	www.lotamorehouse.com

Map 7 Entry 147

Cafe Paradiso & Paradiso Rooms
16 Lancaster Quay, Cork, Co. Cork

The breakfast menu alone is the most devilish temptation to push the door to paradise. Paradiso is the exciting high-class vegetarian restaurant where Denis, who naturally belongs to Slow Food Ireland, has made an enduring name for himself. And now on the 'two floors over the shop' of this city-centre Victorian building they have made three rooms. And what rooms! Not just afterthoughts to be ignored after a feast of aubergine parcels of spinach, pinenuts and Coolea cheese or chard leaf timbale of Puy lentils with four subtle vegetables. They are big with superb modern bathrooms and much character: a generous sofa each, bold yet restful colours, a sophisticated, uncluttered style. Bridget, a warm, friendly New Zealander, has added lots of personal touches and the gentle ethnic influence of Maori motifs, wallhangings and figurines alongside good modern paintings gives a balanced imaginative atmosphere. Two of the rooms overlook the busy road and the River Lee, the other, with no view but masses of sky light, will be quieter. Ask about the local arts and culture scene: your hosts know it all.

rooms	3 doubles.
price	€160.
meals	Lunch or dinner €15-€50.
closed	Sundays & Mondays.
directions	From centre take Washington St/Western Rd towards University College Cork. Paradiso on right between Reidy's Wine Vault & The Thirsty Scholar (10-min. walk from city centre).

Denis Cotter & Bridget Healy

tel	+353 (0)21 427 7939
email	info@cafeparadiso.ie
web	www.cafeparadiso.ie

Restaurant with rooms

Map 7 Entry 148

Ballymakeigh House
Killeagh, Youghal, Co. Cork

If you ask Margaret what time breakfast ends, she'll say "it doesn't, I don't like deadlines ruining my enjoyment"... and breakfast may include strawberry muffins and scrambled eggs with lovage. One of the undisputed grandmasters of Irish hospitality, she is a multi-award-winning Housewife and self-taught Chef, the producer of remarkable country dinners at Ballymakeigh, served with great style in the beautiful candlelit dining room – and she loves it all. Standing at the end of an avenue that wends through a slalom of majestic oak, the 300-year-old farmhouse is immaculate. Bedrooms have bags of old-fashioned comfort, some with views over fields dotted with Michael's dairy herd. Linger in front of a blazing log fire or in the plant-filled conservatory, wander in the prodigious herb and fruit garden, get lost in the secret garden, or work up an appetite on the floodlit tennis court. There's a ghostly ruin on the hill, a riding centre and a 'gastronomic experience' dinner (book ahead). Ingredients, many produced on the Brownes' land, are all fresh. *Tennis on site. Cookery courses in winter.*

rooms	4 twins/doubles.
price	€120. Singles €70.
meals	Dinner, 6 courses, €40–€45.
closed	November–February.
directions	From Youghal N25 for Cork 8km to Killeagh village; at Pub Old Thatch, right up hill between pub and church; first right. Entrance signposted on right, laurel hedge, white gates.

Country house

	Margaret & Michael Browne
tel	+353 (0)24 95184
fax	+353 (0)24 95370
email	ballymakeigh@eircom.net
web	www.ballymakeighhouse.com

Map 7 Entry 149

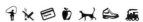

Knockeven House
Rushbrooke, Cobh, Co. Cork

The impressive early Victorian house lifts its pillars to the admiring acres and has a regal interior to match. Red opulence in the main hall, smart golfing wallpaper at the back – a top designer has clearly worked here and you can guess that John is a golfing fanatic (the famous Fota Island golf course is nearby). Pam is a real people person whose warm hospitality will go to your heart: guests send her flowers from home. Having owned and run a successful supermarket, these two have a genuine talent for serving others. Big deluxe bedrooms are richly flounced and draped in florals or toile de Jouy. One has dramatically beautiful long silk curtains and matching throws, another has a superb old half-tester bed, all have fine antiques and the smartest white bathrooms with luscious goodies. Downstairs, white lilies, old timber and modern windows warm the smart sitting room, mahogany glows beneath your linen table mat and silver cutlery, the breakfast spread is sumptuous. But remember the famine-driven thousands who sailed from Queenstown (Cobh) to America in the 1840s; and the Titanic in 1912. Real value.

rooms	4 twins/doubles.
price	€120-€140. Singles €75-€80.
meals	Restaurants in Cobh.
closed	Rarely.
directions	From Cork N25 for Rosslare; 3rd exit R624 to Cobh; pass gates, cross bridge, right to Great Island Motors, left here, first drive on right.

Pam & John Mulhaire
tel	+353 (0)21 481 1778
fax	+353 (0)21 481 1719
email	info@knockevenhouse.com
web	www.knockevenhouse.com

Country house

Map 7 Entry 150

Ballymaloe House
Shanagarry, Midleton, Co. Cork

The iconic Irish country house run by unfailingly caring people, Ballymaloe is a brilliant place to stay – and eat. Superb grounds with memorable trees, modern rugs beneath classic plasterwork, a fine collection of the best 20th-century Irish painters and sculptors, multifarious dining spaces – formal Georgian, relaxed modern, little velvet corner – bringing intimacy to each part of the 100-seat restaurant. The food, much of it home-grown, is unforgettably good and rightly famous throughout Ireland. Some architectural details are amazing: an 18th-century house knitted into medieval walls; a 14th-century keep, reached through an innocuous cupboard behind the bar – like popping into Narnia – and blessed with fine views from the rampart; the ancient gatehouse now a sweet little apartment with a tiny staircase and arrow-slit windows. Bedrooms are all different, unfussy and eminently comfortable with up-to-date bathrooms: in the old house they breathe country-house history, in the extension they are larger, some have private little gardens. *Excellent cookery and organic gardening courses on site. Vegetarian meals available. Tennis on site.*

rooms	33: 15 doubles, 15 twins, 3 singles.
price	€200-€320. Singles from €165.
meals	Lunch €35. Dinner €70.
closed	Christmas; two weeks in January.
directions	From Cork N25 for Waterford 30km; right R630 then R631 through Cloyne for Ballycotton. House 3km after Cloyne.

Country house hotel

	The Allen Family
tel	+353 (0)21 465 2531
fax	+353 (0)21 465 2021
email	res@ballymaloe.ie
web	www.ballymaloe.ie

Map 7 Entry 151

Sunville House
Ballycotton, Midleton, Co. Cork

In all simplicity, Anna pampers her house and guests with fresh flowers, home-baked fruit cake, an enchanting giggle and loving kindness. Pat tends the garden (otherwise those Nicholas Mosse vases go empty), the goldfish pond, the hens for wonderful breakfast eggs and the blooming conservatory. They are a delight, these generous rural Cork folk who love having people to stay. Theirs is a place of contrasts: behind the uplifted modern bungalow (they raised the roof to add a floor) stands the historic granite ruin of William Penn's old house, he who founded Pennsylvania. A favourite colour inside is rusty orange with mellow cream carpets and pretty duvet covers to soften. Laid with Stephen Pearce pottery (do visit the workshop), fresh fruit and jars of nuts permanently on display, oranges squeezed to order, the all-pine breakfast room looks out to spectacular views over the garden (unusual ornaments include a red drill plough and ceramic ducks and hens) to ruins and fields. Bedrooms are pine furnished and thoroughly comfortable with soft carpets and space. Great value, genuine hospitality.

rooms	6: 3 doubles, 1 twin, 2 family.
price	€70-€80. Singles €40-€45.
meals	Choice in Ballycotton, 5-minute drive.
closed	Rarely.
directions	From Cork airport N25 for Rosslare to Midleton; R629 to Shanagarry; right for Ballycotton; over x-roads, right at T-junction; house 2km on right.

Anna & Patrick Casey
tel   +353 (0)21 464 6271
fax   +353 (0)21 464 6271
email   sunvillehouse@eircom.net
web   www.sunville.net

B&B

Map 7 Entry 152

Kilbrogan House
Bandon, Co. Cork

The list of Kilbrogan's owners over its 200 years reads like a summary of Irish upper-class history: a duke, a land agent and a solicitor, a merchant, an electricity maker, a miller and, fame at last, Joseph Brennan, whose signature appeared on Irish banknotes after the war. Catherine escaped from bond-trading to its gracious townhouse peace four years ago and did a brilliant renovation job, giving the house that Georgian vibration of glowing antique beneath delicate cornice, rich dark curtains by tall windows, wooden floors spread with thick decorative rugs hand-made by Catherine's father, stripped doors – all natural materials brought in from the wild to be finely civilised. Beds are modern brass or timber with top-class mattresses, starched Egyptian cotton sheets, soft white duvets. A fine double-glazed conservatory graces the first floor, where armies of geraniums thrive and the garden's serenity pours in. Add her brother's breakfast mastery, the beautiful stone coachhouse – another testimony to this family's talented eye and hand – and you have a triumph of taste and humanity.

rooms	5: 4 doubles, 1 twin.
price	€90–€110. Singles €50–€70.
meals	Restaurants within walking distance.
closed	December & January.
directions	From Cork N71 to Bandon; right at Methodist church, cross river, bear left at statue, follow for Macroom; next right up Kilbrogan Hill; at top, entrance opposite Kays Flowers.

B&B

Catherine FitzMaurice

tel	+353 (0)23 44935
fax	+353 (0)23 44935
email	fitz@kilbrogan.com
web	www.kilbrogan.com

Map 7 Entry 153

Kilbrogan Coachhouse
Bandon, Co. Cork

Renovating this fine Georgian stone coachhouse was a huge job and, with her practical sense and eye for detail, Catherine has done the three apartments beautifully, treasuring all the original features. Two apartments are one above the other, the Circles being windows above the Arches. Up steep iron steps you enter an open-plan garden-view living space: white walls, brown leather sofas, a great mix of modern and old with pristine white and chrome kitchen ware, an intimate pull-out table; then a big pretty bedroom, a high bright bathroom and, oh luxury, a separate shower room. Arches is similar but on the ground floor, with French doors onto the front garden and just one bathroom. Pretty flower boxes deck the Gardener's House window sills, florals abound inside where there's space, a wood-burner in the sitting room, cosy comfort in the darkish bedrooms. Three clear, uncluttered places to stay with lots of clean whiteness – crockery, tiling, walls -, wooden floors, good fittings, crisp linens on excellent beds and great taste. And you are bang in the middle of Bandon with a superb garden.

rooms	3 apartments: 2 for 2, 1 for 4.
price	€400–€650, including heating, electricity & linen.
meals	Restaurants within walking distance.
closed	December & January except by arrangement.
directions	From Cork N71 to Bandon; right at Methodist church, follow signs for Macroom & town centre; right at Court House up Kilbrogan Hill; at top, entrance opposite Kays Flowers.

	Catherine FitzMaurice
tel	+353 (0)23 44935
mobile	+353 (0)86 368 9939
email	fitz@kilbrogan.com
web	www.kilbrogan.com

Self-catering

Map 7 Entry 154

Glebe House
Ballinadee, Bandon, Co. Cork

Gillian's wonderful hearty laugh will greet you at the luscious front door (she changes the colour every year: it's lilac this year) and carry you into her happy, fun house. The old rectory's perfect Georgian proportions create a sense of serenity while Gillian's colour sense and love of art give it a very personal edge. She shares her well-lived-in home with daughter Caroline and her partner. Nothing is fancy or smart, the interest lies rather in her artistic treasures, her lively presence and her divine breakfasts (homemade waffles and rosemary shortbread, date bake with crispy bacon, pickled herrings on toast, fair-trade coffee) and dinners. Old-fashioned rooms are soft pink or blue or green or indigo – or a mixture of all these. There's an antique hobby horse in one bathroom, the warm, inviting sitting room has all the right hi-fi stuff and a fine old piano, from the two lovely oval dining tables you can see the impressive kiwi pergola. Indeed, the big garden has other botanical highlights (a fantastic Chilean flame tree, a wisteria centrepiece) as well as a concealed pizza oven. Great fun. *Vegetarian meals available.*

rooms	4: 2 doubles, 2 family.
price	€100-€120. Singles €65-€75.
meals	Dinner, 3 courses, €35. BYO wine.
closed	Christmas & New Year.
directions	From Cork N71 for Bandon approx. 20km to Innishannon Bridge; left at sign for Ballinadee & Glebe Country House; house in village.

B&B

Gillian Good

tel	+353 (0)21 477 8294
fax	+353 (0)21 477 8456
email	glebehse@indigo.ie
web	www.glebecountryhouse.com

Map 7 Entry 155

Casino Cottage
Casino House, Coolmain Bay, Kilbrittain, Co. Cork

Casino Cottage was once the diminutive gate lodge to Casino House, now a great place to dine and a shining example of European influences entering the cultural life of Ireland. Kerrin is from the German island of Sylt in Friesland, which she says is remarkably similar to this delightful rural backwater in West Cork. Michael is the chef, born in Croatia, brought up in Germany. They stumbled upon the 200-year-old farmhouse one drizzly morning ten years ago and decided to open a restaurant and raise a family. Four children, classy interior design and a reputation for good food followed. They then converted the gate lodge into a delightful snug little hideaway for two. Done with flagstones, tiles and plain colours, the living area is cottage smart with a big heart-warming fireplace (wood provided), books and a good kitchen space. The brass bed is just right, the blue shower room done with shells, coast walks start from the door. The superb restaurant, a mix of old and new, has beamed ceilings, thick walls, worn leather sofas, inspirational local art, even a horse-shaped tricycle. *Min. one week July/August.*

rooms	Cottage for 2 (1 double, 1 shower; sofabed in living room).	
price	€85 per night. €210-€350 per week.	
meals	Casino House Restaurant on the spot (closed 1 January-17 March).	
closed	Never.	
directions	From Bandon R603 south through Kilbrittain; left for Kinsale for about 1.5km; entrance on left at sign.	

Kerrin & Michael Relja
tel   +353 (0)23 49944
fax   +353 (0)23 49945
email   chouse@eircom.net

Self-catering

Map 7 Entry 156

The Glen Country House

The Glen, Kilbrittain, Co. Cork

Old class, new comforts, the ever-inspiring ocean light and a young family – the Scotts are all that. The family has farmed this land between rolling pastures and the Atlantic for 350 years and lived in the house for 100 years. Guy is an easy, laid-back farmer, Diana as friendly and helpful as you could wish. She hasn't hesitated to use good strong colours to tremendous effect and turn her main rooms into perfect backdrops for antique coffee cups, oriental teak dining chairs and old family photographs. Bedrooms are paler in their smart stripey or soft floral wallpapers (magnificent tulips in the 'Versace' room), all beautifully finished and furnished, antique wardrobes sharing the wall space with flat-screen televisions, big beds firm beneath fluffy linen-covered duvets and the modern little bathrooms (with super soapy things) fitting perfectly without destroying the harmony of these old rooms. Stroll in the walled vegetable garden, sit on the lawn, gaze past the cows, soak up the peace – if you can resist the call of the many and various local attractions.

rooms	5 + 1: 4 twins/doubles, 1 suite for 4 (1 double, 1 twin). Cottage for 4.
price	€120-€130. Suite €175. Cottage €300-€450 per week.
meals	Pub within walking distance, 3 restaurants within 3 miles. Children's supper available.
closed	November-March.
directions	Midway between Kinsale & Clonakilty: signs on R600.

Country house & Self-catering

	Guy & Diana Scott
tel	+353 (0)23 49862
fax	+353 (0)23 49862
email	guyscott@eircom.net
web	www.glencountryhouse.com

Map 7 Entry 157

The Cottage
Kilbrittain, Co. Cork

Allow yourself a sigh of pleasure as you arrive: with its sash windows, slate roof and sensitive extension, this charming seaside cottage on a beautiful part of the coast is all you hope for and seldom find. Set below the road in its own simple, private garden, it comes with long soft views of the beach and Courtmacsherry Bay. You go through the traditional half door straight into the sitting room to be greeted by an open fire, simple, well-chosen country furniture and plenty of space for four in Elizabeth's hallmark cosy-comfy décor. The new part is an accurate reflection of the old, walls are painted white or done with attractive limed tongue-and-groove timber, original watercolours and decent prints alongside check and gingham fabrics all emphasise the cottagey look, the neat little bedrooms have new beds, the bathrooms (one in a heated outhouse) have new showers, the traditionally furnished dining/kitchen area has good natural light – indeed the whole cottage is exceptionally well-lit. Ideal for a couple or a family with young children looking for a classic seaside holiday.

rooms	Cottage for 4-6
	(1 double, 1 twin, mezzanine for 2).
price	€250-€550 per week,
	including linen.
meals	Self-catering.
	Pubs & restaurants 1km & 5km.
closed	Never.
directions	12 miles west of Kinsale.
	Directions on booking.

	Elizabeth Connolly
tel	+353 (0)87 261 8418
fax	+353 (0)59 972 2332
email	vconnolly@eircom.net

Self-catering

Map 7 Entry 158

Pier House

Pier Road, Kinsale, Co. Cork

The wide estuary light floods this immaculate designer-modernised 200-year-old house. In the luxury of a simple décor, be warmed by the lovely Irish welcome you will unfailingly get from Ann and Pat. Even the stripped old doors, witnesses to the dockside bustle of Kinsale's past, contribute to the solidly contemporary marine look of Pier House, generously decorated as it is with driftwood carvings, scatterings of seashells and lots of paintings by an artist friend. Natural is the key word: wicker chairs, feather duvets and crisp white linen on polished sleigh beds, dark timber floors and white walls, taupe and wine-coloured fabrics, slate-tiled bathrooms and nothing to shock or jolt. Pat, formerly a master carpenter, oversaw the building of the clever storage spaces for hiding clothes and television sets. Big beds throughout, a private, plant-graced balcony for almost every room, the latest in power showers and one vast bath with telly in the master room. What more? Well… a hot tub on the deck, a sauna, a pretty garden, fabulously knowledgeable local hosts. A wonderful find right at the heart of lovely Kinsale.

rooms	10: 8 doubles, 2 twins.
price	€100–€140. Singles from €100.
meals	Choice in town. Guests may picnic on balcony.
closed	Rarely.
directions	From Cork into Kinsale; follow road round to left by Supervalu; 1st left at Tourist Office. House on right opposite car park.

Hotel

		Ann & Pat Hegarty
tel		+353 (0)21 477 4475
fax		+353 (0)21 477 4475
email		pierhouseaccom@eircom.net
web		www.pierhousekinsale.com

Map 7 Entry 159

Boland Townhouse
Emmet Place, Kinsale, Co. Cork

Built in 2001 beside Tony and Colette's own house, Boland House is immaculate and designed for comfort, a place you can slip into without a second's anxiety over cobwebs or broken chairs. Indeed, beside the realistic gas-fired logs, the red leather reclining armchairs and matching sofa are brand new, the pictures modern, the books and mags up to date. Your quarters are on the first and second floors with boot, rod, golf-club and surfboard storage below. The gleaming tile-and-pine kitchen has just about everything. In colour-coordinated rooms, you will find masses of storage as well as floor-length paisley curtains for cosy softness but... dilemma: which to choose, the power-shower or the jacuzzi bedroom? Nearby, Tony and Colette run a successful Irish crafts and clothing shop and a delicatessen (your welcome pack includes a Mange-Tout Deli voucher) but they are present and attentive for guests. With all the resources of buzzing Kinsale on your doorstep, you can choose the quiet privacy of the roof-garden patio that opens off your kitchen. *Off-street parking. Not suitable for small children.*

rooms	Apartment for 4 (2 twin/doubles, 1 bath, 1 shower).
price	€435–€840 per week, plus electricity & gas.
meals	Self-catering.
closed	Never.
directions	From Cork R600 into Kinsale centre. House opposite Post Office & Tourist Office.

Tony & Colette Boland
tel	+353 (0)21 477 7584
mobile	+353 (0)87 210 8974
email	boland@iol.ie
web	www.bolandkinsale.com

Self-catering

Map 7 Entry 160

Walton Court Country House
Oysterhaven, Co. Cork

Paul and Janis achieve wonders in stone, in gastronomy, in sense of welcome. A charming, modest and irrepressibly energetic couple, they took a restoration course then rebuilt the ruined 18th-century manor (removing 92 tons of soil from the hall) and its courtyard buildings; they filled the house with colour, comfort, myriad intriguing objects and works of art, Africana from their time in Kenya, plus a French dogwheel that's best left to your imagination, then opened the doors to lucky visitors. The view down to Oysterhaven harbour is perfect today but they arrived to a dense jungle — not a dot of blue could be seen and the sea is 150 yards from the front door. Paul has built a jetty down there and now a marina, and a seawater pool in the courtyard garden, and an old railway station in the woods (see opposite), and... they rear their own wasps to keep bugs off their kitchen garden. The courtyard catches the setting sun and you eat, extremely, subtly, well, in the shimmering conservatory or the dark suggestive dining room. A remarkable place in so many different ways.

rooms	6 twins/doubles.
price	€140-€165. Singles €86-€132.
meals	Dinner, 4 courses, €42. By arrangement.
closed	December-February except by prior arrangement.
directions	From Kinsale R600 for Cork to Belgooly; right at Huntsman Bar for Oysterhaven. Enter Oysterhaven over causeway. As you go up hill, house on right.

Guest house

	Paul & Janis Rafferty
tel	+353 (0)21 477 0878
fax	+353 (0)21 477 0932
email	enquiry@waltoncourt.com
web	www.waltoncourt.com

Map 7 Entry 161

Walton Court Cottages

Oysterhaven, Co. Cork

The stone outbuildings that enclosed the sloping courtyard of Walton Court were as ruinous as the rest when Paul and Janis arrived. With their remarkable conversion, the old stables, grain store and estate bakery have sprung to new life. Each 'terraced cottage' has its own front space for basking as the sun fades: admire the Italianate pergola on its way down to the house or soak up your children's laughter in the pool. Supremely well designed and finished, the cottages have everything you need for full enjoyment of this quiet backwater – and nothing you don't: fitted kitchen, toaster, radio, kettle; no telly or dishwasher; the telephone is a bakelite antique. A wood-burning stove, thick curtains and tempting sofa promise cosy, civilised evenings, pretty bedrooms upstairs suggest quiet rest, table and chairs await sunny breakfasts on the terrace. On its own in the woods, the 'summerhouse' is in fact the original Clonakilty Junction station where young and old can relive the age of steam – huge fun. The Raffertys want guests to have restful, organic holidays – and they cook superbly.

rooms	4 cottages for 3-8. Summerhouse for 4.
price	€500-€1,400 per week.
meals	Dinner, 4 courses, €42. By arrangement. Restaurants 1.5-10km.
closed	Christmas.
directions	From Kinsale R600 for Cork to Belgooly; right at Huntsman Bar for Oysterhaven. Enter Oysterhaven over causeway. As you go up hill, house on right.

Janis & Paul Rafferty
tel +353 (0)21 477 0878
fax +353 (0)21 477 0932
email info@waltoncourt.com
web www.waltoncourt.com

Self-catering

Map 7 Entry 162

Hanora's Cottage
Nire Valley, Ballymacarbry, Co. Waterford

The cottage is still in there, overtaken by magnificence. Around it, the Walls designed and decorated a refuge of luxury on the banks of a crystal-clear brook deep in the beautiful Nire valley where the road stops and nature takes over, rising into the Comeragh Mountains and up to majestic Knockanaffrin. The ever-singing brook is floodlit at night, to stupendous effect. Rooms have all the modern guest could want: thick carpet, lavish bed, superb jacuzzi bathroom, fresh fruit basket, all the spoiling extras; and a small gym downstairs for "the exercise you can't take because it's too wet". Mary thinks of everything, the place runs like clockwork and the food is outstanding. Sadly, Seamus died, but his legacy lives on in his bread recipes and special bakes. Son Eoin performs culinary magic with his wife Judith and dinner here after a day in the mountains is a long, lingering, candlelit delight. Next morning, the breakfast table deserves a photograph: every variety of fruit, muesli and bread; creamy porridge, scones, cheeses, smoked salmon… not to mention scrambled eggs, sweet bacon and coffee. Total indulgence.

rooms	7: 1 double, 5 twins/doubles, 1 triple.
price	€170–€250. Singles from €95. Short half-board breaks.
meals	Dinner about €50. No dinner Sundays. Free picnic for walkers.
closed	Christmas; 1 week in spring; 1 week in autumn.
directions	From Clonmel south bank R671 for Dungarvan to Ballymacarbry; left by Melody's Lounge, over small bridge; house 5.5km up twisty road by Nire church.

Hotel

Mary Wall

tel	+353 (0)52 36134
fax	+353 (0)52 36540
email	hanorascottage@eircom.net
web	www.hanorascottage.com

Map 7 Entry 163

Glasha

Ballymacarbry, Clonmel, Co. Waterford

Kindness itself, Olive is formidably houseproud, her hall slathered in framed awards testifying that she gives herself 110% to her guests. Breakfast is the greatest demonstration of her mastery: just try homemade rhubarb and strawberry compote with home-baked courgette and walnut bread for a taster – there's masses more in the basket. It's a feast served on the renowned Stephen Pearce crockery. Her colour mixes are joyous and bright – regal red, cranberry cream, blue, mustard, burgundy and buttercup – and her fanciful spirit is personified in the quirky statues and water features that decorate the garden: it gurgles and bubbles at every turn. Olive's standards shine forth inside, too: the sitting room is so luxurious in its cream sofas and gold candelabras that you feel bound to be on your best behaviour. No dust from the log fires: they're electric! The all-seasons conservatory is a lovely room, more appealing for that breakfast experience than the rather dark dining room. Colourful welcoming bedrooms, comfortable bathrooms and superb walks into those beckoning mountains.

rooms	8: 2 doubles, 4 twins, 2 triples.
price	€100-€120. Singles €50-€60.
meals	Dinner €25-€40.
	Packed lunch on request.
closed	1-28 December.
directions	From Clonmel R671 for Dungarvan 13km; right at sign for Glasha Accommodation 1.5km.

Olive & Paddy O'Gorman

tel	+353 (0)52 36108
fax	+353 (0)52 36108
email	glasha@eircom.net
web	www.glashafarmhouse.com

Guest house

Map 7 Entry 164

Sliabh gCua Farmhouse
Touraneena, Ballinamult, Dungarvan, Co. Waterford

Altogether a wonderful place with views to die for but come to Sliabh gCua (pronounced 'sh-leeve-goo-a') above all for Breeda and Jim, the most wonderfully hospitable couple. Jim, a beef farmer, is softspoken and humorous while Breeda, warm and full of energy, could talk about anything until the oxen came home. She makes her own bread, scones, muesli and jams, keeps her well-loved farmhouse clean and fresh, the roaring fire in the drawing room is gorgeous, the beautifully-laid-out dining room looks over Jim's fine lawn and outhouses ("the neatest farm we've seen in Ireland", a visitor said). Breeda has cleverly fitted little shower rooms into the bedrooms without compromising their good proportions. They all have lovely furniture, tall windows, impeccable bedding and a heart-warmingly nostalgic atmosphere. You are welcome to play the piano, son Jamie may be persuaded to play the accordion, Irish-dancing guests have been known to tread the boards. This is a house of light and laughter where the shyest child will join in; there's even a treehouse in the much-pampered garden, which is even better than ever.

rooms	4: 2 doubles, 2 family rooms.
price	€80. Singles €45.
meals	Pub 5km; restaurants in Dungarvan, 16km; Clonmel, 24km.
closed	November–March.
directions	From Dungarvan R672 for Clonmel about 10km. House 1km off road near village of Touraneena; clearly signposted.

B&B

	Breeda & Jim Cullinan
tel	+353 (0)58 47120
email	breedacullinan@sliabhgcua.com
web	www.sliabhgcua.com

Map 7 Entry 165

Glencairn Inn & Pastis Bistro
Glencairn, Co. Waterford

Glencairn Inn exudes that incomparable mixture of old wood, delicious food and warm friendly chat, all gathered in the small pub, restaurant and B&B that Fiona and Stéphane have taken over from the renowned Buggys. Fiona has come home to her native Ireland to apply her outgoing nature and organisation skills to this marvellous place; her quietly chatty French husband is absolutely the right man in the kitchen. Perch on a stool in the snug old heavy-beamed pub, joyfully eavesdropping on the local gossip while waiting for dinner. The even cosier restaurant has more stone floors, old pictures – including Stéphane's ancestral farmhouse – and a definite French *auberge* flavour. As has the really good food: no jumped-up fussiness, just excellent ingredients, most of them local and fresh, treated with care and inspiration. After coffee, amble back to the bar for a nightcap and more chat. Upstairs, an eclectic mix of non-precious antiques wonderfully put together makes for utterly charming bedrooms: patchwork quilts on super beds, lots of pictures and books. Early sleepers may need their earplugs.

rooms	4: 3 doubles, 1 twin.
price	From €120. Singles from €80.
meals	Dinner from €35.
closed	Christmas & all January.
directions	From Lismore N72 for Tallow 1km; right at Horneybrooks car showroom for Glencairn. House 3km on right in village, opp. T-junc.

Stéphane & Fiona Tricot
tel   +353 (0)58 56232
fax   +353 (0)58 56232
email   info@glencairninn.com
web   www.glencairninn.com

Inn

Map 7 Entry 166

Richmond House
Cappoquin, Co. Waterford

Since Paul and Claire took over from his parents, they have put huge energy into the restaurant and been showered with praises. Paul trained in Switzerland and is relaxed yet very professional about things. In the attractive, fresh-looking dining room with its white linen and red carpets beneath Georgian mouldings and modern mirrors, he offers high-quality local produce – Waterford lamb, Dunmore East scallops, their home-grown chicken and the freshest vegetables – cooked to simple perfection in a gloriously light version of country cooking. Beautifully served, too. The harmonious ground-floor Georgian rooms of this impressive three-storey house, built in 1704 as part of the great Lismore estate, have lots of very fitting heavily-carved furniture, chintz, wallpapers and plush – and a stuffed owl on the staircase. Up those stairs are the lovely bedrooms. The prize goes to the huge master room but all are freshly redecorated in smart country style with a feminine touch and longing views of the Knockmealdown Mountains – and four have king-size beds. A helpful, attentive couple, the Deevys know how to receive.

rooms	9: 2 twins/doubles, 5 doubles, 1 twin, 1 single.
price	€140-€240. Singles €85-€135.
meals	Dinner, 4 courses, €50. Early Bird menu 6.30pm, €30.
closed	Two weeks Christmas & New Year.
directions	From Cappoquin N72 for Dungarvan 1km; house signposted.

Restaurant with rooms

Paul & Claire Deevy
tel	+353 (0)58 54278
fax	+353 (0)58 54988
email	info@richmondhouse.net
web	www.richmondhouse.net

Map 7 Entry 167

Powersfield House

Ballinamuck West, Dungarvan, Co. Waterford

The glowing highlight here is Eunice's cooking: she's a national hero, a Slow Food adept, runs courses at Powersfield, appears on television and, of course, cooks succulent organic dinners. And breakfasts. Which may include goats-cheese and bell-pepper croustade, if you please. All that plus looking after three young children and busy farmer Edmund — how does she do it? An inextinguishable ball of fire, she says "this is a night house" and the atmosphere in the evening is supremely relaxed among the flickering candles. The dining room is a gem, intimate, modern, with polished floors and Eunice's art collection on the walls — Barry Fitzpatrick's head is always a talking point and dinner is a revelation. For someone who didn't know the difference between a tagine and a daube until a few years ago, she brings food to life: piadina with goat's cheese, crispy roast duck, maybe sticky pear and ginger cake. Nothing seems beyond her ken. The deeply comfortable bedrooms are pretty funky, too, with Eunice's plates a constant theme — she just loves plates. Come for lots of fun and fabulous eating.

rooms	4: 3 doubles, 1 twin.
price	€110–€120. Singles €65–€75.
meals	Dinner, 3 courses, €27–€37. 24 hours' notice required.
closed	Rarely.
directions	From Dungarvan centre R672 for Killarney; over Kilrush roundabout; 2nd left; 1st house on right.

Eunice & Edmund Power

tel	+353 (0)58 45594
fax	+353 (0)58 45550
email	eunice@powersfield.com
web	www.powersfield.com

B&B

Map 7 Entry 168

The Castle Country House
Millstreet, Cappagh, Dungarvan, Co. Waterford

These are the kindest, genuinest country people you could imagine. Emmett
runs the large dairy farm and is passionate about his undulating garden watered
by the River Finisk, Joan does mountains of baking (fresh cakes arrive in your
room every day) and grows her own berries and vegetables, both ooze warmth
and friendship. But why the name? Because it is just that: an 18th-century house
built onto the remains of the McGrath clan's 16th-century round stone tower
house. The grand gilded gates are original, you will see one old arch in the long
thin dining room, thick walls and high ceilings in Lady Mary's room, part of the
old tower on the way to the McGrath room, the rest has the gentle proportions
of a later age. Joan and Emmett have been caring for guests for almost 20 years,
brilliantly, and have passed the gift to daughter and daughter-in-law, now part of
the team that produces imaginative breakfasts and fresh local dinners. No grand
décor here but a fine new sitting room and soft-coloured bedrooms with a sitting
space each, snow-white linen and candles. Time-warp Millstreet is a must-see.

rooms	4: 3 doubles, 1 twin.
price	€100-€120. Singles €50-€60.
meals	Dinner, 3 courses, €30. BYO wine. Packed lunch on request.
closed	November to mid-March.
directions	From Dungarvan R672 then N72 for Lismore 15km; right R671 for Millstreet; first right, first house on right.

Country house

	Emmet & Joan Nugent
tel	+353 (0)58 68049
fax	+353 (0)58 68099
email	castle@castlecountryhouse.com
web	www.castlecountryhouse.com

Map 7 Entry 169

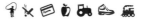

Arlington Lodge Country House & Restaurant

John's Hill, Waterford, Co. Waterford

Maurice Keller, "a fine stamp of a man", is utterly charming, enjoying the company of his guests. His staff are just as delightful, just as efficient. So, although Arlington Lodge may look like another sleek little up-market hotel, it has none of the stuffed-shirt formality you might expect, there is laughter in the air – and really good food in the conservatory restaurant. As far as possible, Maurice and his two assistant chefs use local produce. And the waiters are lovely. Your host's conversion from building to hotel-keeping is almost a vocation, inspired by this Georgian mansion that used to house the Catholic bishop and is perfect for the historic city centre. He has renovated, refurbished, refurnished, reproduced to the hilt, it glitters and gleams, draws you in and keeps you there in the luxury of country-house comfort and top-quality, unobsequious service. Rooms are opulent, the Bishop's Room doubly magnificent: rich draperies, carved furniture, gilt-framed oils – and fake fires so that you shan't burn out. Only room 318 over the kitchen is to be avoided. Relax in style and enjoy your host.

rooms	20: 14 doubles, 4 twins, 2 four-posters.
price	€150–€230.
meals	Lunch €15–€40. Dinner €27–€50.
closed	Christmas.
directions	From Waterford quay for Cork; at 3rd lights on Parnell St, left; over next lights; up John's Hill, hotel on right.

Maurice Keller

tel	+353 (0)51 878 584
fax	+353 (0)51 878 127
email	info@arlingtonlodge.com
web	www.arlingtonlodge.com

Hotel

Map 8 Entry 170

Sion Hill House & Gardens

Ferrybank, Waterford City, Co. Waterford

George and Antoinette are a gentle, modest couple – until it comes to Sion Hill, when they wax totally, enthusiastically passionate about their historic house and garden. It's easy to see why. In ten years, they have re-created this fabulous garden from jungle using old plans discovered in Waterford Library. The result is a living encylopædia of botany with over 1,000 species of rhododendron, azalea, rose, hydrangea and more. Pathways lead to fragrant groves, a walled garden, a pond among ancient tree ferns and an 11th-century Coptic monk lodged in an old wall – how he got here remains a mystery. Such a flower fiesta outside must mean a colour and pattern fiesta inside: the house is alive with embossed wallpapers, bright paintings, porcelain, gilt, carved ornaments, interesting memorabilia – nothing arrived without a story, everything 'fits'. Good-sized, gently chintzy bedrooms have lovely antiques, large beds with fresh white linen and fine views of the wonderful garden and river. That beautiful position overlooking Waterford city and the River Suir gives you pride of place for yacht-watching.

rooms	4: 1 four-poster, 3 family.
price	€80–€116. Singles from €55. Reductions for longer stays.
meals	Restaurants within 15-minute walk.
closed	Christmas & New Year.
directions	From Waterford city centre, N25 over bridge for Wexford & Rosslare; entrance on left, 100m after Ardri Hotel, before Shell filling station.

Country house

	George & Antoinette Kavanagh
tel	+353 (0)51 851 558
fax	+353 (0)51 851 678
email	info@sionhillhouse.com
web	www.sionhillhouse.com

Map 8 Entry 171

Brown's Townhouse

29 South Parade, Waterford, Co. Waterford

Síobhán is young, enthusiastic and fun, a well-travelled spirit with a soft spot for Spain and its gracious people. Happily puncturing pomposities, she brings a light and laughing atmosphere to this pleasant Victorian townhouse whose elegantly-proportioned rooms deserved her refreshments. The sitting and dining rooms have welcoming open fires and breakfast is served at a big convivial table. You will be summoned by the smell of just-baked brown bread, porridge and pancakes, fresh-ground coffee and a very proper full Irish fry. The first-floor double rooms over the street are attractive with their fine old beds and good floral fabrics and one of the other doubles has its own roof terrace looking over the back. At the top of the house, reached by a tiny staircase, is the funky orange and blue family room where the style is more modern and you can be nicely private. Brown's is on a quiet residential street with easy parking and only a short walk from Waterford's lively historic centre and waterfront. And it's ideal for the Waterford Show and the Opera Festival.

rooms	6: 3 doubles, 1 twin/double, 1 family, 1 suite.
price	€80–€100. Singles from €45.
meals	Restaurants within walking distance.
closed	Christmas & January.
directions	Arriving in Waterford from Dublin, cross bridge, left down quayside, follow round to right, left at 2nd lights after Tower Hotel, over hump-backed bridge, past park; house on right.

Síobhán McConnell

tel	+353 (0)51 870 594
fax	+353 (0)51 871 923
email	info@brownstownhouse.com
web	www.brownstownhouse.com

B&B

Map 8 Entry 172

Foxmount Country House
Passage East Road, Waterford, Co. Waterford

The Kents have been looking after guests in their peaceful 17th-century farmhouse for more than 30 years – brilliantly well, they deserve a medal. David and their son work the 200-acre farm while Margaret, whom some call a domestic goddess, greets you with a friendly confidence that comes of years of practice and flourishes her magic wand over breakfast of local free-range eggs, fresh herbs and unsprayed fruit. She is justly proud of her home, its smart family-comfortable feel and lush gardens. A house-party atmosphere often develops as guests mingle, after a day's hard gaze at Waterford's renowned sparkling crystal and an exploration of the town's many and various eating places, for a beautifully-served cup of tea or coffee in the big drawing room, warmed by the grand marble fireplace. The lovely fresh, thick-carpeted bedrooms are the highlight, with split levels, nooks and crannies, cosy bathrooms and creeper-clad windows overlooking a valley on one side, the farmyard on the other. And Foxmount is only three miles from the sea. No wonder people come back time and again.

rooms	5: 2 doubles, 3 twins.
price	€110. Singles €60.
meals	Choice in town.
closed	November-February.
directions	From Waterford R684 for Dunmore East 5km; left for Passage East & follow signs to house.

Country house

	Margaret & David Kent
tel	+353 (0)51 874 308
fax	+353 (0)51 854 906
email	info@foxmountcountryhouse.com
web	www.foxmountcountryhouse.com

Map 8 Entry 173

Coast Townhouse
Upper Branch Road, Tramore, Co. Waterford

Turlough and Jenny's former high-flying lifestyle has left echoes in this, the coolest, hippest young place to sleep and eat in County Waterford. They are young, cute and adorable, Coast is the child of their desire to come home and live differently. Turlough's front-of-house touch, Jenny's cooking genius and their flair for combining ultra-modern with traditional Irish styles in design and food have brought people flocking to the clean-cut, chocolate-and-cream restaurant with its lively funky bar, fashionable dishes and terrace for fine days. On polished floors stand plain benches backed by thin mirrors to show off your haircut, wonderful antique sofas, small drawing-room tables. A love of light shines through, the two Italian chandeliers are hypnotic, the breakfast menu alone is irresistible. Big, sleekly white bedrooms, sensual in their velvety cappucino carpets and silky red cushions, contemporary in their lighting and curvy daybeds, sport startling glass-box bathrooms: fabulous chrome fittings, peat-brown woodwork, long muslin veils for hazy privacy (one is opaque). Ask for a bay-view room.

rooms	4 doubles.
price	€100–€150.
meals	Dinner, 3 courses, €30; à la carte €25–€45. Sunday lunch €28.
closed	2 weeks in January.
directions	From Waterford R675 to Tramore; through first roundabout, first right up hill, 200m on left.

	Turlough McNamara & Jenny McNally
tel	+353 (0)51 393 646
fax	+353 (0)51 393 647
email	coastrestaurant@eircom.net
web	www.coast.ie

Restaurant with rooms

Map 8 Entry 174

Gaultier Lodge
Woodstown, Co. Waterford

The other side of this 18th-century hunting lodge almost tips you onto a clean, sandy beach and the estuary that separates Waterford from Wexford – a fabulous spot. On sunny days, walk for a mile with the sand between your toes; on bracing days, let the wind and crashing surf inspire you. Built on rock, surrounded by impregnable walls breached by one stone entrance under the gnarled boughs of an evergreen oak (there's an entrance for cars beyond), the house is intriguingly 'upside down' with exceptionally horse-loaded décor. Bill is American, a keen carriage driver and has bred Arabs; Sheila is Irish, energetic and equally horse-mad. They make a fun couple. The square, whimsical hall with its antique table, books, games and other busy things to look at opens onto two very fine bedrooms, both with sweeping sea views, and the rich, dark and luxurious four-poster room with painted floorboards, tall windows and an astounding great wardrobe. In the living room you'll find a log fire, more big views and a bountiful brunch. Sheila also runs painting courses. *Children over eight welcome.*

rooms	3: 1 double, 1 twin, 1 four-poster.
price	€110-€120. Singles €95. Discount for 3 nights or more.
meals	Restaurants in Dunmore East & Passage East.
closed	Rarely.
directions	From Waterford R684 for Dunmore East 9.5km; left for Woodstown; towards beach, right at T-junc. Lodge 0.5km on left, drive through gates at end.

		Sheila Molloy
B&B	tel	+353 (0)51 382 549
	fax	+353 (0)51 382 549
	email	castleffrench@aol.com
	web	www.gaultier-lodge.com

Map 8 Entry 175

Tir na Fiúise Cottages

Terryglass, Borrisokane, Co. Tipperary

In utter peace on an organic farm whose very air vibrates with health and things natural. Lovingly restored and painted with non-toxic organic paints, these three stone cottages are ideally placed for learning rural Ireland hands-on, touring the west and discovering great Lough Derg. Lime Kiln even has an enclosed patio that makes it safe for young children. The strong red paintwork follows you inside for a bright cheerful splashing against clean white-washed walls and original stonework. Each cottage has a welcoming wood-burning stove, lots of books to flick through, simple country furnishings and tempting easy chairs. The neat tiled kitchens have all the equipment you could wish for on a holiday while the shared laundry is at the end of the block. Living rooms and bedrooms are warmly floored in wood, the odd rug, furniture is clean-limbed pine clothed with light natural fabrics. Just two miles away in Terryglass you will find Paddy's pub, for genuine Irish atmosphere, and the Derg Restaurant for excellent food. And, of course, the Heenans will supply deliciously fresh organic things in season.

rooms	Granary for 2 (1 double, bathroom). Stables for 4 (2 doubles, bathroom). Lime Kiln for 6 (1 twin, 1 family, bathroom).
price	Granary €200–€350. Stables €300–€640. Lime Kiln €270–€480. Prices per week; electricity & heating extra.
meals	Self-catering. Pub & restaurant 3km.
closed	Never.
directions	Directions given on booking.

Niall & Inez Heenan
tel	+353 (0)67 22041
fax	+353 (0)67 22041
email	info@countrycottages.ie
web	www.countrycottages.ie

Self-catering

Map 4 Entry 176

Kylenoe House

Ballinderry, Nenagh, Co. Tipperary

Coming to Kylenoe, set in this beautiful wooded spot near Lough Derg, is like coming to visit a favourite aunt: Virginia will spoil you rotten with tea, sympathy and myriad bathroom smellies. And moreover, she draws your curtains and turns down your bed in the evening, those little attentions that are going out of fashion. You are immediately made to feel part of the family in her cosy old farmhouse. Pets are very welcome, too – they've won an award for being the most pet-friendly B&B in Ireland – though Virginia's special love is the thoroughbreds she has been breeding professionally for years. You will see the mares from the window of your cosy, antique-furnished, lacey-covered bedroom. One room has a balcony onto the surrounding woods. Sitting and dining rooms wear the same family-worn antique-comfortable air, all utterly relaxing and easy. Virginia's other great strength is cooking: readers have told us about her delicious country dinners. Kylenoe also has its own pier on the lake where you can swim or take a boat out, and the pretty harbour village of Terryglass is a short drive.

rooms	3: 2 doubles; 1 double with separate bath.
price	€110–€140. Singles €60.
meals	Dinner, 4 courses, €38.
closed	Rarely.
directions	From Nenagh N52 to Borrisokane 17.5km; left for Ballinderry 8km; pass village store on left, continue 3.5km, entrance on right: house in trees up drive.

B&B

Virginia Moeran

tel	+353 (0)67 22015
mobile	+353 (0)86 275 6000
fax	+353 (0)67 22275
email	ginia@eircom.net

Map 4 Entry 177

Ashley Park House
Nenagh, Co. Tipperary

Refreshingly Irish and old-fashioned, Ashley Park bathes in its 18th-century time warp by the trout-filled waters of Lough Ourna, blissfully detached from modern madness. A giant trout greets you in the hall; the sweet smell of endless turf fires wafts over quiet, ornate rooms, dark polished floors and deeply carved 17th-century furniture. The circular reading room with its exquisite Chinese art is lighter. Big bedrooms rejoice in heavy curtains, old-style linen on fine old beds, armchairs for quiet gazing over vast swathes; fadedly Victorian bathrooms have chequered floors and original fittings. Take tea on the crumbling colonial veranda, ponder the ruins of the island castle or listen to Sean's inexhaustible repertory of stories: he is a true character, an ever-present force here while daughter Margaret applies all her drive and imagination to reviving house and garden. Children love the cobbled farmyard with its peacocks, guinea fowl and doves; there's a walled garden, a nature reserve where ancient woodland protects red squirrels, dreams to dream. An authentic, unsmart delight – the kind of place we love.

rooms	5: 3 doubles, 2 family.
price	€100–€110. Singles €50–€60.
meals	Dinner €38–€45.
closed	Never.
directions	From Nenagh N52 for Borrisokane 5.5km; entrance on left after big lake.

	The Mounsey Family
tel	+353 (0)67 38223
fax	+353 (0)67 38013
email	margaret@ashleypark.com
web	www.ashleypark.com

Country house

Map 4 Entry 178

Bayly Farm

Ballinaclough, Nenagh, Co. Tipperary

These terrifically kind and welcoming people whose sons have grown and flown (one of them was the 2001 world champion Mirror-dinghy sailor), are still hard at work on their 130-acre farm and love entertaining guests in the comfortable family atmosphere of their Georgian farmhouse, owned by Baylys for 200 years. Enjoy breakfast at the fine mahogany table, once used to store harnesses, lounge by the crackling drawing-room fire, sleep in huge, handsome bedrooms with good beds, a few antiques, family pictures, wonderful views. Bathrooms are another pleasing mix of old and new, smart modern fittings, black-and-white floors, underfloor heating. The house stands among beautiful trees and well-tended shrubs, the south-facing patio is a real sun trap on a fine day, beyond lie the dramatic Silvermines Mountains. It is a tranquil, lovely spot. A stay in this caring, intelligent house would cheer and comfort any weary traveller – or indeed enthusiastic sailor, fisherman, golfer, hill-walker, castle-gazer: all will find grist to their mills within half an hour's drive. *Dogs welcome to sleep in the boot room.*

rooms	3: 1 double, 1 twin; 1 twin with separate bathroom.
price	€80–€90. Singles €50–€55.
meals	Dinner €30. BYO wine. By arrangement.
closed	Rarely.
directions	From Nenagh R498 for Thurles; over r'way 600m; over river, imm'ly right for Ballinaclough 2km; lane on right (sign); house 800m along.

B&B

	Jacqueline & Desmond Bayly
tel	+353 (0)67 31499
mobile	+353 (0)87 648 1752
email	bayly@eircom.net
web	www.baylyfarm.ie

Map 4 Entry 179

Saratoga Lodge
Barnane, Templemore, Co. Tipperary

Valerie is hospitable, funny, full of chat and extremely talented: one of Ireland's great characters, she does the heart good. She lives on the stud farm where she restores ceramics, bronzes and stoneware, organises hunting, shooting and fishing parties (there are some magnificent bogs here), and great cookery courses when required. An accomplished cook, she uses fresh things from her garden, eggs from her hens, honey from her bees, meat and game from local farms whenever possible: meals are a treat. In its fine big garden, she designed this practical Georgian-style house herself. Books, racing and hunting memorabilia, soft sofas, antiques and log fires make it relaxed and homely; bedrooms are simple and inviting with deeply sleep-inducing beds. Beneath the the Devil's Bit mountain, Saratoga lies on 120 acres of rolling pastureland in the lovely Golden Vale where mares and foals and cattle graze in peace. There's sailing on Lough Derg; walks and hunts start from the door. Bring your own horse and ride or walk out to explore the castle-strewn, legend-laden heart of Ireland. *Pets by arrangement. Vegetarian meals available.*

rooms	3: 2 doubles, 1 twin.
price	€90–€100. Singles €45–€50.
meals	Dinner €30. BYO wine. Packed lunch €7.
closed	23 December–3 January.
directions	From Templemore R501 for Borrisoleigh 3km; 2nd right 1.5km; left at T-junc.; entrance with white gate 300m on left.

Valerie Beamish

tel	+353 (0)504 31886
fax	+353 (0)504 31886
email	saratogalodge@eircom.net
web	www.saratoga-lodge.com

B&B

Map 7 Entry 180

Inch House

Thurles, Co. Tipperary

Emerging stately from its beech stand, Inch House promises elegant comfort. The Egans have tirelessly renovated this fine Georgian house, creating a generous temple of ease and good taste – country living in the grand style. In the chapel, recently finished, you may find a family relation saying Mass. John and Nora work well together, she the neat and practical nurse, he the farmer bursting with grand plans; the rest of the family lend unflagging support. Lovely features stand out: the fine relief of the serpent ceiling rose, the 44-foot pitch-pine floorboards in the William Morris-papered blue, white and gilt drawing room, the wide double oak staircase, the rich stained glass of the Ryan family with its motto, "Death before Dishonour". Mysteriously, the Ryans survived where fellow Catholics were dispossessed by Cromwell's penal law. Today, this is a place happily free of intrigue where you can recline in finest linen in a Prince Albert bed or beneath an antique lace canopy, then soak in a wood-panelled bathroom before an exquisite breakfast or dinner served on silver in the public restaurant.

rooms	5: 1 four-poster, 2 doubles, 2 twins.
price	€116-€120. Singles €68-€70.
meals	Dinner, 7pm-9.30pm, €50. Restaurant closed Sunday & Monday.
closed	Christmas.
directions	From Dublin N7 to Port Laoise; N8 for Cork 50km; N75 to Thurles; through town square, R498 for Nenagh 6.5km. Stone entrance just past 'The Ragg' crossroads.

B&B

	John, Nora & Máirín Egan
tel	+353 (0)504 51348/51261
fax	+353 (0)504 51754
email	mairin@inchhouse.ie
web	www.inchhouse.ie

Map 7 Entry 181

Derrynaflan

Ballinure, Cashel, Co. Tipperary

The eye-catching collection of glistening cranberry glass in the cosy sitting room reflects the fire crackling in the grate and the cheerful smile that Sheila bestows at the ever-open door of her most welcoming 300-year-old farmhouse. In this haven of old Tipperary charm — antique chests, pianos, ticking clock, even a wind-up gramophone — she makes her own farmhouse cheese (one of the best in Ireland), her preserves and chutneys festoon the magnificent dresser where china sparkles, the living room groans with books and photographs. Bedrooms are extremely comfortable: patchwork quilts on wooden beds, fireplaces with original mosaic surrounds, spotless bathrooms. Some have views of Slievc Adagha, framed by the tangle of creeper that cascades down the front of the house. Sheila's cooking is a hearty affair: fresh beef, lamb and salmon from the farm, a dizzy variety of warm winter puds, homemade yogurt, her prize-winning cheese. Great value and a top-class welcome from someone who really cares about her guests. Don't miss the nearby Rock of Cashel and Glen of Agherlow.

rooms	5: 1 double, 1 single, 2 family, 1 triple.
price	€80. Singles €40.
meals	Restaurants 15-minute drive.
closed	November-February.
directions	From Port Laoise N8 for Cashel 61km; left at Horse & Jockey village; right in Ballinure following signs to house. Entrance on right on sharp bend through green iron gates.

Sheila & Edmund O'Sullivan

tel	+353 (0)52 56406
fax	+353 (0)52 56406
email	info@derrynaflanhouse.com
web	www.derrynaflanhouse.com

B&B

Map 7 Entry 182

Dualla House
Cashel, Co. Tipperary

A poem hangs in the hall: "Go placidly amid the noise and haste and remember what peace there may be in silence." Maireád knows it by heart – and lives it. She and Martin love welcoming guests to their splendid, well-lived-in Georgian house, its marvellous views across pastures to the mountains, its romantic ruined coach house. Farmers come from afar to learn about pedigree sheep breeding: there are over 1,000 ewes here and you can watch the lambing and shearing in season; it's instructive fun for children, too. Irish racehorses are another passion: Tipperary is the cradle of Ireland's thoroughbred industry and the 1926 Irish Grand National winner Amberwave lived here. Well-proportioned rooms are furnished in a traditional farmhouse style, with some antiques, original polished floorboards in the breakfast room, fresh flowers, paintings brought back from Korea by Maireád's sister, who is a nun. Big, comfortable bedrooms have good mattresses and clean, modern bathrooms. Come to walk, visit The Rock, enjoy the country peace, not to see perfect Georgian architecture.

rooms	4: 1 double, 2 twins, 1 family.
price	€90-€100. Singles €50-€60. Discount for children.
meals	Restaurants in Cashel, 5km.
closed	December-February.
directions	From Dublin N8 into Cashel. Take R688 300m, pass church on left, left R691 for Dualla 5km. Entrance on left as road dips.

	Maireád Power
Country house	
tel	+353 (0)62 61487
fax	+353 (0)62 61487
email	duallahse@eircom.net
web	www.duallahouse.com

Map 7 Entry 183

Mobarnane House
Fethard, Co. Tipperary

There is nothing fake about Mobarnane, its architecture, people and atmosphere are all products of Ireland's history with that tinge of Jane Austen Englishness. In 1740, a farmhouse was built over an old tower house; in 1820 a Georgian half with Doric columns was added. Both from Tipperary, Richard and Sandra lived in England and dreamt of coming back to somewhere like Mobarnane, the lake, the trees, the soaring ceilings. At last it was theirs and their renovation shows their love of the place: outstanding curtains fall the full height of huge windows, the biggest heirloom sideboard ever sits perfectly in the dining room, the elegant drawing room gazes over fields to mature woodland. Bedrooms, two with sitting rooms, two with lake-view window seats, large and immaculately finished, have wooden shutters, deep carpets, watercolours by Sandra's great-grandfather. Sandra smiles a lot, Richard is passionate about cooking ("something I inherited from my mother"), so dinners beneath the beautiful friezes are superb and convivial, everyone at one big table. A sociable, civilised and eco-friendly house.

rooms	4: 1 double, 1 twin, 1 suite (double), 1 suite (twin).
price	€160-€190. Singles from €110.
meals	Dinner €45. Supper by arrangement.
closed	November-February, except to groups of 4-8.
directions	From Cashel for Clonmel 1km; left R692 for Fethard 9km; left for Ballinure and Thurles; entrance 2.5km on left.

Richard & Sandra Craik-White
tel +353 (0)52 31962
fax +353 (0)52 31962
email info@mobarnanehouse.com
web www.mobarnanehouse.com

Country house

Map 7 Entry 184

Bansha House
Bansha, Co. Tipperary

A very special lady with years of B&B behind her, Mary offers warmth, talk and *cráic* to your heart's content in the kitchen of her handsome early Georgian farmhouse. Chat away as long as you like, soaking up the gentle atmosphere. The conversation will inevitably turn to horses, they're sacred at Bansha, second only to guests, and John's mares, foals and racehorses decorate the 100-acre estate. Life feels so settled here. The house cloaked in creeper, the gently swaying trees, the horses lazily grazing in the field: it's worth packing some watercolours and a sketchbook. A row of Norman Rockwell prints leads upstairs to pastel bedrooms with thick walls and small but comfortable showers. The huge family room with separate bathroom is possibly the nicest; the twin, if rather cramped, has the advantage of being downstairs; breakfast, eaten at one table, is vast and wholesome. Thoughtful touches include thick bathrobes and fresh flowers. The informal drawing room is warmed by a log fire, walking in the nearby Galtees and the Glen of Aherlow is superb. "My retreat from this modern crazy world," wrote a reader.

rooms	5 + 1: 2 doubles, 1 twin, 1 single; 1 family with separate bathroom. Cottage for 5.
price	€90–€180. Singles €55. Cottage €400–€550 p.w.
meals	Dinner €27. By arrangement.
closed	Christmas.
directions	From Limerick N24 south. 8km after Tipperary entrance to house signposted on left.

B&B & Self-catering

John & Mary Marnane
tel	+353 (0)62 54194
fax	+353 (0)62 54215
email	banshahouse@eircom.net
web	www.tipp.ie/banshahs.htm

Map 7 Entry 185

Rathellen House
Raheen, Bansha, Co. Tipperary

Set in an amphitheatre of mountains and four green acres, this generous 'Georgian' house has the elegance of the 18th century and the comforts of the 20th: it was built in 2005 and not a drop of oil passes its lips. Underfloor heating smooths the air, fed by a wood-chip boiler and solar panels, plumbing is state-of-the-art silent, beds are dreamy memory foam and fine Egyptian cotton. After years in marketing, Eamonn is loving his new life, taking after his vivacious, hospitable grandmother Ellen (hence the name) who lived in the cosy-comfy Coopers Cottage: he's a Ballymaloe-trained cook, his artisan food promises delight in the lush dining room. He and Stella have created a sensitive blend of classic and modern: super books are strewn on beautiful antique tables, Waterford crystal chandeliers wink at you from ceilings, big mellow bedrooms are palely splendid with Ulster carpets and more antiques. The mahogany four-poster is a collector's dream, it's jacuzzi bathroom a hedonist's indulgence. This extraordinarily welcoming place has a most attractive ethos and utterly charming owners.

rooms	7 + 1: 4 doubles, 2 twins, 1 four-poster. Cottage for 6 (1 double, 2 twins, 2 bathrooms).
price	€100-€160. Singles from €65. Cottage €300-€500 per week.
meals	Dinner €30-€35. By arrangement.
closed	Rarely.
directions	From Tipperary N24 through Bansha; continue for Cahir 1.5km; left for Rathellen House & Coopers Cottage; house 1.5km on right.

Stella & Eamonn Long
tel	+353 (0)62 54376
fax	+353 (0)62 54376
email	info@rathellenhouse.com
web	www.rathellenhouse.com

Country house & Self-catering

Map 7 Entry 186

Kilmaneen Farmhouse

Ardfinnan, Newcastle, Clonmel, Co. Tipperary

A magic spot. Look out onto a landscape untouched for centuries: not a pylon in sight, wonderful lush hedgerows, fine trees. Its totally unspoilt beauty makes Kilmaneen very special, in large part thanks to the O'Donnells' loving care of their land, their animals and their rivers. The Tar and the Suir flowing through the farm to meet at one corner of the property have inspired them to develop model environmental practices (superb trout fishing: book a ghillie). You are welcomed by the gentle grace of this family – Kevin, Bernadette and three student children – to their compact and crisply modernised farmhouse where discreet mod cons hide behind country antiques, pretty wallpapers match the unintrusive floral fabrics and lovely watercolours by a local artist give you reason to pause on the landing. The peace outside is reflected in the house and cottage and Bernadette's attention to detail shines out; her succulent breakfasts have won awards. These are open, genuine, warm people. All set against the breathtaking backdrop of the Knockmealdown Mountains and their great hill walks (book a guide).

B&B & Self-catering

rooms	3 + 1: 1 double, 1 twin/double, 1 twin. Cottage for 2-5 (1 double, 1 family).
price	€80-€85. Singles €45-€50. Cottage €250-€500 p.w.
meals	Dinner €25. BYO wine. Picnic on request.
closed	December-February.
directions	From Cahir R670 or from Clonmel R665 to Ardfinnan; through village to 'Hill Bar'; left up hill; Kilmaneen Farm signposted.

Kevin & Bernadette O'Donnell

tel	+353 (0)52 36231
fax	+353 (0)52 36231
email	kilmaneen@eircom.net
web	www.kilmaneen.com

Map 7 Entry 187

Irish Proverbs

Ni he la na gaoithe la na sgolb
The windy day is no day for thatching

Is geall leis an bhfiach dubh a ghearrcach féin
To the black crow its offspring is bright

Bionn adharca fada ar an boidh thar lear
Foreign cows have long horns

Ní dheanfaidh an saol capall ráis d'asal
The world can't make a racehorse out of a donkey

Ólann an cat ciúin bainne leis
The quiet cat also drinks milk

Briseann an duchais tri shuile an chait
Nature breaks through the eyes of the cat

Ar Mhaite leis féin a Dheinnean an cat crónán
It's for its own good that the cat purrs

Is minic a bhí fear maith i seanbhriste
Good men can often wear worn britches

Is cuma le fear na mbróg cá cuireann sé a chosa
The man with boots does not worry where he puts his feet

Ní hí an áileacht a chuireann an corcán ag fiuchaidh
Beauty does not boil the pot

Chuirfeadh sé cosa faoi chearca duit
He would put legs under a chicken (he's talkative)

Is fearr focal sa chúirt ná punt sa sparaán
A good word in court is better than a pound in your purse

Ta tir na n-Og ar chul an ti
The land of youth is at the rear of the house

Ni feidir ceann crionna a chur ar ghualainn oga
You can not put an old head on young shoulders

With thanks to Seán Fhocail/O'Neill

Leinster

Woodlands Country House
Killinierin, Gorey, Co. Wexford

Philomena is everyone's dream hostess, sweet, old-fashioned and cosy. She still loves doing B&B after 20 years. She'll do anything to help, even spending hours tracing family roots with visiting Americans. The Irish Georgian farmhouse and its pretty courtyard stand in the loveliest setting: two acres, a copse, a river and a little lake, all kept trim and inviting by John's hard work, when he's not out chairing something or other. Light peeps into the cosy farmhouse bedrooms to show off the fresh white sheets that hug the wooden beds. They have florals and crochet and proper old furniture and a good shower room each; three have balconies, the four-poster is the most striking but even the smaller ones are appealing and eminently sleep-worthy. If you prefer a bath, you may use the free-standing tub in the gorgeous main bathroom. The sitting room feels like the best old-world parlour with its velours and brass and fox-furs draped over the chaise-longue; Philomena's breakfast menu includes fresh fruit, her own brown bread, scones and jam on crochet cloths in the cheerful dining room.

rooms	6: 3 doubles, 1 twin, 1 single, 1 four-poster; extra bath.
price	€100-€110. Singles €65-€70.
meals	Pub in village, 1.5km; restaurants in Gorey, 8km.
closed	October-March.
directions	From Dublin Airport M50 then M11, N11 past Wicklow & Arklow, through Inch; 5km north of Gorey right at fruit farm & follow signs 1.5km.

Country house

	John & Philomena O'Sullivan
tel	+353 (0)402 37125
fax	+353 (0)402 37133
email	info@woodlandscountryhouse.com
web	www.woodlandscountryhouse.com

Map 8 Entry 188

Woodbrook House
Killanne, Enniscorthy, Co. Wexford

The long sweeping drive, the massive old hardwoods, the pillared entrance flanked by two marble lions. So far, so Anglo-Irish. Yet… lions? in Ireland? Walk into the hall with its painted frieze: the mood here suggests a hotter climate. Giles and Alexandra are no strangers to the wider world. She is half-Italian, he capped a diplomatic career as British ambassador to Venezuela, they toured Italy and India before starting the restoration work on their intriguing 1770s Georgian house which has Ireland's only 'flying staircase' — it quivers as you climb. The lions are from Florence, Alexandra has used subtle Italian washes and trompe-l'œil to transform the interior; painted furniture from Rajasthan and a wide-striped bath with its claws on polished boards add style and fun; rooms are big, relaxed, unposh. Giles, a seasoned character, well-travelled and well-read, has strong convictions, a wry humour and eco-friendly attitudes, while Alexandra and their four children lend youth and vitality to this memorable family home. They are part of the local opera-à-la-carte circuit: picnics with Mozart.

rooms	3: 2 doubles, 1 twin.
price	€150–€160. Singles €80–€90.
meals	Dinner €35.
closed	November–April. Groups off season by arrangement.
directions	From Enniscorthy R702 to Kiltealy. Through village for Rathnure 2.5km; left down small lane with tall trees; entrance 300m on left down drive.

Giles & Alexandra FitzHerbert
tel	+353 (0)53 925 5114
fax	+353 (0)53 925 5114
email	fitzherbert@eircom.net

Country house

Map 8 Entry 189

Monfin House
St John's Road, Enniscorthy, Co. Wexford

Sheer indulgence, a place of peace to revel in the best of everything. Chris, the lively host (and a wine merchant the rest of the time), and Avril, the quiet one, have restored their 1832 listed Georgian house with pride and taste, old-world charm and all modern luxuries. Handmade Indian carpets, original oak floorboards, gold taps, Czech chandeliers: no expense has been spared. The immaculate bedrooms are colour-coded: *Peach* is huge with an impressive four-poster, *Green* has a beautiful roll-top bath, *Yellow* a chaise-longue and *Blue* looks onto rhododendrons that burst into bloom in spring. This is not a duvet house, Avril prefers crisp sheets and handmade bedcovers, all on fine new mattresses. She also provides fruit, fresh flowers, bathrobes and Occitane smellies. Breakfast is served in the smart cranberry-coloured dining room. There's an orchard, a walled garden where ponies now graze but they plan to restore it, there's talk of a gazebo and a pond, the surrounding fields grow grain to make Guinness, the air is clean and fresh and riding, hunting, shooting, massage can all be arranged.

rooms	4: 1 double, 1 twin/double, 2 four-posters.
price	€110–€130. Singles €85.
meals	Restaurants in Enniscorthy & Wexford.
closed	December & January.
directions	From Enniscorthy N30 for New Ross; after big, grey mill, next left up hill; entrance signposted 1km on right.

B&B

Chris & Avril Stewart

tel	+353 (0)53 923 8582
fax	+353 (0)53 923 8583
email	info@monfinhouse.com
web	www.monfinhouse.com

Map 8 Entry 190

Ballinkeele House
Ballymurn, Enniscorthy, Co. Wexford

Every part of this 19th-century house has a sense of easy lived-in grandeur: the columned portico sets the tone. At the bottom of the stately staircase, Mercury lifts and enchants the whole atmosphere on his winged heel. The play of heavy and light follows you. Ballinkeele was designed for John's ancestor by an Adam son-in-law with space and light in mind. Not at all pretentious, John and Margaret are a good team: his delight in his family seat and "all the things his grandfather collected on the Grand Tour", her modest pride in her sense of colour and texture (she has green fingers too); her cooking skills, his splendid butler act. Each huge room is adorned with old family pictures and Margaret's paintings. Bedrooms are exquisite, the gem being the superb four-poster room. John supervises garden and forestry. Margaret, something of a perfectionist, presides over succulent meals (that includes breakfast) in the heavy red dining room, just the right period feel. A splendid place to relax and walk round ponds and lakes, where coarse fishing may be on offer, in 360 acres of grounds.

rooms	5: 2 doubles, 1 twin/double, 1 twin, 1 four-poster.
price	€150–€220. Singles €90–€110.
meals	Dinner €40. Book by noon the same day.
closed	December–January.
directions	From Rosslare N25 to Wexford, then N11 to Oilgate. Right at lights in village for Ballinkeele 6.5km; left in Ballymurn, 1st black gates on left.

	Margaret & John Maher
tel	+353 (0)53 913 8105
fax	+353 (0)53 913 8468
email	john@ballinkeele.com
web	www.ballinkeele.com

Country house

Map 8 Entry 191

Healthfield Manor
Killurin, Co. Wexford

As Irish and as eccentric as they come, Mayler and Loreto are warm, helpful, full of stories – and Healthfield is matchless. Built in 1820, it lies above the languid River Slaney. When Cromwell sacked Wexford in 1649 the people fled upriver to escape the plague and found an untainted well in a field: health field. You reach the house via a tunnel of overgrowth that winds uphill to a stunning view of the river and the towering house. Inside is an incredible mix of antique and kitsch; the ornately-framed oil painting of Princess Diana seems perfectly normal here, as do the dated floral wallpapers and fake flowers. Beds, breakfast and welcome are as huge as the old-fashioned rooms. Loreto is lovely, her style of B&B almost theatrical. Mayler, a bearded ex-shot-putter, farms the estate with ingenuity, selling eels to the Dutch, growing reed-beds for thatch – and creating a water garden in what was probaby Ireland's first heated outdoor pool. The walled garden rambles past wild potting sheds, ancient vineries and a perfect fig tree. Utterly original and great fun. *No smoking in bedrooms. Children over seven welcome.*

rooms	3: 1 family suite, en suite; 2 twins, each with separate bathroom.
price	€90. Singles €58.
meals	Restaurants in Wexford, 3km.
closed	Mid-November to Easter.
directions	From north, N11 for Wexford; over River Slaney; right for Heritage Park; under r'way bridge, sharp right; follow river 3km. Entrance on right, signpost; up long drive.

B&B

	Mayler & Loreto Colloton
tel	+353 (0)53 28253
fax	+353 (0)53 28253
web	www.healthfield.8k.com

Map 8 Entry 192

Kilmokea Country Manor & Gardens
Great Island, Campile, Co. Wexford

With its incomparable heritage gardens and long history, Kilmokea is hard to fault. Mark and Emma could not be nicer: gracious, welcoming and so very helpful, they somehow find time to bring up three young children as well. Bedrooms, four in the main house, two in the converted courtyard suite, are in luxurious good taste: thick carpets, lovely beds, smart antiques, voluminous towels. In the evening guests meet over a drink and your hosts make sure everyone is introduced before sitting down in the formal Regency dining room. Cooked to order by the chef, whose speciality is seafood, many ingredients come from the organic walled kitchen garden, eggs from hens that graze the pretty apple orchard: integral parts of Kilmokea's chemical free botanical treat. Breakfast is deliciously fresh and unusual, too. The gardens cover seven acres, peacocks strut by the Italian loggia, paths and bridges lead past a trout lake to a hide whence you can watch coastal birds swoop over the estuary. Plus the heated pool, gym, jacuzzi, sauna. Like staying in a five-star hotel owned by friends – quite remarkable. *Pets by arrangement. Tennis. Vegetarian meals available. Bikes for hire.*

rooms	6 + 2: 3 doubles, 1 four-poster, 1 family; 1 twin with separate shower. 2 apts: 1 for 2, 1 for 4-8.	
price	€190-€300. Singles €100. Apartments €750-€1,150 per week.	
meals	Lunch €7-€25. Dinner €45-€55.	
closed	Mid-November to January. (Self-catering open all year.)	
directions	From Waterford to Passage East; R733 north 2.5km; at sharp right bend, straight on for Great Island; left at T-junc. 2km to house.	

Mark & Emma Hewlett

tel	+353 (0)51 388 109
fax	+353 (0)51 388 776
email	kilmokea@eircom.net
web	www.kilmokea.com

Country house & Self-catering

Map 8 Entry 193

Glendine Country House
Arthurstown, Co. Wexford

Standing on a hill in 50 acres of private farmland and looking over the Barrow Estuary to the hills beyond, Glendine is a lively family home with a farm zoo feel to it: scenic Jacob sheep, Highland cattle, Silka deer hang around for all to love. The farm bustles, Tom sells most of his corn crop to a well-known Dutch brewer. The 1830s house has grown and the four bedrooms in the new extension are really big with superb sea views, the King's Bay Suite has a fabulous bathroom, a Victorian repro bed and rich colours fit for… a king. Those warm colours, Victorian-style beds, glowing pitch-pine floors give all the rooms their old-style atmosphere. Relax in the big drawing room with just the right amount of family photographs and antiques. Annie serves home-grown organic rhubarb, bread and scones, organic porridge and strawberries, and masses more – all part of her gourmet breakfast that will sustain you along the spectacular coastal walk to the Hook Peninsula. On deciding to land at the Hook or at Crookhaven further up the coast, Cromwell exclaimed "by Hook or by Crook, we'll do it".

rooms	6 + 2: 2 doubles, 2 twins/doubles, 1 family, 1 suite. 2 cottages for 5.
price	€90-€120. Singles €60-€85. Cottages from €350 p.w.
meals	Hotel restaurant & pubs within walking distance.
closed	Christmas.
directions	From Rosslare N25 for Wexford 8km; left 1st r'bout; left 2nd r'bout R733 for Wellington Bridge 32km. Entrance on right as road dips into Arthurstown.

Tom & Annie Crosbie

tel	+353 (0)51 389 500
fax	+353 (0)51 389 677
email	glendinehouse@eircom.net
web	www.glendinehouse.com

Guest house & Self-catering

Map 8 Entry 194

Aldridge Lodge
Duncannon, Co. Wexford

Billy is a brilliant, inventive chef with an easy sense of humour and Joanne a charmingly friendly and efficient organiser. The perfect couple. Together they have built this clean-limbed elegant inn overlooking the town and the estuary of the Suir and Barrow Rivers (also known as Waterford Harbour) – a shimmering spot. The food alone is worth the journey: Aldridge Lodge is becoming a household word in the area. The finest, freshest ingredients are cooked and presented with loving care and no fiddle-faddle. The décor follows the ethos: white walls, solid timber beams and gleaming floors, plain under-designed furniture that looks smart but is warm and comfortable and a sleek modern finish to everything. Bedrooms are in the same vein: white walls, pine furniture, pristine bathrooms. The largest room ("mini-suite") looks out to sea, the others give onto the quiet road. Dinner here is a must (book ahead, it's often full), the people are a delight, Duncannon beach is a short walk away and there are so many things to do and see in Co. Wexford – or over the estuary in Co. Waterford.

rooms	4: 3 doubles, 1 twin.
price	€90–€100. Singles from €45.
meals	Dinner €35. Sunday lunch €22.50. Restaurant closed Monday.
closed	Every Monday. Christmas week; last 3 weeks in January.
directions	From Wexford R733 for Duncannon 30km; at junc. left R737 to Duncannon centre; at South Beach Holiday Homes, right for Aldridge Lodge.

	Billy Whitty & Joanne Harding
tel	+353 (0)51 389 116
fax	+353 (0)51 389 116
email	info@aldridgelodge.com
web	www.aldridgelodge.com

Restaurant with rooms

Map 8 Entry 195

Churchtown House
Tagoat, Rosslare, Co. Wexford

Although it looks like a small hotel, this is the Cody's family home and they create the mix exceptionally well. They have gradually added pieces onto the 300-year-old house, often using old materials and keeping the grounded solidity of the old farm (it belonged to the same family for 250 years). The giant cedar that rules the smooth front lawn is pretty ancient too. Bright-coloured pristine rooms have a cosy elegance while tall windows and an atrium draw in the sunshine. Bedrooms vary greatly; some have bay windows, some have views over the countryside. The garden room looks onto an open courtyard where a chiminea (a Mexican brazier) gives off a haze of heat on cooler evenings. The Codys are relaxed, generous hosts, Austin being the admin 'mechanic', Patricia bringing it all to life. Nothing is too much trouble: they will find a spot for your bike, your trailer, even your boat – just ask when booking. Ideal for the Rosslare ferry but do stay longer for an abundance of super walks on unspoilt beaches, bird-watching and historic sites as well as riding, sea fishing and the Wexford opera festival. *Vegetarian meals available.*

rooms	12: 6 doubles, 3 twins, 1 family, 1 suite, 1 single.
price	€110–€160. Singles €65–€75.
meals	Dinner, 4 courses with sherry, €39.50 (Tuesday-Saturday). Packed lunch €15. By arrangement.
closed	Mid-November to early March. Off-season by arrangement.
directions	From Rosslare ferryport N25 for Tagoat 5.5km; right on R736. House 1km on left.

Guest house

	Austin & Patricia Cody
tel	+353 (0)53 913 2555
fax	+353 (0)53 913 2577
email	info@churchtownhouse.com
web	www.churchtownhouse.com

Map 8 Entry 196

Kelly's Resort Hotel & Spa
Rosslare Strand, Co. Wexford

Yes, a vast 'resort' hotel – and it's wonderful! Family-grown by four generations of Kellys beside five miles of safe sandy beach, it is ideal for children yet has a priceless collection of modern art perfectly hung as if in a private home – and never more than 50 children present; all the latest in spa, aqua, gym and games things yet aiming to become carbon neutral. Not only is Bill the greenest man in Irish business today, he's a perfectionist whose life's work is to make and keep Kelly's superb. He runs the place with common sense, an excellent eye, the easiest manner – chatting to all and sundry, including little kids – and endless lovely staff. The décor is cool, funky, bright and bold, there are myriad sitting and eating rooms, a teenage hang-out room, no false pomp, nothing tacky, and breathtakingly high standards. So if you love a buzzy, happy-families atmosphere and everything to hand (library, hairdresser, snooker, more), disregard the ugly block of a face, step into the light and colour of the great hall and learn why some people talk of Kelly's with almost religious fervour. *Tennis on site. Vegetarian meals available.*

rooms	99: doubles, twins/doubles, twins & family rooms.
price	Full-board €310 p.p. + 10% service charge.
meals	Full-board only. Lunch €25-€28. Dinner €45-€48.
closed	Early December to late February.
directions	From Wexford N25 for Rosslare Strand 16km & follow signs.

	Bill Kelly
tel	+353 (0)53 913 2114
fax	+353 (0)53 913 2222
email	kellyhot@iol.ie
web	www.kellys.ie

Hotel

Map 8 Entry 197

Cuasnog

St John's Road, Wexford, Co. Wexford

Catriona has the warmest smile, the twinkliest eyes – and she sings in three choirs. Many musicians stay for the Opera Festival. Sociable, helpful and hugely caring of her guests, she cannot possibly let you leave for the early ferry without breakfast. You'll like Miss Ellie, too, even though she's a mongrel. Catriona's small 1930s house, inherited from her great-aunt, is a simple, comfortable, easy place to be. Breakfast is as organic as she can make it, the brown bread, scones and muffins (made with home-grown raspberries) are her own, her herby vegetarian omelette is made with a friend's free-range eggs whose shells are then baked, crushed and returned whence they came – as hen food. She is a fanatic recycler. In the living room great-aunt's antique sideboard holds the packets of cereals, the wood-burning stove glows and there's a soft sofa, CD-player and books. Bedrooms are pine-simple, print-pretty, cottagey and intimate and have good new bathrooms. And you'll discover the fine modern kitchen with its stainless steel and black looks – and try Catriona's fancy coffee-maker. She is a lovely person.

rooms	3: 2 doubles, 1 twin.
price	€70-€100.
meals	Restaurants within walking distance.
closed	Rarely.
directions	From Rosslare N25 to Wexford. House in town centre. Map provided on request.

B&B

Caitriona Ni Chathain

tel	+353 (0)53 912 3637
mobile	+353 (0)87 292 2679
email	cuasnog@eircom.net
web	www.cuasnog.com

Map 8 Entry 198

Butler House

16 Patrick Street, Kilkenny, Co. Kilkenny

A high-class Russian-doll experience: through a rather unexciting façade you enter what looks like a grand country house built on the estate of a medieval castle. Next morning, you walk through superb formal gardens to the estate's refurbished stables for breakfast – then step out into the heart of an historic city. Those stables now house the Kilkenny Design Centre which masterminded the 1970s renovation of Butler House. Originally home to the Earls of Ormonde, it is now owned by the Kilkenny Civic Trust. Grandeur is all about you: those fluted columns, high ceilings, fabulous plasterwork and floods of light that the Georgians loved so much, none of it spoilt by frills or curlicues. Furniture in the big high bedrooms (the four best overlook the gardens) is sleekly, discreetly modern, fabrics are understatedly stylish, muted colours are enhanced by the occasional deep-hued cushion or good-looking rug. A plushness that will make you feel distinguished and exclusive. Gabrielle Hickey is a most attentive host and her staff are both friendly and efficient. *They also do seminars & company events.*

rooms	13: 12 twins/doubles, 1 suite.
price	€120–€200. Singles €80–€155.
meals	Restaurants within walking distance.
closed	Christmas week.
directions	From Dublin N10 into Kilkenny; cross river, over High Street/Parade crossroads, hotel on left.

	Gabrielle Hickey
tel	+353 (0)5677 65707/22828
fax	+353 (0)5677 65626
email	res@butler.ie
web	www.butler.ie

Guest house

Map 8 Entry 199

Blanchville House
Dunbell, Maddoxtown, Co. Kilkenny

Monica and Tim found trees growing inside this big Georgian farmhouse in 1970 so they lived in the dining room while renovating – beneath the benign eye of Sir James Kearney, the creator of Blanchville – preserving original wallpaper, intricate plasterwork and golden pelmets in the graceful drawing room. They are practical people, Tim a shy and busy farmer, Monica a perfect host who generates an atmosphere of relaxed sophistication that you won't forget. Working hard behind the scenes, they are restoring the clock tower, dusting the antiques, checking the leaping draperies, adjusting the fine paintings. Large bedrooms have half-testers and thick carpets but the luxury is in the detail – the enamelled taps warrant a photograph – while glorious pastoral views belong in an oil painting. Breakfast round the huge dining table, beautifully laid with silver and white linen, is a delight. Monica cannot bear the thought that guests might feel neglected: she looks after you with natural, unfussy ease and runs a holistic centre here, too. Blanchville is a place you'll remember, and there's masses to do in Kilkenny.

rooms	6 + 3: 3 doubles, 2 twins, all en suite; 1 twin with separate bathroom. 3 houses for 4-6.
price	€110-€120. Singles €65-€75. Houses €350-€650 p.w.
meals	Dinner €45. By arrangement only.
closed	November-February.
directions	From Kilkenny N10 for Carlow/Dublin; 1st right 1km after Pike Inn; left at next x-roads; 1st large stone entrance on left.

Country house & Self-catering

		Monica & Tim Phelan
tel		+353 (0)56 772 7197
fax		+353 (0)56 772 7636
email		mail@blanchville.ie
web		www.blanchville.ie

Map 8 Entry 200

Lawcus Farm Guesthouse
Stonyford, Co. Kilkenny

An imperious setting. Leave the lane, drop down to the end of the track and find the King's River pottering along at the bottom. Woodlands rise on the far bank, fields encircle you. A smooth arc of stone on the river bed creates a small weir and a heron fishes here most mornings. So can you – Mark bought Lawcus for its exceptional fishing – or follow the river, looking out for otters, badgers, foxes, leaping salmon, kingfishers, swans and ducks – but no tourists. Mark is the star: down-to-earth, instinctively generous, a man who has found his slice of heaven. He'll cook your wild trout for breakfast if you've been lucky, tell you where to go (don't miss the fortified Augustinian monastery at Kells). Incredibly, he renovated this 200-year-old cottage single-handedly, adding a wing, a conservatory/kitchen, an elaborate water garden. It's perfect – rustic, comfortable, quietly indulging: stone walls, pretty rooms, compact showers, lots of wood. Sit out on the deck with a glass of wine, picnic by the river, you can even barbecue. Red Rum was born up the road and there's golf galore on your doorstep.

rooms	5 + 2: 2 doubles, 1 twin, 1 triple, 1 family. 2 cottages: 1 for 2, 1 for 4-5.
price	€100. Cottages €450-€800 p.w.
meals	Dinner €25. By arrangement. BYO wine.
closed	Rarely.
directions	From Kilkenny N10 south to Stonyford. Enter village & immed'ly right for Kells; house signposted right down lane at top of hill.

Mark Fisher

tel	+353 (0)56 772 8949
email	info@lawcusfarmguesthouse.com
web	www.lawcusfarmguesthouse.com

B&B & Self-catering

Map 8 Entry 201

Ballaghtobin
Callan, Co. Kilkenny

Silver mirrors and clothes brushes on the dressing table can tell no lies, you are in a genuinely gracious house. Ballaghtobin is a beacon of contented hospitality amid the lush pastures of County Kilkenny. Catherine, warm and efficient, and Mickey, relaxed and funny, are renowned for their entertaining: be it friends, colleagues or guests, everyone is treated with the same easy-going generosity. Mickey farms 450 acres, growing cereals, blackcurrants and the Noble Fir commercially. In his spare time, he competes in classic car rallies: ask to meet the prized automobiles. Catherine is also a doer, full of energy and ideas, the kind of person who puts you in a good mood. Together they are great fun. Their elegant Georgian home feels nicely lived in with its period furniture and the Herend china they've been collecting since they got married. Gorgeous bedrooms are all done with taste and luxurious country-house style: fabrics chosen for subtle matching, beautiful beds, the best linen and spoiling extras. Walk in lovely grounds, play tennis, or wander off down the lane. It's all authentic.

rooms	3: 1 double, 1 twin/double, 1 family.
price	€100. Singles €50.
meals	Pub 6 miles.
closed	December-February.
directions	From Callan ring-road R699 for Knocktopher; over x-roads at bridge; past Golf Club on left; 3.5km; bear left at Y-junc. as main road turns sharp right; entrance on left opp. lodge.

Country house

	Catherine & Mickey Gabbett
tel	+353 (0)56 772 5227
fax	+353 (0)56 772 5712
email	catherine@ballaghtobin.com
web	www.ballaghtobin.com

Map 8 Entry 202

Ballyogan House
New Ross Road, Graiguenamanagh, Co. Kilkenny

Robert and Fran live beside the beautiful stretch of the River Barrow that cast its spell on them many years ago. They waited 25 years to live there but they're making up for it now and want you to enjoy their good fortune, too. Hidden down a narrow lane just outside the tongue-twisting town of Graiguenamanagh ('demesne of the monks'), Ballyogan looks over the river to the Blackstairs Mountains. Built by the Joyce family around 1830, it was 'the Joyce house' until the last in the line, a local vet, died in 1998. Redecorated throughout with conservative good taste, the whole place feels at ease. Bedrooms are comfortable, Lilac the prettiest. The thick tick-tock of the grandfather clock sets a genteel pace. Walk past the well-used croquet lawn down a wooded path, with cats and hens in tow, to where their boat, *La Brouette* ('wheelbarrow'), is moored. Robert may take you on a gentle picnic cruise, just as he and Fran first did in 1973. Fran serves hearty home-cooked food, the large garden delivering lots of produce, even melons, and Robert knows a properly authentic Irish pub for afters.

rooms	4: 1 double, 2 twins, 1 family.
price	€90-€100. Singles €55-€60.
meals	Dinner €35-€40. By arrangement.
closed	November-March.
directions	From Graiguenamanagh R705 for New Ross 4km; sharp left down lane, signposted.

	Robert & Fran Durie
tel	+353 (0)59 972 5969
fax	+353 (0)59 972 5016
email	info@ballyoganhouse.com
web	www.ballyoganhouse.com

B&B

Map 8 Entry 203

Ballyduff House
Thomastown, Co. Kilkenny

Ballyduff is B&B heaven. The gentle curved drive, the graceful, spaceful Georgian architecture fringed with wisteria and the big lawn surrounded by truly superb trees call you in. So ring the bell: Brede will come and wrap you in lively smiles. This human dynamo runs the show single-handedly, plus two children, 240 acres of farmland and a pony club. She has genuine warmth, possibly the product of 10 years in the restaurant business in America, while the house is the epitome of Anglo-Irish refinement with legions of Thomases in view, Regency furniture, Venetian glass, the odd Napoleonic teddy. The library is a sort of aristocratic rumpus room with ancient tomes in the four corners and comfy lived-in sofas — "just the place to kick back in," she says. You'll see. Lovely bedrooms are all generously big and different with beautiful antiques, Colefax & Fowler wallpaper and linen from the White Company in London. Two are prettily cottagey, two are grander with views of the River Nore that runs past the house; you can fish here and Brede can organise children's pony rides. *Whole house available.*

rooms	4: 1 double, 1 family suite, both en suite; 1 double, 1 twin, sharing bath.
price	€90. Singles €45.
meals	Restaurants in Thomastown.
closed	November-February.
directions	From Thomastown R700 for New Ross 5km. After Brownsbarn Bridge, immed'ly right; right at x-roads; entrance on right after 200m: white gates, no sign.

Country house

	Brede Thomas
tel	+353 (0)56 775 8488
email	ballydhouse@eircom.net

Map 8 Entry 204

Cullintra House

The Rower, Inistioge, Co. Kilkenny

Standing in 230 acres of field and woodland at the foot of Mount Brandon, 250-year-old Cullintra House has gorgeous views, thronging wildlife and Patricia is an artist: her energy and eye for detail come with dramatic gestures and a direct manner; her eccentricity has created the Cullintra legend. It suits those who can go with her flow. Breakfast till noon, walk the woods on restored paths, visit the ancient cairn, meet the myriad cats, the fox who comes to be fed, the suckling cows. Stay two nights with dinner, or more. Patricia has a sense of occasion and dinner is an unforgettable, possibly very late, event; beneath all the theatre is an very talented cook who gives each course due respect: don't expect clockwork service, it isn't her way. She adores soft olive green and her lovely house is a thrilling mix of zany and classic – Accommodation Art with brilliantly Irish bedrooms, from the theatrical conservatory to the gallery rooms in the converted barns. Wonderful breakfasts, not before 9.30am (continental at any hour). Do say: surprise, humanity, taste. Don't say: hunting.

rooms	6: 2 doubles, sharing bathroom; 1 family room for 6 with shower, separate wc; 3 doubles en suite.
price	€60–€100. Singles from €50–€90. Minimum stay 2 nights, with dinner.
meals	Dinner, 5 courses, €35. BYO wine.
closed	Rarely.
directions	From Rosslare ferryport N25 to New Ross then R700 for Kilkenny 9.5km. House up road on right, signposted.

Patricia Cantlon

tel	+353 (0)51 423 614
email	cullhse@indigo.ie
web	indigo.ie/~cullhse

B&B

Map 8 Entry 205

Ballin Temple
Ardattin, Co. Carlow

The only tracks beaten here are those of generations of Butlers, the ghosts of the Templars who preceded them, and eager fishers on their way to the Slaney. This is a family of entertaining, intelligent, caring people. Tom and his Canadian wife Pam, a yoga teacher, turned away from investment banking to run the estate salvaged by Tom's parents, creating a nature sanctuary and an organic farm. Recently renovated, the semi-detached cottages are sweetly cosy and true to their origins in their pastel colours and simple, neo-rustic furnishings. You will find a glowing wood-burner, books and games, a barbecue, a laundry and a complete kitchen: they are open-hearted, warm and wonderful hideaway houses and you may even be able to pick your own fruit and veg in that great organic garden. The main garden is slowly being rejuvenated, including a rediscovered Victorian aqueduct; the walks are peaceful birdsung experiences; the views are a superb added extra. Both place and people are particularly special and their 'Settlement of Sanctuary' brings you Nature at her most natural. *Vegetarian meals by arrangement.*

Remote? Woodsy? Old-agey? Not entirely. Ballin Temple is connected to the latest thinking in earth protection and spiritual development. Masses of fruit and vegetables, from artichokes and rhubarb to peas and tomatoes, are grown organically; chickens and ducks roam freely; fresh water comes directly from artesian wells; 50 acres of magical 'Ancient Woodland' (not interfered with for 600 years) harbour rare plants and real wildlife such as deer. The Butlers harvest their own wood for heating and run yoga courses and transformation retreats in the Lodge. A living, loving temple to life.

rooms	2 cottages for 3-4.
price	From €500 per week.
meals	Breakfast, packed lunch or dinner by arrangement. BYO wine.
closed	Never.
directions	From Carlow N80 then R725 to Tullow then to Ardattin & follow signs. Detailed directions on request.

	The Butler Family
tel	+353 (0)59 915 5037
fax	+353 (0)59 915 5038
email	manager@ballintemple.com
web	www.ballintemple.com

SPECIAL GREEN ENTRY
see page 16

Self-catering

Map 8 Entry 206

Burgage Courtyard
Leighlinbridge, Co. Carlow

Set in the river-run rolling parkland of a working stud farm, the courtyard flat is a newly-converted stable and grain loft, naturally. The white-washed hall sets the tone: lovely old cobbled floor, antique cupboard, original feed trough. Up you go to the well-lit pine-clad living space, clothed in peaceful lime wash, where antiques and original art contrast with super modern bathrooms, rugs and runners warm the cosy-comfy sitting area and the kitchen is full of new equipment. The two bedrooms are just as inviting, the double has its own claw-foot bathroom, the sofabed in the living room is excellent for overflow. Historic Kilkenny, packed with cultural activity (Ireland's answer to Chester?), is half an hour: catch the bus at the gate. Leighlinbridge has the famous Lord Bagenal Inn beside the marina and Irish folk concerts organised by the postmaster. And it was at history-laden Burgage (built 1760) that Mrs Alexander wrote "All Things Bright and Beautiful". Walk into your childhood images: "the purple-headed mountain (Mount Leinster)", take the kayak on "the river (Barrow) flowing by". Wonderful.

rooms	Flat for 4-6 (1 double, 1 twin, 1 sofabed for 2, 1 bath, 1 shower).
price	€350-€550 per week, inc. linen.
meals	Self-catering. Restaurants 15-minute walk.
closed	Rarely.
directions	On N9 Dublin-Waterford road, 13km south of Carlow, 22km north of Kilkenny.

Self-catering

Elizabeth Connolly

tel	+353 (0)59 972 2332
fax	+353 (0)59 972 2332
email	vconnolly@eircom.net
web	www.burgage.net

Map 8 Entry 207

The Lord Bagenal Inn
Main Street, Lieghlinbridge, Co. Carlow

In the thirty years since James Kehoe, a dynamo of charm and energy, created his wayside inn by the ancient bridge of this pretty Heritage Town, it has become *the* place for young and old to meet, eat, drink and enjoy the old-style *craíc*. There's even a small crèche. That's the old-oak part. With the next generation moving in – son George to introduce high-end dining standards, having cut his chef's teeth at some of Dublin's finest eateries, son Patrick to greet and guide guests – they have spread their wings along the bucolic river bank where the Barrow opens itself for boating and fishing. In magnificent modern contrast to the memory-strewn pub, the cleancut new wing looks from a timber-decked veranda onto fields of famous racehorses and stud mares. One of Ireland's leading designers has made rooms of quiet sophistication in elegant tones of colour-splashed beige with matching bathrooms. Here are new and old Ireland hand in hand, an exceptional marriage and an exceptionally lively, intelligent family to inspire and carry it. Plus lovely countryside, great old castles, buckets of pre-history.

rooms	39 doubles & twins.
price	From €130. Singles €110–€115.
meals	Dinner €25–€45. Lunch from €15.
closed	Christmas Day.
directions	On N7 Dublin-Waterford road between Carlow and Kilkenny: on right in town centre.

	James & Mary Kehoe
tel	+353 (0)59 972 1668
fax	+353 (0)59 972 2629
email	info@lordbagenal.com
web	www.lordbagenal.com

Hotel

Map 8 Entry 208

Lorum Old Rectory
Kilgreaney, Bagenalstown, Co. Carlow

Step through the door and feel instantly at home. Bobbie is cosy and warm, her three daughters, all professionals in their own fields, live across the yard, the family atmosphere is tangible. Bobbie will usher you into the drawing room to a soft sofa by the lovely fireplace for the compulsory tea and chat; the piano is there for all to talk to. Up the creaky stairs are bedrooms full of character with a carved four-poster, interesting antiques and peaceful views of the Blackstairs Mountains. The best treat of all is dinner at the big old dining table. Bobbie, an exceptional cook – and exceptionally modest about it despite her awards – uses locally-sourced meat and organic produce to stunning effect, and her Irish cheeseboard must be one of the most comprehensive in the country. She also turns her hand to stained glass in her workshop in a converted outbuilding. There's a heart-soothing walk by the nearby Barrow River, or you can hire bicycles and explore the sunny south-east where it's said the climate is as gentle as the hills. Even cycle to another lovely house, with your luggage taken on ahead.

rooms	4: 2 doubles, 1 twin/double, 1 four-poster. Extra bathroom available.
price	€150-€160. Singles €90.
meals	Dinner, 6 courses, €45.
closed	December-March.
directions	From Bagenalstown R705 for Borris 6.5km; house signposted on left.

Country house

Bobbie Smith

tel	+353 (0)59 977 5282
fax	+353 (0)59 977 5455
email	info@lorum.com
web	www.lorum.com

Map 8 Entry 209

Mulvarra House
St Mullins (Graiguenamanagh), Co. Carlow

On one of the most sensational spots in Carlow, this angular building stands above the River Barrow, facing the tree-clad mountains that fold in over the river as it meanders below and protects the ancient marvel that is St Mullins with its famous abbey, graveyard and aura of spirituality. With determination and amazing open-heartedness – extended to all guests plus four rescue dogs and three pet goats – the owners have transformed a fading B&B into an unpretentious, deliciously Irish haven. Nothing is too much trouble for Noreen: you can to be collected from the station in Bagenalstown, go chad fishing for a day, join her in preparing a huge barbecue for that special evening. Each pretty, freshly-painted room has a little balcony onto the river, flower-embroidered duvets and a crisp clean shower room. The food is genuine home-cooking, organic where possible: do book dinner. On dimmer days when cultural Kilkenny, great hill walks, sport fishing or river swimming (for the brave) cannot tempt you, indulge in Noreen's brand new treatment centre. Remarkable value and such lovely people.

rooms	5: 2 doubles, 2 twins, 1 family. Extra bathrooms.
price	€80. Singles €48.
meals	Dinner, 5 courses, €30.
closed	Rarely.
directions	From Carlow N9 for Kilkenny 16km; left R724 for Bagenalstown 1km; right R705 thro' Borris; R729 for New Ross; in Glynn right at Post Office for St Mullins; left, left again, follow signs to house.

	Noreen & Harold Ardill
tel	+353 (0)51 424 936
fax	+353 (0)51 424 969
email	info@mulvarra.com
web	www.mulvarra.com

B&B

Map 8 Entry 210

Ivyleigh House
Bank Place, Church Street, Port Laoise, Co. Laois

A house of modern comforts and care, Ivyleigh was built in 1845 as a townhouse 'in the Georgian style' and Dinah pursues the tradition of elegance and refinement in every detail, all carefully chosen for your greater comfort. There's an æsthetic pleasure here, too: Italian towels and bed linen, Mason tableware, Newbridge silver cutlery, rather special wallpaper, and one lovely Chippendale double bed – others are comfortably normal. But nothing frighteningly perfect. The big drawing room calls you to relax with its modern sofas and Victorian ancecdotes, antiques collected over the past 20 years. Next door is the superb Chippendale dining table with its beautifully carved ball and claw feet. Dinah's breakfast is more than a match for it. Choose from a dizzy array of delicious breakfast alternatives including surprises such as yogurt with geranium jelly and Cashel Blue cheesecakes. Port Laoise has good restaurants and a theatre within walking distance. Dinah and Jerry are friendly, down-to-earth people who work hard to look after you. An ideal staging post en route to the south-west.

rooms	6: 2 doubles, 3 twins/doubles, 1 single.
price	€130. Singles €85.
meals	Restaurant in Port Laoise.
closed	Christmas.
directions	Follow signs for Church Street, multi-storey car park; house 25m on right.

B&B

	Dinah & Jerry Campion
tel	+353 (0)57 862 2081
fax	+353 (0)57 866 3343
email	info@ivyleigh.com
web	www.ivyleigh.com

Map 4 Entry 211

Roundwood House

Mountrath, Co. Laois

Frank has a dry chuckle that makes you feel he knows all the jokes Ireland has ever told. He and Rosemarie are lovely people, as relaxed as the dogs that lie around outside, and have endless time for visitors. Which doesn't mean they neglect the cooking: Roundwood's reputation for good food and wine is reliable and deserved. That supremely harmonious Palladian façade, built by Quakers in 1680, hides an unpretentious family house which the Kennans have loved and lived in for 20 years. Elegance salutes you in the building's fabric, old family portraits in the hall, old oils in the drawing room – so what matter a few cracks or some worn upholstery? The six rooms in the main house are big and bright and not over-furnished, the four in the scented herb-garden courtyard, one a four-poster, are newly dressed in rush matting and all-white bedcovers. Need to exercise your mind? there are books and board games galore; your fresh-air craft? the croquet lawn challenges. Then dine with your garrulous, poetic hosts by the fire in the cosy dining room. You won't regret or forget a single human moment.

rooms	10 + 3: 9 twins/doubles, 1 four-poster. 3 cottages for 4.
price	€150–€170. Singles €95. Cottages €280–€500 p.w.
meals	Dinner €45.
closed	January.
directions	From Portlaoise N7 to Mountrath 13km; right R440 for Birr & Slieve Bloom Mountains 5km; signpost & gate on left.

Frank & Rosemarie Kennan

tel	+353 (0)57 873 2120
fax	+353 (0)57 873 2711
email	roundwood@eircom.net
web	www.roundwoodhouse.com

Guest house & Self-catering

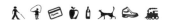

Map 4 Entry 212

Ballaghmore Manor House & Castle
Borris-in-Ossory, Co. Laois

Grace by name, graceful by nature — and grand fun. An endlessly fascinating fount of Irish history, Grace will hold you spellbound with the story of Ballaghmore, and more. She has put a lifetime into this extraordinary house, bought as a ruin 'last lived in by the King of Ossory', and the 15th-century tower castle in its back garden which you can rent for a medieval experience week (inc. mod cons). Chieftain Macgiollaphadraig, who grew up at the court of Henry VIII, got his castle back from the usurping Butlers with classmate Edward VI's backing, on condition that he normanise his name to FitzPatrick. Grace tells the history with a scholar's enthusiasm while making absolutely sure you are looked after. A gilder and gallery owner before moving here to restore the house and castle, she's one special, unusual lady. Her daughter Sorrel breeds Connemara ponies on the manor's 30 acres. Ballaghmore is surrounded by golf courses, there's riding, fishing, boating and even swimming in the lake, for the hardy. The elegant bedrooms and the smoked salmon and scrambled egg breakfasts are peerless.

rooms	3 + 1: 1 twin, 1 four-poster, both en suite; 1 family suite with separate bath. Castle for 10-20.
price	From €120. Singles from €60. The Castle €2,000 p.w.
meals	Restaurants 1 mile.
closed	Rarely.
directions	From Dublin N7 for Limerick through Borris-in-Ossory for Roscrea. House signposted 5km after Borris; entrance on right.

Country house & Self-catering

	Grace Pym
tel	+353 (0)57 862 1453
email	gracepym@eircom.net
web	www.castleballaghmore.com

Map 4 Entry 213

The Manor Cottages
Manor Kilbride, Blessington, Co. Wicklow

There are four charming granite cottages here, hidden from the world in the grounds of a Victorian Revival heritage house at the foot of the Wicklow Mountains, a glorious place for nature-lovers. Herds and Wood Cottages stand at opposite ends of the pretty mid-18th-century courtyard; Anvil Lodge and River Lodge – the latter a romantic retreat for two at the river's edge by the entrance gate – are out on the wonderful 40-acre estate with views over pastureland and the river. The whole setup is great for children. All the cottages have little gardens and flagstoned open-plan interiors, beautifully done by Margaret with exposed stonework, beams and comfy sofas round an open fire – a super mix of old and new. Kitchens are equipped with all the modern bits, the village shop is a five-minute walk and good restaurants and pubs are nearby. Take long walks with mountain views around two lakes – with some trout – or explore Dublin and Wicklow from this tranquil spot. *Swimming can be arranged in the owner's pool in summer. French & Spanish spoken. Pets by arrangement.*

rooms	3 cottages for 4 (2 doubles, 1 bathroom). Cottage for 2 (1 double, 1 bathroom).
price	From €360-€740 per week.
meals	Self-catering.
closed	Rarely.
directions	From Dublin N81 through Brittas, left 3km after village R759 for Kilbride; left at T-junction for Sally Gap. Entrance 150m on right at next junction.

	Margaret Cully
tel	+353 (0)1 458 2105
fax	+353 (0)1 458 2607

Self-catering

Map 5 Entry 214

Rathsallagh House & Country Club
Dunlavin, Co. Wicklow

The easy-going, utterly professional O'Flynns still run this growing place as if it were just another country house: each guest feels individually welcome in the soft sofas of the panelled drawing room. Family photographs set the tone, carved elephants stand guard, logs crackle, flowers flutter; 'Big' Joe, supremely laid-back, delights with his endless stories and songs, charming 'Little' Joe is the front runner, the staff are in the same mould. Yet it's a luxury hotel: championship golf course, superb classy food that people come for miles to enjoy, spa bathrooms. Breakfast will bowl you over. Organic veg and fruit are plucked from the unforgettable walled garden, home to a full-grown sequoia, herbs bursting from the courtyard walls. But before the dinner menu, get the bath menu and choose your scented oils and soft music! Posh, quilty bedrooms, all with DVD players and bathrobes, are huge in the courtyard wing with intimate garden views, smaller in the main house with long parkland vistas. No two are alike, some have their own door to the garden. A lovely, peerlessly friendly small hotel. *Tennis on site.*

Country house

rooms	29: Inner Courtyard: 11 doubles, 6 twins. Outer Courtyard: 12 twins/doubles.
price	€270-€320. Singles from €135.
meals	Dinner from €60-€70.
closed	Never.
directions	From Dublin N81 through Blessington & continue 9.5km; right R756 to Dunlavin; through village for Colbinstown 4km (signs); entrance on left.

	The O'Flynn Family
tel	+353 (0)45 403 112
fax	+353 (0)45 403 343
email	info@rathsallagh.com
web	www.rathsallagh.com

Map 5 Entry 215

Barraderry House
Kiltegan, Co. Wicklow

John and Olive are adorable: Irish farming folk who will go out of their way to make you feel at home. The house has a properly solid farmhouse feel, too, where life hums along to a cheery tune in a peaceful, bucolic setting in the shadow of Lugnaquilla, Ireland's second highest mountain. The main house – early Georgian with Victorian additions – is approached along a drive that dips and curves through an avenue of trees. At the back, tree enthusiasts will gasp at the amazing grafted Siamese beech tree. After the last of six daughters left home, Olive decided to spruce it all up; she did a wonderful job. The large uncluttered hall, warmly coloured with a lively black and white floor, leads to a dining room where silver gleams and breakfast is served at a huge table, and a drawing room with beautiful porcelain, a century-old rosewood grand piano and a bay window to the garden. Unfussy bedrooms have pretty fabrics, good prints, the odd fireplace, cleverly-squeezed-in showers. Olive is friendly and easy-going, John has been known to sing at the piano when the mood takes him, the setting is lovely.

rooms	4: 1 double, 1 twin, 1 twin/double, 1 single.
price	€90-€100. Singles €50.
meals	Restaurant 4 miles.
closed	Mid-December to mid-January.
directions	From Dublin N81 through Blessington to Baltinglass (56km); left R747 for Kiltegan. Entrance on right just before village.

Olive & John Hobson

tel	+353 (0)59 647 3209
fax	+353 (0)59 647 3209
email	jo.hobson@oceanfree.net
web	www.barraderrycountryhouse.com

Country house

Map 5 Entry 216

Clone House
Aughrim, Co. Wicklow

If you are a cat-lover, you'll be purring all the way. Coming up the drive you'll see other four-footed, cud-chewing friends, a huge monkey puzzle tree, a courtyard of terracotta pots and a smiling Carla at the door. Born in Tuscany, she met Jeff in America and they came here to bring up their children. Her sunny Mediterranean taste colours this remote and delightful corner of the Wicklow Mountains with a warm ochre finish to the sturdy building. The original house was burnt down in the 1798 rebellion – once the lady of the house had been carried out on her bed! Lovely bedrooms mix rural Italy with a touch of the baroque as rich colours, Regency fabrics and voile dress glowing floorboards and textured bricks; some have open fires lit before you arrive. It's simply pleasing, not luxurious. But food remains Carla's great passion: stuffed quails wrapped in pancetta, *osso bucco*, maybe white chocolate cheesecake to follow. It's all organic and GMO-free and her focaccia bread is irresistible. There's a folksy Irish snug, a small waterfall, even a sauna, but Carla is the true star here.

rooms	7: 5 doubles en suite; 1 double, 1 four-poster, each with separate bath.
price	€140-€200. Singles €110-€200.
meals	Dinner, 3-5 courses, €45-€55. 24 hours' notice required.
closed	Rarely.
directions	From Aughrim, R4747 for Tinahely. On village outskirts, left at low black and yellow wall & follow signs to house; entrance on right.

Country house

Jeff Watson & Carla Edigati Watson
tel	+353 (0)40 236 121
fax	+353 (0)40 236 029
email	stay@clonehouse.com
web	www.clonehouse.com

Map 8 Entry 217

Ballyknocken House

Glenealy, Ashford, Co. Wicklow

Catherine is a joy, the heart and soul of Ballyknocken, creating a great atmosphere with her family and her charming staff. Her cooking skills – on woodchips if you please – are lively too: do taste her sublime modern-Irish country dinners, made with imagination and local produce, served on white linen in the dining room where pot and kettle still hang in the old fireplace (calling each other names?). Such is her pleasure in food that she has opened a cookery school in the old milking parlour. The antiques, paintings and utterly personal style of the sweet old 1850s manor farmhouse will delight you. It feels rich in its deep red carpets, fine old dressers and strong colours. Bedrooms have brass beds or gauzy overhead canopies, more antiques and ornaments, good little bathrooms, some with big Victorian baths decorated in Catherine's stencils. Outside this hive of activity lie 300 acres of pasture, the lovely forested hills of Wicklow for superb walking, the Carrig Mountain on the doorstep – peace by the basinful. Or catch the DART at Greystones for a day in swinging Dublin. *Tennis on site.*

rooms	7 + 1: 4 doubles, 2 twins, 1 triple. Loft for 4-6.
price	€118-€130. Loft €140 p.p. per week.
meals	Dinner, 4 courses with aperitif & canapés, €39.50 (Tuesday-Saturday). Book ahead.
closed	December-January.
directions	From Dublin N11 to Ashford 48km; there, right after Chester Bealty pub for Glenealy 5km. House on right signposted, 4km.

Catherine Byrne-Fulvio

tel	+353 (0)40 444 627
fax	+353 (0)40 444 696
email	cfulvio@ballyknocken.com
web	www.ballyknocken.com

Guest house & Self-catering

Map 5 Entry 218

The Cottage
Ballybetagh Hill, Kilternan, Co. Dublin

This perfect little cottage for combining fabulous hill walking (the Wicklow Way is two miles away), golf (12 courses within 5 miles: 'golf heaven') and Dublin's buzzy culture and night life (the station is five minutes' drive) was built in the 1800s – and looks brand new. It has all the finish and fittings of modern life yet is bright, cheerful and comfortable, just as a cottage should be, with incredible views of the sea from its five acres. Hilary, a warm, caring person, provides the basic foodstuffs any kitchen needs and all possible guidance to make your stay a complete success. Inside, the rooms are surprisingly light: the low windows are bigger than in most Irish cottages, the light bounces off the fresh flowers that always greet new arrivals from the solid-pine kitchen table, the open-plan living space has a pleasing rustic-pine simplicity. You could happily read all day here in dimmer weather. Bedrooms are equally easy and comfortable, with excellent new bedding, and there's a little private garden for balmy days. Don't miss the original Saturday-morning Irish country market in Kilternan. *Minimum stay three nights.*

rooms	Cottage for 3 (1 double, 1 single, 1 shower).
price	€735 per week.
meals	Self-catering. Pub/restaurant within 5km.
closed	Rarely.
directions	Directions given on booking.

Self-catering

Hilary Knott
tel   +353 (0)86 846 2450
email   ballybetaghhill@eircom.net

Map 5 Entry 219

Druid Lodge

Killiney Hill Road, Killiney, Co. Dublin

Is this magnificent house on the cliff a parody? a museum? a crazy concoction?
A Titian-copy cardinal glares down upon innumerable pieces of art and artefacts,
Irish, African and Italian, that hang, lie, squat in his shadow. Ken is an unstoppable
collector of the unusual, the arcane, the merely beautiful. He was a sociologist in
Africa (hence the Macondi carvings) and now paints – he has the temperament.
Cynthia, a maths teacher who brought up six children here once they had put a roof
on the crumbling mansion, welcomes guests with her gently efficient manner into
the grand Georgian rooms upstairs (book early for their high views to the almighty
ocean and the purifying east wind) or the smaller inward-looking basement retreats
with more African interest to admire and barred windows to the roots of the
tangled garden and the 'Spite' Tower that stands there. All are pleasingly personal in
their quiet fabrics, family antiques, good beds and bathrooms. In winter, the warm
dark drawing room is superbly atmospheric, in summer the conservatory elf
enlivens the green space, and breakfast is a feast all year round.

rooms	4: 2 doubles, 2 twins/doubles.
price	€80-€100. Singles €60-€70. Children under 7, €20.
meals	Restaurants in Dalkey.
closed	24 December-28 December.
directions	From M50 southbound exit 16 for Dun Laoghaire onto dual carriageway; right at top of hill, imm'ly left into Killiney Avenue; at T-junc. right; next T-junc right; next gate on left opp. white stones.

Ken & Cynthia McClenaghan

tel	+353 (0)1 285 1632
fax	+353 (0)1 284 8504
email	dlodge@indigo.ie
web	www.druidlodge.com

B&B

Map 5 Entry 220

Aberdeen Lodge

53 Park Avenue, Ballsbridge, Dublin 4, Co. Dublin

Pat fought hard to start his super little hotel amid the Regency mansions and embassies of leafy Ballsbridge. He won the neighbours over by promising to protect their peace and quiet and Aberdeen Lodge is indeed a refuge from the hullabaloo of Dublin city, yet the metro is close enough to catapult you back into the fray within minutes. Pat is a friendly hotelier, with a quiet deferential manner and his logo on the bathrobes, for whom nothing is too much trouble. His Irish staff have helpful charm, too. This modest Victorian villa has been cleverly converted into a variety of contemporary rooms with all mod cons and Egyptian cotton sheets. Candy-striped curtains remind you that the seafront is only 200 yards away and Biedermeier-style furniture adds a touch of luxury. Rooms at the back look over the good big garden onto a cricket pitch, an unusual sight in a country devoted to Gaelic football. Everything seems to run effortlessly and Pat's partner Ann's award-winning breakfast to piped classical music is deeply revitalising. Ideal for those wanting the best of both worlds in this fair city.

rooms	17: 11 twins/doubles, 2 family, 2 triples, 2 suites.
price	€120–€160. Singles €99–€119. Suites €199–€249.
meals	Room service menu €15–€30.
closed	Never.
directions	From city centre by DART railway. From Merrion Square, Northumberland Rd to Merrion Rd; left into Ailesbury Rd, cross Sydney Parade DART Station, 1st left into Park Avenue; house on left.

	Pat Halpin
tel	+353 (0)1 283 8155
fax	+353 (0)1 283 7877
email	aberdeen@iol.ie
web	www.halpinsprivatehotels.com

Hotel

Map 5 Entry 221

Number 31
31 Leeson Close, Dublin 2, Co. Dublin

Radically revamped, visibly and invisibly, into a real little city-centre hotel, Number 31 holds fast to its essential family-run Irish personality. A leading designer did fabrics and fittings, old beds and bathrooms were swept away, the comfort is top class, the service professional, the attitude remains upbeat and friendly. Like its owners, this place doesn't take itself over-seriously: Noel employs intelligent young staff and knows that in an anonymous city the personal touch makes all the difference. The coach house sitting area is sunken and funky and the art is modern. Across the garden in the more demure Georgian townhouse on Fitzwilliam Place there are some huge rooms with original plasterwork – and a couple at lower ground floor level – but your favourite may be a cosy den with its own secluded patio in the coach house. As someone once said, it's an aesthetic jungle with a split personality to suit all tastes. Attention to detail and a genuine enjoyment of what they do make the Comers wonderful hosts. *Children over 10 welcome. Secure parking. Self-catering cottage in Mayo, entry 65.*

rooms	21 doubles, twins & triples.
price	€140-€300.
meals	Restaurants close by.
closed	Never.
directions	From St Stephen's Green past Shelbourne Hotel, up Merrion Row, right Pembroke St to end, left Leeson St; Leeson Close, 1st left. Entrance on right through arched wooden gate in high wall.

Noel & Deirdre Comer
tel	+353 (0)1 676 5011
fax	+353 (0)1 676 2929
email	info@number31.ie
web	www.number31.ie

Hotel

Map 5 Entry 222

Waterloo House

8-10 Waterloo Road, Ballsbridge, Dublin 4, Co. Dublin

On a peaceful Georgian terraced street close to St Stephen's Green, Trinity College and the city centre, Waterloo House is in fact two large 1830s Georgian townhouses melded into one hotel whose shiny twin doors say 'come right in'. It is extremely well run – not surprising given that Evelyn spent years in the hospitality 'industry' before striking out on her own, but what sets it apart from many similarly-priced places in Dublin is the sincerely friendly welcome, a relief from busy urban anonymity. Helpful staff go out of their way to make sure you're treated as an individual. The converters preserved the lofty ceilings and elegant big windows. Bedrooms, all similar in layout, are neat, clean and in perfect working order, with thick carpets, repro furniture and good-sized bathrooms. On the street side, you will find useful noise-reducing shutters and heavy curtains. The reception area doubles as a comfortable sitting space or there's the conservatory. Good breakfasts, served in the plush dining room, set you up for a day of sight-seeing. *Parking for eight cars in front of house.*

rooms	17: 12 doubles, 5 twins.
price	€99–€199. Singles €76–€130.
meals	Restaurants within walking distance.
closed	Christmas.
directions	From Merrion Row, near St Stephen's Green, to Baggott St into Upper Baggott St. 1st right after bridge into Waterloo Rd; house on left. 15 minutes walk from city centre.

Hotel

Evelyn Corcoran

tel	+353 (0)1 660 1888
fax	+353 (0)1 667 1955
email	waterloohouse@eircom.net
web	www.waterloohouse.ie

Map 5 Entry 223

Belcamp Hutchinson

Malahide Road, Balgriffin, Dublin 17, Co. Dublin

This was deep country when Francis Hely-Hutchinson built the house in 1786. The encroaching city now encircles it but, lying off the busy road that leads to the lovely village of Malahide, Belcamp is still an extraordinary oasis within its high walls. Its four acres of garden are full of birds, flowers – and a maze (harder than it looks: take Ariadne with you); there's even a pet cemetery. Doreen and her good-natured old dogs will usher you into this beautiful Georgian home which feels like a small country-house hotel. The antique furniture and old paintings tell of another age, the drawing room takes in the peace of the garden, the green dining room has one fine big table for convivial breakfasts. Doreen is tireless in her efforts to make sure guests are well looked after, getting up at all hours to see that they catch their early flight home. Super-comfortable bedrooms are immaculately tidy with polished floors, big zip-link beds, strong colours and modern furnishings. Escape the city to peace and quiet. *Dublin airport 10 mins, St Stephen's Green 20 mins. Children over 10 welcome.*

rooms	8: 5 doubles, 3 twins/doubles.
price	€150. Singles €75.
meals	Restaurants in Malahide.
closed	20 December to end January.
directions	From Dublin, Malahide Road out of centre for about 6.5km. House signposted on left; entrance 2nd left.

Doreen Gleeson & Karl Waldburg

tel	+353 (0)1 846 0843
fax	+353 (0)1 848 5703
email	belcamphutchinson@eircom.net
web	www.belcamphutchinson.com

Guest house

Map 5 Entry 224

Redbank House & Restaurant

6 & 7 Church Street, Skerries, Fingal, Co. Dublin

Terry epitomises all that's good about Ireland. A true Irish original with an infectious sense of humour and a love of cooking, he has won awards galore, especially for his seafood. In his spare time, he sails dinghies and champions the cause of this pretty fishing village. He has built an excellent reputation for food and service and his small hotel is just as unpretentiously good. Hotel-style rooms with old-look furniture, classic colour schemes and all the mod cons are split between the Old Bank House, next to the restaurant, and a new extension. The restaurant is the mainstay of this converted bank, the old safe complete with original vault door is the wine cellar, bright-coloured walls easily make up for the lack of natural light. Terry sources locally: fresh fish from Skerries harbour, Dublin Bay prawns and, more unusually, razorfish, whose long fluted shells are collected from local beaches. Take a train to Dublin for the day, play some great golf, or come for one last good meal before leaving: the ideal place to start or end your trip to Ireland. *Dublin airport is a 20-minute drive.*

rooms	18: 12 doubles, 4 twins, 2 family.
price	€120–€140. Singles €70–€85.
meals	Dinner from €50, 6.30pm. Sunday lunch €33, 12.30-4pm.
closed	Never.
directions	From Dublin N1 to Blake's Cross; right for Skerries about 11km; under bridge, 1st left, continue. Church St on right opp. AIB.

Hotel

	Terry McCoy
tel	+353 (0)1 849 1005
fax	+353 (0)1 849 1598
email	info@redbank.ie
web	www.redbank.ie

Map 5 Entry 225

Martinstown House

The Curragh, Kildare, Co. Kildare

Martinstown! A Neo-Gothic flight of fancy unlike any other, a *cottage orné*, no less, sitting grandly on an immaculate green sward, reigned over by tall trees and the inimitable Meryl. Full of great energy and character, a committed animal-lover with a flair for interiors and gardening, she settles easily into conversation with guests. Son Edward's dinners are proper country-house style at one big table with solid silver cutlery and superb vegetables grown in the fine walled garden. His wife Roisín is a gentle helpful presence. The pastorals and pillars mural in the hall is riveting; the drawing room, twice as high as the rest of the ground floor, garlands galore, good furniture, is staggering – a room fit for a king; the Blue Room bathroom blows you away: it's covered in clouds. The beautiful bedrooms are superbly country-house, the whole wonderful place bubbles with vitality, style and elegance yet remains comfortably informal, the garden provokes the same admiration. A perfect mix of old-fashioned hospitality, modern comfort, and a working farm nearby. *Horse racing locally. Unsuitable for young children.*

rooms	4: 1 double, 1 twin/double; 1 double, 1 twin, both with separate bathroom.
price	€190-€240. Singles €115-€140.
meals	Dinner €55. By arrangement. Restaurants 4km-5km.
closed	December-January.
directions	From Dublin N7 south onto M7/M9; 1st exit for Athy onto N78 1.5km; right for Martinstown 2.5km; left at sign 1km; entrance on left.

	Meryl Long, Edward & Roisín Booth
tel	+353 (0)45 441 269
fax	+353 (0)45 441 208
email	info@martinstownhouse.com
web	www.martinstownhouse.com

Guest house

Map 5 Entry 226

Coursetown House
Stradbally Road, Athy, Co. Kildare

You could talk natural history and plants for hours with both Iris and Jim: she's a plantsman whose passion is gardening, he's an agricultural scientist – lovely, real, eco-friendly people. Their early Victorian farmhouse stands in one of the best-tended gardens in Ireland, full of colour, texture and, most important of all, scent; just smell those old-fashioned roses. Jim has a library of natural history books and grows crops on 270 acres, working closely with agri-researchers from University College Dublin. From the front bedrooms the woodland garden bursts into life in the spring. Well-sprung mattresses, electric blankets, crisp linen and luxurious pillows ensure the soundest sleep; soft towels and classy smellies lie in wait in all the bathrooms. From the yellow-washed breakfast room you look over groomed lawn and teeming border; from the fully wheelchair-friendly ground-floor bedroom, too. Over a slice of delicious homemade cake, you can ask about the sea bean or the huge whale bones in the yard. Engaging company and a great example of Irish hospitality. *Children over eight welcome.*

Country house

rooms	4: 2 doubles, 2 twins/doubles; extra bath.
price	€120. Singles €75.
meals	Restaurants in Athy, 3km.
closed	Mid-November–mid-March.
directions	From N78 at Athy, or N80 at Stradbally onto R428. House 3km from Athy & 9.5km from Stradbally, signposted.

Jim & Iris Fox
tel	+353 (0)59 863 1101
mobile	+353 (0)87 207 2070
fax	+353 (0)59 863 2740
web	www.coursetown.com

Map 4 Entry 227

Griesemount
Ballitore, Co. Kildare

Carolyn and her handsome Georgian house mirror each other: adventurous, funny, oozing with taste and a touch of the wild, a treasure-trove of goodies and style. Within five minutes of arriving you may find yourself talking about the strangest things, Mongolian red tape, for example. There is nothing neat or fussy here, she is not afraid to mix Robert's beautiful Irish antiques with her lovely African prints and furniture, prizes from an earlier life in Zimbabwe, to create an eclectic atmosphere that is both happy and charming. The four-poster bed is incredible, echoes of the Princess and the Pea: guests ask to take it home, once they've dragged themselves out of the book-stocked bathroom; the Topiary Room is freshly, brightly decorated and gorgeous with its painted shutters and hidden bathroom, the twin has a touch of Africa. Also, a well-lived-in drawing room with furniture crowded round the fireplace and a piano, superb views perfectly framed by the tall windows: paddocks or old rooftops, the walled garden or the River Griese and its ruined mill. Inimitable. *Shaker furniture for sale in village.*

rooms	3: 1 double, 1 four-poster; 1 twin with separate bathroom.
price	€80–€140. Singles from €50.
meals	Dinner €25–€30, on request. Restaurants nearby.
closed	Rarely.
directions	From Dublin N7 off M50 for Naas 32km; N9 for Carlow 19km. After Texaco garage right for Ballitore; left in village 1.5 km past mill, over bridge; 3-storey yellow house, no sign at gate.

	Robert & Carolyn Ashe
tel	+353 (0)59 862 3158
mobile	+353 (0)86 830 8676
fax	+353 (0)59 914 0687
email	griesemount@eircom.net

Country house

Map 5 Entry 228

Whigsborough House
Five Alley, Birr, Co. Offaly

The daffodil door and spreading fanlight give Whigsborough a lovely face. You walk from that uplifted porch straight into the living room – almost improper in a Georgian house. Sofas surround a roaring fire and soft red wallpaper soothes. Then there's the joy in Anna's welcome as she leads you in: she loves this place deeply and is calmly determined to make it work. Born in Sweden, she moved to Ireland in 1988 and married Eamon, who breeds steeplechasers in his spare time. They now have four young daughters and organise high-class private dinner parties using lots of home-grown delights. The house was built in 1714 by the Drought family who lived here and altered it for 250 long years, once in 1780 and again in the early 1800s to add a ballroom. Guests have the ground and first floors to themselves and improvements are constant. The staircase takes you cleanly, grandly up to the bedrooms. Anna has filled it all with old-world charm: huge beds, one massive four-poster, modern bathrooms that look across lawn and woodland, handmade rugs, ancient maps and beautiful wallpaper everywhere.

rooms	6: 1 double, 2 triples, 1 single, 1 four-poster, 1 family suite.
price	€80-€120. Singles €40-€60.
meals	Dinner €35. 24 hours' notice required. Packed lunch €7.
closed	Christmas. Dinners by arrangement only.
directions	From Birr N52 for Tullamore to Five Alley; left for Banagher, immediately left. House 1km on right.

Country house

	Anna Heagney
tel	+353 (0)57 913 3318
mobile	+353 (0)87 994 3390
email	whigsborough@eircom.net

Map 4 Entry 229

Spinner's Town House
Castle Street, Birr, Co. Offaly

Between the ruins of St Brendan's church and the high walls of the thoroughly lived-in castle, surrounded by graceful Georgian Birr, Spinner's is a modest terrace of five houses and an old wool mill, all skilfully gathered into a delightful place to stay – and eat. Its new owners, two eager multi-talented young couples, have redone the public rooms in their signature biscuit-and-chocolate colours – restful and warm – adding a hot red dash in the bar and a chiminea out on the exotic-feel deck. Sitting here with your tea or aperitif, you overlook the beautifully patterned and planted stone courtyard, sheltered by the old stones. Upstairs, bedrooms breathe anew after their quiet magnolia refreshments, again with a wall of brave contrast each while the entertaining 'gothic' rooms have an iron and ogive look. Canvas wardrobes are discreet and adequate, linen is impeccable, shower rooms are snug. And good food – Rory is the clever chef – is served in a happy, relaxed atmosphere. Do visit the 3rd Earl of Rosse's monster telescope in the castle park, a triumph of engineering and science... in 1845.

rooms	12: 3 doubles, 3 twins/doubles, 3 family, all en suite; 1 double, 2 twins/doubles, each with separate bath.
price	€80–€120. Singles €55–€75.
meals	Dinner €16.95; à la carte around €35. Restaurant closed on Tuesdays.
closed	Hotel open all year.
directions	From Mountrath R440 to Birr. From Emmet Sq, down Main St to Market Sq, right at monument, house 500m on right, opp. Birr Castle.

	Clare & Fearghal O'Sullivan, Ruth & Rory Dunne
tel	+353 (0)57 912 1673
fax	+353 (0)57 912 1673
email	spinnerstownhouse@eircom.net
web	www.spinnerstownhouse.com

Hotel

Map 4 Entry 230

Brendan House
Brendan Street, Birr, Co. Offaly

A place of joy for creative spirits and full of unexpected marvels, Brendan House is a listed building that spans history and culture in one generous human brushstroke – poets, artists, musicians flock. Nepalese prayer flags flutter outside, fabulous masks enchant the corridors, art and antiques jostle. French, Tudor, Victorian bedrooms have canopy beds, reclining cushions and no telly. Shutters and sash windows are original, as is the amazing 19th-century bath, the second to be fitted in Birr, with its crazy history, gaudy looks and Rosalind's loving restoration. Catch the sun in the small courtyard garden or snuggle up to the roaring fire in the drawing room. Derek the explorer, poet and accomplished walking guide, has a bushy red beard and the dress sense of a Victorian gentleman. Rosalind the designer and occasional writer, prefers the ethnic look, gives art classes and castle tours. Both are engaging, unusual company and are doing their best to protect the planet. Breakfast, fulsome, hearty or healthy, is totally memorable. 6th-century transatlantic sailor St Brendan had his monastery nearby.

rooms	3 + 1: 1 double, 2 singles, sharing bathroom. Artist's studio for 3.
price	€65-€75. Singles €42-€45. Studio €22-€25 p.p.
meals	Dinner €35. Supper €15. By arrangement (minumum 2). Cream tea €12.
closed	Rarely.
directions	Arriving in Birr from Dublin, left at central square, down main street, then left by Market House Tavern. House on right.

B&B & Self-catering

Rosalind & Derek Fanning
tel +353 (0)57 912 1818
mobile +353 (0)87 668 1783
email tinjugstudio@eircom.net
web www.tinjugstudio.com

Map 4 Entry 231

Ardmore House
The Walk, Kinnitty, Co. Offaly

The clear light of the Irish heartland washes into Christina's handsome early-Victorian house and her encouragements to "get out there and walk the Slieve Blooms" become all the more persuasive, though if you don't go to them, the mountains will come to you, sliding in on that light. A quietly attentive host, Christina, who used to be a teacher, belongs deeply to her beloved Midlands, living in the house that she always wanted (even though it had a purple face), chairing the local development society, organising walking holidays great and small, nurturing biodiversity, playing fiddle in a traditional Irish band. Her rooms illustrate her calm take on life: lots of white, a well-worked quilt here, an amazing carved bedend or a fine oval-mirrored wardrobe there. In the same vein, the house sits sure and square in its large plot of well-tended trees, shrubs and borders: space to sit out in summer (the little dog is too old to do much romping now but the swallows liven things up). On cooler days, turf brings a warm aroma to the living room where breakfast may include prize-winning cheese.

rooms	5: 1 twin, 2 doubles, 2 family rooms with double sofabed.
price	€74-€80. Singles from €50.
meals	Choice in village.
closed	Rarely.
directions	From Tullamore N52 for Birr 1.5km; fork left R421 for Kinnitty 13km; right at T-junction 10km; house on right entering Kinnitty.

	Christina Byrne	
tel	+353 (0)57 913 7009	
mobile	+353 (0)86 278 9147	B&B
email	info@kinnitty.com	
web	www.kinnitty.com	

Map 4 Entry 232

Viewmount House

Dublin Road, Longford, Co. Longford

Beryl and James have spent the past decade restoring this house, built in 1750 by the Cuffe family and later used as a base to administer the Earl of Longford's estate. Now, unstoppable enthusiasts that they are, they have converted the old coach house into a small, refined restaurant. James gave up pedestrian accountancy to devote himself full-time to the house and grounds and he rejoices in realising his dream of running a restaurant (with a professional chef, of course). Young and eager to please, they have done the guest wing with flair and lots of colour. The elegant spiral staircase climbs past warm red walls to the fine green library and excellent bedrooms with a good mix of old furniture, big antique beds, wooden floors, woven rugs and garden views. Each has its own character. Breakfast is served in a stunning Georgian-blue vaulted dining room. James is working on an ambitious Japanese garden, too. The Kearneys are a sincere, friendly couple who laugh easily; so does Oisín the Irish wolfhound. An ideal staging post for Mayo and Donegal, and do stop by Ardagh village before you go.

rooms	5: 3 doubles, 1 twin, 1 suite.
price	€110–€160.
meals	Dinner around €40.
closed	Rarely.
directions	In Longford R393 for Ardagh 1km; right up sliproad following signs to house; entrance 200m on right.

Country house

	Beryl & James Kearney
tel	+353 (0)43 41919
fax	+353 (0)43 42906
email	viewmt@iol.ie
web	www.viewmounthouse.com

Map 4 Entry 233

Knockbrack Grange
Oldcastle, Co. Meath

The views here must be hard to beat for beauty: this is the lovely heart of County Meath, its gardens and historical treasures. Having lived all over the world, Kitty and Richard are happy to be home. Her effervescent enthusiasm will pick you up at the door and carry you into her love for Ireland, her family furniture and portraits and her B&B summers. She's an inspired cook, too, while Richard knows all the history. They have repointed, repainted and recurtained the solidly proportioned rooms and big 1930s extension of this friendly late-Georgian rectory, furnishing it with good pieces that have old charm and no arrogance. The library's picture windows may be 'out of period' but they capture the ancient burial grounds to perfection and the yellow and white bedroom has the hugest dressing/bathroom. Upstairs, rooms are their proper original shapes – one with a red four-poster, the other done in beautiful blue fabric from America – and as Kitty refuses to spoil them by putting in bathrooms the yellow cast-iron bath and clean fresh shower are across the landing. Leave time for the amazing multiple beech tree.

rooms	3: 1 four-poster; 1 double, 1 four-poster, each with separate bath.
price	€100. Singles €60.
meals	Dinner €30.
closed	October-May except by arrangement.
directions	From Kells R163 for Oldcastle; after Ballinlough ignore sign to Oldcastle; 800m after Loughcrew gardens, house on right (beech trees, stone wall).

Kitty Kinsella-Bevan
tel   +353 (0)49 854 1771
email   kittybevan@eircom.net

Country house

Map 4 Entry 234

Loughcrew House
Oldcastle, Co. Meath

Inspired by peerless views and their fabulous historic gardens down by Oliver Plunkett's church, Emily and Charlie are an artistic couple, bursting with non-stop creative and organising energy, and excellent company. As well as the B&B, Emily runs a gilding school in the beautiful Grecian-style yard and a family castle in Wales; Charlie designs, prints, engineers (the chip-fat generator…) and writes. This was the orangery: the mansion burned down, the victim of a priest's curse, it is said; bits of its grand entrance stand in classical ruin nearby. The Napers took over the derelict, sheep-run remains of the old family home and, with ingenuity, artistry and patience, created a house that oozes style and things from Emily's showroom – French furniture, gilded pineapples, small masked faces peering from pelmets. The 17th-century gardens now have a water feature, fairies in the grotto and a wooden coffee pavilion. Do explore their megalithic tombs, too. An exceptional experience in a stunning history-steeped place. They do weddings, of course, and their annual opera season is a music-lover's must. *Tennis on site.*

Country house & Self-catering

rooms	5: 1 double, 2 twins, each with separate bathroom. Courtyard house: 2 doubles, sharing bathroom.
price	€150. Singles €75–€95. Courtyard house also available for self-catering, €400 p.w.
meals	Restaurants 3 miles.
closed	Christmas.
directions	From Kells R163 into R154 for Oldcastle 17.5km; ignore turn to Oldcastle, 3km until blue railings on left. Signed opp. gatehouse.

Charlie & Emily Naper

tel	+353 (0)49 854 1356
fax	+353 (0)49 854 1921
email	info@loughcrew.com
web	www.loughcrew.com

Map 4 Entry 235

Boltown House
Kilskyre, Kells, Co. Meath

Set back among fields of peace, Boltown has solid Georgian serenity. Inside it oozes personality. Susan, ever artistic and professional, has prepared her family home impeccably, leaving pictures, hunting and fishing stuff, old rugs on creaking floorboards and good furniture that is not worryingly precious. Up the unusual double staircase, four bedrooms, one at each corner of the square, have masses of soft-coloured old-world charm with working shutters, pretty fabrics, books and country views. The fifth room has its own staircase and a sitting room/study. Good baths grace the big country bathrooms. The Aga-warmed kitchen, where the delightful eating nook looks onto the stable yard, is the place for breakfast, the back room is ideal for wet clothes, boots and dogs, while the dining room is properly formal and the blue-upholstered drawing room invites an instant sofa-flop (both have working fireplaces). Photographs, memorabilia and a wood-burner warm the terracotta-cosy sitting room, ideal for cooler evenings. A wonderful light-filled peace-loving place for family and friends to gather.

rooms	House for 10 (4 doubles, 1 twin, 5 bathrooms).
price	€1,000-€1,900 per week.
meals	Self-catering. Catering & housekeeping can be arranged.
closed	Rarely.
directions	From Kells R163 for Oldcastle 6km; 2nd left after petrol station for Kilskyre. House 1km on right, white iron gate.

	Susan Wilson & Jean Briscoe
tel	+353 (0)46 924 3036
mobile	+353 (0)87 672 3268
fax	+353 (0)46 924 3036
email	boltown@eircom.net

Self-catering

Map 4 Entry 236

Clonleason Gate Lodge
Fordstown, Co. Meath

Clonleason sets the standard for self-catering in Ireland. Sinead has converted the Georgian lodge into the dandiest cottage that indulges the senses and yet, despite the luxury and attention to detail, never feels overly perfect: roses meet honeysuckle, country-house elegance meets cosy cottage. It lies secluded among trees at the end of her drive with only the odd tractor to interrupt the peace. You enter by the kitchen: hand-printed wallpaper, a Welsh dresser storing patterned Portmeirion china, red deal cupboards distressed to create a limewash effect, a hob but no oven, all the basics generously provided. Left is the sitting room: books, paintings and a comfy cream sofa in front of an open fire – so civilised. The sabre is purely for decoration. French doors open onto a terrace and a beautiful secret garden that leads to a small stream and the wild fields. The bedroom has lots of storage, fresh white linen on an excellent bed, coir matting and a pretty shower room. If you can drag yourself away, there are lots of fabulous gardens to visit, too. Enchanting. *Linen, logs and turf included.*

rooms	Lodge for 2 (1 double, 1 shower).
price	€300–€480 per week, plus electricity & heating.
meals	Self-catering.
closed	Christmas week.
directions	Directions given on booking.

Self-catering

	Sinead Connelly
tel	+353 (0)46 943 4111
fax	+353 (0)46 943 4134
email	clonleason@iol.ie
web	www.clonleason.com

Map 5 Entry 237

Rossnaree

Slane, Co. Meath

Through Georgian picture windows, echoes of prehistoric spirituality shimmer onto the languid elegance born of centuries of family life. Here at Rossnaree ('headland of the king') the High Kings of Tara waited to cross for ceremonies at sacred Newgrange, the magician's cauldron rose and fell with the river: one of Ireland's most evocative views. The neolithic burial grounds are clearly visible – you can walk there, over the river, past fish weirs built by 12th-century Cistercian monks (get a ticket first). And an exceptional welcome. The Law family, the fourth owners since 1150…, have been here for 80 years. Poetic and generous, Aisling is an artist, has an eye for graceful family interiors with a personal touch and plans to fight the addiction to oil by heating Rossnaree with its own timber. Extended in the 1850s in the Italianate style, the house has a 'campanile', a rarity in Ireland, a genuine roulette table in the fantastic library, enticing bedrooms, local produce, a waist-high soft-hearted wolfhound, a huge pet pig. Marvellous. *Three miles of private fishing. 40-minute drive from Dublin Airport.*

rooms	4: 2 doubles, 1 four-poster; 1 twin with separate bath.
price	€140-€160. Singles €70-€90.
meals	Dinner €35, by arrangement (min. 4 people).
closed	Christmas. House available for rent during this time.
directions	From Dublin Airport 40 mins: M1 to Brú na Boinne (Newgrange) exit; after 11km, white gates to house on right.

	Aisling Law
tel	+353 (0)41 982 0975
email	rossnaree@eircom.net
web	www.rossnaree.ie

Country house

Map 5 Entry 238

The Cottages
Seabank, Bettystown/Laytown, Co. Meath

Once through the 'village gate' you are secluded, safe in magical surroundings. Not a car can be seen from the cottages, the beautiful organic flower gardens wind through the thatched hamlet and you can walk along the near-private beach to pubs and restaurants. Liz's family has been letting cottages beside this safe seven-mile sandy beach since 1910 and her warm Irish welcome, possibly with hot scones from the oven, proves she inherited the hospitality gene. She and Roger, whose background is engineering, have impeccably refurbished the cottages, making them state-of-the-art practical, dressing them with a sense of luxury in oak and pine. With their quilted bedcovers on excellent beds, modern bathrooms, CD players, local art and pottery, comfy sofas and fully-fitted kitchens, everything is just so: you will surely be content. All you can hear is the sea. There's even a thatched Wendy house for children, a barbecue, a gourmet farm shop at the gate, those head-clearing beach walks, sand-yachting,... The best antidote to city madness, 25 minutes from Dublin Airport. *Min. stay three nights.*

rooms	6 cottages: 2 for 2 (1 double, 1 bath); 2 for 4 (1 double, 1 twin, 2 baths); 1 for 5 (2 doubles, 1 single, 1 bath); 1 for 6 (2 doubles, 1 twin, 1 bath).
price	€900-€2,700 per week. €65 p.p. per day. 3-night break €390-€1,170.
meals	Self-catering.
closed	Rarely.
directions	Directions given on booking. 25 minutes from Dublin airport.

Self-catering

Roger & Liz Pickett

tel	+353 (0)41 982 8104
fax	+353 (0)41 982 7955
email	info@cottages-ireland.com
web	www.cottages-ireland.com

Map 5 Entry 239

Annesbrook
Duleek, Co. Meath

The narrow entrance to Annesbrook is called 'the pockets'. Dive in between them and emerge into peace: the drive cuts a swathe through dense undergrowth, turns back and there, suddenly, is the house, gazing across open countryside. The effect is stunning. Inside, this slightly eccentric Georgian house has fine proportions; a vast banqueting hall was added for George IV's visit in 1812; Voltaire and Shakespeare eye each other across the hall. Kate is a great ambassador for the house, a thoughtful, calmly relaxed host who makes her own jam, muesli and bread. Flop in soft sofas round a carved marble fireplace beneath the turquoise ceiling, investigate the surprisingly purple dining room. Works by contemporary Irish painters, including Kate's daughter, crowd the walls as you make your way down corridors and landings. Bedrooms are enormous, uncluttered, full of light; one has a terrific German Art Nouveau sleigh bed. Those at the front have the gorgeous view, the others look onto a courtyard with an old and rare meat safe. Ideal for the historic Boyne Valley. *Art & photography courses.*

rooms	5: 1 double, 2 twins, 2 family.
price	€106-€110. Singles €66.
meals	Restaurant in Duleek.
closed	October-March. Groups by arrangement in winter.
directions	From Dublin N2 for Derry through Ashbourne 4.5m/7km. Right R152 for Drogheda & Duleek; entrance 7km on left.

	Kate Sweetman
tel	+353 (0)41 982 3293
fax	+353 (0)41 982 3024
email	sweetman@annesbrook.com
web	www.annesbrook.com

Country house

Map 5 Entry 240

Ballymagarvey Stud
Ballymagarvey Village, Balrath, Co. Meath

The 18th-century house has a round battlemented tower, no pomposity, oodles of charm and a flax-mill village behind, all in cut stone, all superbly, sensitively restored. With Vincent's energy and vision and the eye of a talented designer, the house has become an intimate, opulent country-house hotel whose rich warmth will wrap you in silks, velvets and brocades falling to ripe walnut-coloured floors or thick pale carpet in swathes of soft gold and orange, old rose and burgundy. The furniture is a stylish mix of old and new, Irish and continental, lampshades are feathered and beaded, there's nothing plain anywhere – and ten lovely, luxurious bedrooms. A fine conservatory growing Mediterranean fruits and vines opens onto the walled garden, you can walk the 100-acre grounds and out into the forest or wallow here in gym, sauna and spa. The mill buildings, coach houses and two-storey workers' houses round the tranquil 'village square' are now beautifully converted self-catering cottages but "tenants" can eat out... on the spot. Just the place for a small wedding or your special party. *Tennis on site.*

rooms	10 + 8: 10 twins/doubles. 8 cottages for 4-8.
price	€150-€250. Cottages €440 p.p. per week.
meals	Pub & restaurant on the premises. Dinner €20-€50. Lunch €5-€20.
closed	Rarely.
directions	From Dublin N2 for Newgrange & Monaghan; through Ashbourne; continue 11km; at bottom of slight hill, enter large white gates on left.

Country house & Self-catering

Vincent Callan

tel	+353 (0)41 982 1450
fax	+353 (0)41 982 1410
email	vcallan@oscdesign.ie
web	www.ballymagarvey.ie

Map 5 Entry 241

Lough Bishop House
Derrynagarra, Collinstown, Co. Westmeath

Helen's vitality is infectious. She breeds rare Irish Draught horses and loves cooking (preserves galore). Christopher, with equal enthusiasm, deals with myriad sheep, tends the pretty young orchard and the beginnings of a rare-breed cattle herd. Lough Bishop is a slice of quintessential Irish country life, including a view of the lake and the hills rolling round. The typical 19th-century, white-painted, red-tipped Irish farmhouse has a delightful courtyard and a checquered hall floor. Cosy rooms come in warm pinks, greens and yellows without an ounce of twee and some lovely old furniture. Everything is well loved and cared for, done with natural fabrics and a mix of styles that carry the Kellys' story. They share their super sitting room with you, friendly with its family-worn leather sofa, open fire and many books. Guest rooms are bright and pretty, the old furniture feels just right, interesting pictures to intrigue, no clutter to annoy and lovely views over the stable yard or the countryside to draw you out into the peace. A great house to stay in, fresh, charming, interesting people to stay with.

rooms	3: 1 double, 1 single, 1 family.
price	€100. Singles €50-€60.
meals	Dinner €30. Book before noon.
closed	December.
directions	From Castlepollard R394 for Mullingar. At Whitehall church & school, left up country road 3km; sign on gate on right.

Helen & Christopher Kelly
tel	+353 (0)44 966 1313
mobile	+353 (0)87 680 8298
email	chkelly@eircom.net
web	www.derrynagarra.com

B&B

Map 4 Entry 242

Mornington House
Multyfarnham, Nr. Mullingar, Co. Westmeath

Seclusion here is absolute. With the shutters closed on your bedroom windows you could sleep all day, provided the jackdaws did too. You approach Mornington through a gap in the trees, the manifold guardians of the property that protect it on all sides. The central section was built in 1710, the front in 1897, the wing in 1906: the concerted efforts of the founders (the Daly family). The first O'Haras took up residence in 1858. Most of the bedrooms are large, done in bright colours, with big bathrooms, oval baths, brass beds and views that include the mighty solitary oak tree on the front lawn. A path has been cut through the meadow to Lough Derravaragh with Knock Eyon in the distance. Downstairs, carpets fade as they approach long ranks of park-facing windows, lovely velvet cushions are sprinkled over a variety of antique sofas and chairs and a huge potted lime tree in the dining room catches the sunlight in the morning. Warwick and Anne are genuinely dedicated hosts and produce the most delicious meals, growing many of their vegetables in the walled garden behind the house.

rooms	5: 4 twins/doubles; 1 single with separate bathroom.
price	€130–€150. Singles from €80.
meals	Dinner, 4 courses, €42.50.
closed	November-March.
directions	From N4/Mullingar bypass R394 for Castlepollard 8km; left at Wood Pub in Crookedwood 2km; right at 1st junc. House 1.5km on right, down long drive.

Country house

	Anne & Warwick O'Hara
tel	+353 (0)44 937 2191
fax	+353 (0)44 937 2338
email	stay@mornington.ie
web	www.mornington.ie

Map 4 Entry 243

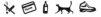

Lough Owel Lodge
Cullion, Nr. Mullingar, Co. Westmeath

So often in Ireland, you only need to turn off a main road to find yourself in beautiful countryside. Lough Owel Lodge is just off a dual carriageway north of Mullingar, yet you are deep enough in the country to forget the road is there. Nothing spoils the view from this nature-surrounded 1940s house. The open-plan sitting/dining room has full-length, timber-framed windows that seem to draw the outside in. In winter you can also see writer JP Donleavy's house through the trees. There is nothing to spoil this view for miles. The Lodge's land stretches past terraced garden and tennis court to the lake below. Unusually-shaped rooms are scrupulously clean with some lovely beds, including a four-poster and a 150-year-old half-tester. Walkers will appreciate the library of books on the region known as the 'Land of Lake and Legend' – fishing fans will know the name already. Trout fishing can be arranged with ghillies and boats. Aideen and Martin are easy-going hosts, he busy with his farm, she a competent painter and mother of teenagers. A good-natured, unpretentious family home and ideal for children.

rooms	5: 1 double, 1 twin, 2 four-posters, 1 family suite.
price	€70-€75. Singles €40-€45.
meals	Restaurants in Mullingar, 3km. Packed lunch €6.
closed	November-April. Off season by arrangement.
directions	From Dublin N4 for 80km. Just past Mullingar, as lake comes into view, left at sign; entrance on right.

	Martin & Aideen Ginnell
tel	+353 (0)44 934 8714
fax	+353 (0)44 934 8714
email	aideen.ginnell@ireland.com
web	www.angelfire.com/tx/aginnell

B&B

Map 4 Entry 244

Wineport Lodge
Glasson, Athlone, Co. Westmeath

Step down from the quiet little road, through a strip of flourishing garden and onto the deck of a glorified boating club. Low-slung, weather-boarded Wineport Lodge is designed to be utterly discreet against the spreading lake – and a glorious spot for birds. A watery peace washes the gorgeous rooms and their balconies (only a couple miss the lake view). The décor shares the philosophy: solid pieces of real timber, gleaming white cotton, simple classy furniture by Jane's designer brother, all natural, respectful and yet contemporary, furnishings and fabrics as genuine as the timber. It's a lesson in "sober needn't be boring". An easy-going, efficient couple, Ray and Jane have firm good taste and show their knowledge of modern art in the public spaces where ceiling heights can bring a touch of drama. The harmony of this organic building is palpable against the unparallelled, changing waterscape. Swim if you're tough enough, boating can be organised, Fearghal O'Donnell's cooking is said to be divine, a small decanter of Jameson is waiting in your room. *Dublin Airport under 2 hours.*

rooms	29: 24 twins/doubles, 1 family, 4 suites.
price	€195–€275. Singles €139. Suites €295–€395. Half-board available.
meals	Dinner €59 or à la carte. Snack lunch available for residents.
closed	Christmas.
directions	From Athlone ring-road N55 for Longford & Cavan 4km; entering Glasson village, left at the Dog & Duck, 1.5km on left.

Hotel

	Ray Byrne & Jane English
tel	+353 (0)90 643 9010
fax	+353 (0)90 648 5471
email	lodge@wineport.ie, ray@wineport.ie
web	www.wineport.ie

Map 4 Entry 245

The Bastion
2 Bastion Street, Athlone, Co. Westmeath

Old Athlone, an historic staging post between Dublin and Galway on the banks of the Shannon, is now the trendy 'culinary capital of the Midlands'. On the Left Bank, around King John's 13th-century castle, the houses are ancient, the narrow streets full of good restaurants and swinging pubs. *Sean's* is so old it's mentioned in the 9th-century Clonmacnoise Annals. At the Bastion, brothers Vinny and Anthony have turned the house above the family shops into a very special B&B that meanders from level to landing. Their slightly bohemian style is gentle and definitely 'green': space to recline, happy plants, an eclectic collection of original art, globetrotters' mementoes. The snug bedrooms, where apprentice tailors once lived, have a clean spartan elegance, crisp white linen, floorboards, oak dressing tables, hangers on hooks, designer lamps, modern art – impeccable. A healthily natural buffet breakfast, a welcome change from Irish Fry, is served in the colourful communal room over the street. Great fun, delightful easy people. Ask about boat trips to prehistoric Clonmacnoise, bog walks and nearby Lough Ree.

rooms	6: 2 doubles, 2 family; 1 double with separate bath. Annexe: 1 double studio.
price	€70. Singles €40–€50.
meals	Restaurants within walking distance.
closed	Rarely.
directions	From Dublin N6 for Galway to Athlone; follow signs to town centre; cross bridge to Left Bank, left round castle, follow street round, house 100m on right.

Vinny & Anthony McCay

tel	+353 (0)90 649 4954
fax	+353 (0)90 649 3648
email	info@thebastion.net
web	www.thebastion.net

B&B

Map 4 Entry 246

Ghan House
Carlingford, Co. Louth

Enter the low, beamed hall with its blazing log fire – and know 18th-century Ghan House for the much-loved family inn that it is. Yet Joyce, who started her cookery courses here, and son Paul who is taking over (he's a honey), give more than just love: attention to detail is paramount. Food is important, too, so do book dinner. Enclosed within the ancient walls of Carlingford, probably the best-preserved medieval town in Ireland, the house looks over the pond, the road and Carlingford Lough to the distant Mourne Mountains. Some guests prefer a room in the creaky timeworn old house, others the peace and quiet of the new annexe. There are arched doorways, mouldings, old-style velvet with tassels, proper bathrooms – everything is impeccably done, everywhere you find thick wool carpets, family antiques, personal bits, a sense of deep comfort, plus books in the cosy little sitting room. The Carrolls know and enjoy what they are doing and are genuinely friendly with it. You won't be short of things to do, either. Restaurants, pubs, watersports, hill-walking or the simple pleasure of sitting by a turf fire.

rooms	12: 11 twins/doubles, 1 single.
price	€190-€200. Singles from €75.
meals	Dinner €30; 5-course menu €47. Book ahead. Restaurants within walking distance.
closed	Christmas & New Year.
directions	From Dublin N1 north 85km; right at 1st r'bout after Dundalk for Carlingford. House 1st on left entering village, 10m after 50kmph sign.

Guest house

Paul & Joyce Carroll
tel +353 (0)42 937 3682
fax +353 (0)42 937 3772
email ghanhouse@eircom.net
web www.ghanhouse.com

Map 2 & 5 Entry 247

Fine Breakfast Scheme

By accepting their pledge, we are relying on owners' integrity and honesty to keep to the points listed below. It's not a perfect scheme but the message is right – that it is important to choose food carefully and support local economies. Over 90 owners have signed the pledge. Please understand that those who have not signed the pledge have done so for a variety of reasons and this does not mean they do not provide delicious breakfasts, too.

Fine Breakfast Scheme – Pledge

1. I agree to serve breakfasts of only the best available ingredients – whether organic or locally sourced.

2. Any certified organic ingredients will be named as such. (Note that the word 'organic' is a legal term. Any uncertified 'organic' ingredients cannot be described as organic.) Where there is a choice of organic certifier I will prefer the Soil Association if possible, recognising that their standards are generally the most demanding.

3. All other ingredients will be, whenever reasonably possible, sourced locally from people and institutions that I know personally and have good reason to believe provide food of the best quality.

4. Where I have grown food myself, I will say so.

5. I will do my best to avoid shopping in supermarkets if good alternatives exist within a reasonable distance.

6. I will display the Fine Breakfast cards in the breakfast room or, if I prefer, in the bedrooms. (We accept that some of you may not want to use the cards.)

7. I know that the scheme is an imperfect instrument but accept its principles.

Photo Paul Groom

Gardens of Ireland

With the mild air and gallons of soft rain that cover this island, Ireland's gardens are possibly the lushest in Europe. With such heavenly gifts, many houses in this book have wonderful gardens, big and small, ancient and modern, some of them open to the public, most of them known only to the initiated. Our seven two-page 'greener' entries all have interesting gardens, from the sweeping hillside at Iskeroon to the Mustard Seed's organic vegetable 'patch', and are easy to consult - just look for the green edge on their pages. It is impossible to list all the others so here is a selection.

Private gardens
Hilton Park (entry 48) The gardens here can be seen as a metaphor for the history of 18th and 19th-century Ireland. The five great indigenous oaks at the front were already mapped in the 1780s and are probably 400 years old. A century later, the great conifers and thuyas were brought back from America - as tiny seeds - by a Victorian Madden,

as was the towering Wellingtonia. His descendents are restoring the formal areas, the walks, the herb garden to their inspired Georgian plans.

Newforge House (entry 26) has a listed formal garden that is almost all one man's work. It is worth making the journey to see his handiwork and, above all, hear him talk about it.

At Ashley Park (entry 178) they are ever restoring what was a fabulous two-acre walled garden. It is wonderful again with its wide borders and glorious clumps of colour through the spring and summer, its peaceful sitting spot by the gazebo, its rare old fruit trees that still produce basketfuls for the kitchen.

Ardtarmon House (entry 50) Restoration continues within a long-established framework of

**Photo left Hilton Park
photo above Ashley Park**

compartments over 16 acres: formal avenue, walled garden, tennis lawn, flower beds, borders, walkways, arches, Japanese garden. Spring and early summer see a blast of colour from deutzia, lilies and hydrangeas. Vegetables and an orchard have been planted, a Jersey cow keeps the grass under control, a sow and her piglets help with the growing process... and wildlife rejoices.

At Ballinkeele House (entry 191) the garden is nurtured by John and Margaret's commitment to its past and present. House and garden were designed by Daniel Robertson in the days when it was considered poor taste to have the garden near the house: one had to work up an appetite for lunch by walking miles to the flowers. The revival has given a large formal garden, a reclaimed lake, a pond surrounded by water-lovers and all the fruit and vegetables you could imagine.

Photo above left Ballinkeele House
photo above right Clone House

Clone House (entry 217) has four acres of loveliness, done with imagination and care, peppered with thousands of bulbs (the birch and bulb grove by the stream is magical in spring), specimen plants and shrubs among the rockery and ruled by the largest monkey-puzzle tree in this part of Ireland.

Cashel House (entry 75) stands at the head of Cashel Bay in fifty glorious acres of flowering shrubs, fine great trees and woodland walks which have won many awards.

Ard Na Sidhe (entry 108) was built and its gardens laid out in the early 20th century by a keen gardener, Lady Edith Gordon. In time, the wrinkles of age covered most of her youthful ideas, apart from the rock garden, so typical of her time. New plantings and projects include the Tree Fern Glade whose damp shade shelters tree ferns, bamboos and rhododendrons.

Gardens of Ireland

Gardens open to the public
Bantry House's (entry 126) seven
world-famous terraces in the Italian
style seem to lift the extraordinary
house as they flow down towards
the bay.

At Enniscoe House (entry 64) the
great Victorian gardens are being
restored with knowledge and
determination: the walled garden is
as sheltered as you could wish, the
ornamental garden centres on its
fern-fuzzed stone arch and the
pleasure gardens are nearing
completion.

Kilmokea (entry 193) has two parts,
the organised and the wild: the
variety of tender plants and shrubs,
the classical loggia and the
rediscovered old flowering plants lie
in contrast to the woodland area with
paths that curl through imported
exotica and hot-spice colours.

These gardens have been worked
on for two generations with
spectacular results.

Sion Hill House (entry 171) George
and Antoinette Kavanagh have
studied the old Victorian plans deeply,
dug and delved untiringly and
nurtured their many plants
intelligently - they have every right
to rejoice in the flourish of success
that their tree ferns, rare
rhododendrons and old roses have
brought.
At Loughcrew House (entry 235),
sweeping 17th-century elegance goes
hand in hand with modern ideas of
entertainment and the old pleasure
gardens, medicinal beds and water
features have been shaped into
'mystery' walks that keep the young
happy while others enjoy the beauty,
the history – and the sheer
gardening.

Glin Castle's (entry 95) gardens
attract gardeners and horticultural
groups with their specimen plants
and trees in the park and formal
gardens, fruit and vegetables in the
walled garden and some judiciously-
placed follies - quirky mementoes of
our Victorian heritage.

For the great gardens that are open
to the public - the Mount Stewarts
and Derreens of this world - there are
plenty of web sites to consult. Try
www.visitireland.com.

Photo Kilmokea

Suggested reading

Contemporary Ireland
- *The Pope's Children: Ireland's New Elite*
by David McWilliams
The author, a popular lecturer and television journalist, has been described as "an extraordinary brainbox with a sense of humour" and his book as "a brilliant survey of Ireland today." *Meet the huge new Irish middle class, young, sassy and making out like bandits. Meet the Pope's Children folks. Meet your new bosses!*

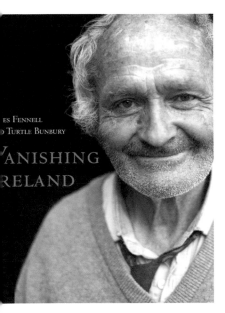

ES FENNELL
TURTLE BUNBURY
ANISHING
RELAND

- *Vanishing Ireland*
by Turtle Bunbury and James Fennell:
Combining insightful interviews and stunning photographs, this book captures 64 characters of senior vintage from all over Ireland. Blacksmiths and farmers, fishermen and horse dealers unite with housemaids, lacemakers, publicans and musicians to bring to life a world which is fading fast. Amusing and poignant.

20th-century history
- *Desmond's Rising: Memoirs 1913 to Easter 1916*
by Desmond FitzGerald
Written during the Second World War, *Desmond's Rising* charts his involvement in the Irish Volunteers and the IRB, his arrest and imprisonment in 1915-1916 and his experiences in the GPO during the fateful Easter week of 1916. What strikes the reader most strongly is the unselfconscious heroism of those who took part in the Rising.
- *An Illustrated History of the Gaelic Athletic Association*
by Eoghan Corry
The GAA (Gaelic Athletic Association) is the largest amateur sports body in the world and the most successful voluntary organization in the history of modern Ireland. Its games are played in every parish, village and townland of Ireland; its influence on Irish public life is immeasurable.
- *The Rebels of Ireland (Ireland Awakening)*
by Edward Rutherford.
A tale of fierce battles, hot-

Suggested reading

blooded romances, and family and political intrigues.

• *Parnell: The Uncrowned King of Ireland*
by Katherine O'Shea,
(first published 1914)
Covers her early life, her marriage to Captain O' Shea and her life with Parnell, in a personal and touching way, using many letters and discussions between Parnell and herself.

General history of Ireland
• *A Short History of Ireland*
by Martin Wallace
Traces the invasions of Celts, Vikings and Normans, the Tudor and Stuart settlements and the emergence of the 'Irish Question' in British politics; the failure of the union, the partition of the island and developments in the Republic and Northern Ireland in modern times. Descriptions of prominent figures and major historical sites plus a list of important dates make this an ideal introduction to Ireland.

Origins of people and places
• *Irish Family Names*
by Ida Grehan
Describes 80 well-known Irish family names chosen not merely because they are historically important and still numerous but also because of their outstanding personalities.

• *Irish Place Names*
by P.W. Joyce
Over 2,000 well-known Irish place names with explanations of their various forms and a list of root words from which Irish place names are most commonly formed.

Monuments and Castles
• *Ireland's Ancient Stones: A Megalithic Heritage*
by Kenneth McNally
The Irish countryside is rich in prehistoric reminders and one has only to catch sight of a lone dolmen standing against the sky to appreciate the efforts of the ancient builders. Ken McNally describes over 100 sites from the Neolithic and Bronze Ages, every one beautifully illustrated with photographs, drawings and engravings, many from the 17th and 18th centuries. A beautiful celebration of Ireland's prehistoric monuments and a tantalising glimpse at the lives of her ancient peoples.
• *Irish Castles*
by Terence Reeves-Smyth
A handy pocket guide to Ireland's old castles, great and small.
• *Irish Trees and Shrubs*
by Peter Wyse-Jackson
Describes over 60 common countryside plants, both native and introduced species that have gone wild, with colour illustrations.

Slow Food

Hand-roasted oats, jugs of Jersey cream, 'heirloom' tomatoes, Bantry Bay mussels, wild salmon from the Blackwater River, smoky Gubeen bacon, nutty Coolea cheese, wholegrain sodabread, Kerry lamb – Ireland is a larder like no other. It is as natural a place for the Slow Food movement to flourish as anywhere, and a splendid destination for foodies.

Slow Food was founded in Bra, Italy in 1986: Italy's way of thumbing its nose at multi-national fast foods and fat-friendly meals. Its logo a snail, its membership spanning 50 countries, the movement has inched its way into the countries of the British Isles – most conspicuously to Shropshire's Ludlow and Ireland's County Cork. Fast times call for slow food and food tastes best when it is grown organically, harvested locally and eaten in season. Slow Food not only champions artisan-producers, it also seeks to conserve endangered seeds, breeds (the rare-breed Kerry cow is a notable example), cultivars and processes.

The oldest of the Slow Ireland 'convivia' (community forums) is West Cork whose cheese makers, salmon smokers and organic gardeners have been thriving for 30 years. And among the earliest exponents of the movement are

Slow Food

Myrtle and Darina Allen of Ballymaloe House, Co. Cork (see entry 151), co-founders of Darina's famed cookery school whose inspired courses range from *Game Cooking for the Festive Season* to *How to Keep a Few Chickens in the Garden*. Then there is Powersfield in Co. Waterford (entry 168), run by the exuberant Eunice Power, Heron's Cove (entry 132), a charming small inn down a West Cork peninsula, and the all-vegetarian Café Paradiso (entry 148), a much-celebrated restaurant with rooms in the centre of Cork city. All are passionate exponents of the Slow Food ethos. However, Slow Food championing Irish-style is not limited to restaurants and country-house hotels. It spreads its net wide – in Kerry, as far as the flourishing Community Organic Garden in Shanakill, Tralee, a local authority housing area with high levels of unemployment.

As for farmers' markets, that burgeoning branch of the food revolution – even the tiniest villages are engendering them. They range from Saturday's munificent markets at Dunhill, Co. Waterford and Midleton, Co. Cork (started by the indefatigable Darina Allen) to Sunday's stalls in minuscule Schull. Farmers' markets and the Slow Food movement make natural bedfellows, united in their quest for taste and quality. There is no middleman: the markets' produce is grown, reared, raised, baked, caught or produced by the seller, and is as local and as seasonal as can be.

Jo Boissevain

www.slowfoodireland.com
www.irelandmarkets.com

A brief history of Ireland

Ireland – a brief outline of where it came from and where it is now

Twenty-first century Ireland is a land that astonishes in many ways. Twenty years ago, who would have believed this impossibly romantic island would emerge as one of the most prosperous and influential nations in Europe?

Ireland's history has been nothing but eventful. In 2003, excavations of the central peat bogs revealed the well-preserved bodies of two ancient princes from the Iron Age. One of them famously used hair gel. The Ireland these princes knew was a lush landscape replete with simple stone temples built in tribute to the mysterious complexities of the Universe beyond. The native pagan beliefs merged with those of the Middle East at the time of the Celts and so inspired a new age of industry and commerce, of goldsmiths and storytellers, warriors and druids. With Saint Patrick at the helm,

Christianity swept into the island "of saints and scholars" in the 5th century AD. Monasteries and abbeys rose along the misty riverbanks. For the next 300 years, Irish missionaries carried the Christian spirit east to Germany and west to the unknown. Between the 9th and 12th centuries, Viking longships and Norman armies invaded the island, laid waste the Celtic kingdoms and erected the first towns. In time, the whole island was seized as a colony of the Anglo-Norman crown.

Under Henry VIII, the Catholic Church was abolished and the church lands parcelled out to those loyal to the Crown - native Irish, Norman settler and new Scottish and English planters alike. The redistribution of land to loyal subjects continued under Queen Elizabeth, the Stuarts and Oliver Cromwell; those who protested were cast away to the barren lands of the west. William of Orange's victory at the Boyne in 1689 was the start of more than 200 years of rule by

A brief history of Ireland

an Anglo-Irish elite, primarily Protestant, intrinsically British. A series of disastrous rebellions, economic hardship and the horror of the Great Famine ultimately ignited a war of independence against Britain in 1919. Irish independence came in stages thereafter.

The Republic of Ireland was officially born on 1st April 1949 and consists of 26 of Ireland's 32 counties. The remaining six counties constitute Northern Ireland, an area that still falls under British rule. At the time of the negotiations for Irish independence in 1921, these six northern counties were controlled by wealthy Protestant loyalists who felt a strong attachment to the English crown. They had little desire to unite as an independent nation with the Catholic dominated counties of the south. Partition was deemed the best solution. Tensions between Northern Ireland's Catholics and Protestants erupted in riots and murder in 1969, leading to an often-brutal 30-year war. Peace has returned since the 1998 Good Friday Agreement although attempts to share power between the Catholic and Protestant political parties remain a thorn in the side of amity.

The Republic's extraordinary economic success since the early 1990s has become a blueprint for all members of the European Union. The Republic of Ireland's population currently stands at 4.2 million, its highest level since records began in 1861. This includes more than 400,000 'non-nationals' who have arrived in Ireland from Africa, China and Eastern Europe since the start of the new century. Dublin is booming; the dockland development is just one example of the massive renaissance taking place in the city. Provincial towns and villages are likewise metamorphosing into fresh and contemporary shapes. Away from the roads and suburbs, romance, history and outstandingly good *craic* still permeate the air of this most magical of European islands. In Northern Ireland too, prosperity and peace have paved the way for a new dawn of positivity for the island of Ireland.

Turtle Bunbury

Quick reference indices

On a budget?
These places have double
rooms for £70/€100 or less

Horse
These owners have stabling
for guests' horses

Fragile Earth series

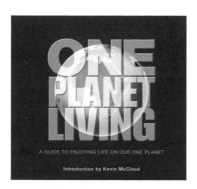

One Planet Living
Edition 1, £4.99
By Pooran Desai and Paul King

One Planet Living is a practical guide providing us with easy, affordable and attractive alternatives for achieving a higher quality of life while using our fair share of the planet's capacity.

The Little Food Book
Edition 1, £6.99
By Craig Sams, Chairman of the Soil Association

An explosive account of the food we eat today. Never have we been at such risk – from our food. This book will help clarify what's at stake.

The Little Money Book
Edition 1, £6.99
By David Boyle, an associate of the New Economics Foundation

This pithy, wry little guide will tell you where money comes from, what it means, what it's doing to the planet and what we might be able to do about it.

www.fragile-earth.com

Where on the web?

The World Wide Web is big – very big. So big, in fact, that it can be a fruitless search if you don't know where to find reliable, trustworthy, up-to-date information about fantastic places to stay in Europe, India, Morocco and beyond....

Fortunately, there's www.specialplacestostay.com, where you can dip into all of our guides, find special offers from owners, catch up on news about the series and tell us about the special places you've been to.

www.specialplacestostay.com

Discover your perfect self-catering escape in Britain... With the same punch and attitude as all our printed guides, Special Escapes celebrates only those places we have visited and genuinely like.

www.special-escapes.co.uk

Order form

All these books are available in major bookshops or you may order them direct.
Post and packaging are FREE within the UK.

Bed & Breakfast for Garden Lovers	£14.99
British Hotels, Inns & Other Places	£14.99
British Bed & Breakfast	£14.99
French Bed & Breakfast	£15.99
French Hotels, Châteaux & Other Places	£14.99
French Holiday Homes	£12.99
Greece	£11.99
Green Places to Stay	**£13.99**
India	£11.99
Ireland	£12.99
Italy	£14.99
London	£9.99
Morocco	£11.99
Mountains of Europe	£9.99
Paris Hotels	£10.99
Portugal	£10.99
Pubs & Inns of England & Wales	£13.99
Spain	£14.99
Turkey	£11.99
One Planet Living	**£4.99**
The Little Food Book	£6.99
The Little Money Book	£6.99
Six Days	£12.99

Please make cheques payable to Alastair Sawday Publishing   Total £

Please send cheques to: Alastair Sawday Publishing, The Old Farmyard, Yanley
Lane, Long Ashton, Bristol BS41 9LR. For credit card orders call 01275 395431
or order directly from our web site www.specialplacestostay.com

Title   First name   Surname

Address

Postcode   Tel

IR6

If you do not wish to receive mail from other like-minded companies, please tick here n
If you would prefer not to receive information about special offers on our books, please tick here n

Report form

If you have any comments on entries in this guide, please let us have them. If you have a favourite house, hotel, inn or other new discovery, please let us know about it. You can return this form, email info@sawdays.co.uk, or visit www.specialplacestostay.com and click on 'contact'.

Existing entry

Property name: _____

Entry number: _____ Date of visit: ___ / ___ / ___

New recommendation

Property name: _____

Address: _____

_____

Tel: _____

Your comments

What did you like (or dislike) about this place? Were the people friendly? What was the location like? What sort of food did they serve?

_____

_____

_____

_____

_____

_____

_____

_____

Your details

Name: _____

Address: _____

Postcode: _____ Tel: _____

IR6

Index by property name

Index by Town

How to use this book

1   Co. Sligo

The Old Rectory
Easkey, Co. Sligo

2 Though Robert and Lorely would call themselves designers, the Old Rectory is somehow a 'work of art'. There's nothing flash about this 1790s house, they have simply brought its warm comforting shapes to life with their vibrant colour sense and family furniture – plus heaps of drawings, paintings, books and china. The courtyard has tangled climbing roses and hurricane lamps — an ideal sun trap for tea and talk. The magical walled garden shelters fuchsias, exotic palms, vast fruit trees, a young orchard, a family-laid cobbled path and a formal kitchen garden. Starry ceilings twinkle over Lorely's imaginative and lovely rooms, their gold curtains, painted shutters and stencilled walls. Views of the River Easkey and the village church are memorable and the beach is world-renowned for surfing. It's a down-to-earth family home with dozy cats and friendly dogs at breakfast in the Aga-warm kitchen, strutting hens, munching sheep and two mellow donkeys outside. Lorely and Robert are easy folk to be with, friendly, creative and devoted to the little paradise they've built together.

3 rooms	3: 2 doubles, 1 family, sharing bathroom & shower room.	
4 price	From €80–€90. Singles from €55.	
5 meals	Restaurants in Easkey & Enniscrone.	
6 closed	Christmas & New Year.	
7 directions	From Dublin for Sligo; leave N4 dual carriageway at Coolooney to Ballisadare; before bridge left N59 for Ballina to Dromore West; right for Easkey 6km; house next to church.	

Robert & Lorely Forrester
tel   +353 (0)96 49181
email   easkey14@eircom.net

8   B&B

10    **9**   Map 3 Entry 51